FEMININE
LEADERSHIP
or
How to Succeed
in Business
Without Being
One of the Boys

FEMININE LEADERSHIP

or

How to Succeed in Business Without Being One of the Boys

Marilyn Loden

BOOKS

Library of Congress Cataloging in Publication Data

Loden, Marilyn.
    Feminine leadership, or How to succeed in business without being one of the boys.

    Includes index.

    1. Women executives. 2. Women in business.
3. Leadership. I. Title
HD6054.3.L63   1985   658.4'09'024042   85-40283
ISBN 0-8129-1240-3

Designed by Doris Borowsky
Manufactured in the United States of America

85 86 87 88 89 5 4 3 2 1

In loving memory of
Dr. Harold Kellner,
whose genius shone like a candle in the rain

Acknowledgments _____

N ow that this book is finally finished, I find it difficult to recount the enormous hours of thought and discussion that went into the task of writing it. But I can vividly recall the many friends and colleagues who helped me along the way by challenging my assumptions and forcing me to think through my ideas; by offering me their insights into the complex issues that working women face today; and by giving me the encouragement and support I so greatly needed to see this project through. It gives me great pleasure to thank them here.

I begin with my dear friend Bernadette Hogan and offer her my thanks for the ideas, generosity, and endless support she has given me. I also want to thank Pat Ferro and Amy Coughlin for helping me sharpen the focus of the book; the many men and women who agreed to be interviewed and who are quoted in these pages; the Downeys and the Lodens for their enthusiasm and interest; Joe Potts and Marilynn

Swenson of NTL for providing me with many good leads; Beth Backman, my agent, for staying committed to this project through its many ups and downs; and Elisabeth Scharlatt, my editor, for helping me find my own voice and for encouraging me to "let the facts speak for themselves."

In the moral support category, I want to thank Tom Attea, Cook Brogan, Clare Browne, Kitty Dearie, the Delta Consulting Group, Pat Dolan, Marcia Feldhaus, Wendy Fleder, Dave Hackett, Terry Limpert, Bob Maul, Vinnie McGuire, Nan Meltzer, Maruta Miluns, Richie Orange, Pat Ryan, Charlie Seashore, and, particularly, Sara Stone. I also want to pay special homage to two women who have been important role models for me and who, in my view, symbolize what feminine leadership is really about: Dr. Estelle Ramey and Edith Whitfield Seashore.

Finally, I want to thank John Loden for being "unique among men." His energy, candor, intelligence, interest, and editing skills played a critical part in making this book a reality. Most of all, I want to thank him for his unflagging support and for having the wisdom and grace to recognize how much better off the world will be when there is ample room in it for feminine leaders.

Contents

Introduction.   xi

PART I

Chapter 1   Leadership in Transition   3
Chapter 2   Masculinism in the Corporation   19
Chapter 3   The Crisis in the Corporation   41
Chapter 4   The Case for Feminine Leadership   58

PART II

Chapter 5   The Use of Power   83
Chapter 6   Setting Performance Standards and
             Taking Risks   100
Chapter 7   Teamwork and Participative
             Management   114
Chapter 8   Interpersonal Effectiveness   133
Chapter 9   Conflict Management   158
Chapter 10   Intuition and Problem-Solving   182
Chapter 11   Managing Diversity, Stress, and
             Boundaries   199
Chapter 12   Pitching In and Professional
             Development   217

PART III

Chapter 13 Making a Real Difference: What
           Women Can Do   229
Chapter 14 Making a Real Difference: What Men
           Can Do   244
Chapter 15 Making a Real Difference: What
           Organizations Can Do   256
Chapter 16 Feminine Leadership and the Future   275
           Notes   281
           Index   291

Introduction

Over the past ten years, hundreds of books have been published about women in management; thousands of articles have appeared in magazines and newspapers; countless seminars have been conducted to counsel women on career-related issues. With all this advice already available, why, you might ask, publish another book on the subject? Very simply, because this book is different.

While virtually every book and article written to date has focused on the weaknesses of women managers, this book focuses on their strengths. In contrast to the general advice to women on how to *change* their natural management style to be more compatible with traditional methods, this book counsels women on how to *develop* their natural skills to benefit themselves and their organizations. While practically every publication has held up the traditional, masculine leadership model as the standard for emulation, this book proclaims that there is a different, complementary, and equally effective feminine leadership style.

In choosing a title for this book, I was very conscious of the negative reactions that many men and even some women might have to the term "feminine leadership." To many men, the terms "feminine" and "leadership" are contradictory, even mutually exclusive. In their minds, leaders must be aggressive, unemotional, and detached. To some women, the term "feminine leadership" causes discomfort because it points out differences between the sexes at a time when people are trying to convince themselves and others that differences do not exist and that, in terms of management style, men and women are completely interchangeable.

Despite these likely reactions, I chose this title because I think it captures both the uniqueness and the strengths of many women managers. In a very real sense, women are born leaders just as surely as men are. The time has come to clearly define the unique style of many women managers and the positive impact it can have on organizations so that more women will understand that they don't have to make themselves over in the image of men in order to succeed.

With each passing day, evidence is mounting of the unique skills and perspectives that women, as a group, bring to business. These skills will complement, not replace, the traditional masculine approach to managing. Sometimes, when looked at on an individual basis, these different managerial skills and perspectives may be subtle and difficult to discern. But when viewed in the aggregate, across large numbers of women, the subtleties disappear and the differences become more clearly defined. Women, as a group, truly have their own leadership style, and this style can make an important contribution to American business.

In corporations today, no reality is more certain than change. Industries, products, the competition, even the work force are changing. Today, for the first time in history, white men are in the minority. According to U.S. Bureau of Labor statistics, women now represent almost 45 percent of all those employed in American corporations.

Amid all this change, isn't it time the traditional concept of leadership began to change, too? Not change for the sake of change, but change for the better—to result in a more productive, more spirited, and more humane workplace. The directions these changes must take are already becoming evident, as is the central role feminine leadership can play in making these changes a reality.

PART
I

Chapter One
Leadership in Transition

This is a book about the future—about potential and possibilities. New ideas will be explored about the contributions women managers can make to the success and growth of American business. The purpose is to raise awareness among men and women of a different type of leadership—feminine leadership—and to discuss in detail what it is, how it differs from traditional management methods, and, most important, how it can enhance and support current efforts to solve productivity problems, improve employee morale, and revitalize stagnant organizations.

The concept of feminine leadership has begun to take shape slowly during the past few years. It is an idea born of the experiences of hundreds of thousands of women who today labor in previously all-male management ranks in the real world of competitive, everyday business. It is a notion based on both their successes and their frustrations, not on some ivory tower academic theory.

While the exact parameters of this different style of leadership are still evolving, the evidence is already overwhelming that it exists and can make a much needed contribution to business and society in general. But before its potential can be maximized, it must first be acknowledged and endorsed by American corporations.

The qualities that define feminine leadership are by no means characteristics limited exclusively to women. These traits can certainly be found among men as well. It is also true that there are individual women who are more comfortable with a predominantly masculine style of leadership, just as there are individual men who find a feminine approach more natural. But the key distinction is that as a class, women exhibit these particular leadership attributes to a far greater degree than do men. The fact that feminine leadership is a generalization, and may not apply to each individual, in no way makes it less valid, relevant, or meaningful.

In discussing the roots of feminine leadership, some people have begun to raise the issue of whether this unique management style is a result of innate differences between men and women or simply a function of socialization. While this is certainly an intriguing question, it is essentially a moot point. Regardless of its origins, this different leadership style is today much more heavily concentrated among women as a group than among men. Therefore, the descriptor "feminine" seems entirely appropriate.

Over the longer term, some of the current distinctions between masculine and feminine leadership may begin to blur as both sexes benefit from exposure to the other's style of management. However, it seems unlikely that basic differences between men and women managers will ever completely disappear. It is difficult to accept the notion of one "visionary" who said recently, "In fifty years, I can see a situation where there will be no differences between men and women as classes within organizations. There will be lots of differences, but they will be individual differences."

On the contrary, just as gender differences persist in virtually every other aspect of life, it seems very likely that a distinctive feminine management style will also persist. And this will be to everyone's benefit because the feminine style of leadership is not a replacement for the traditional style. Both styles have their own strengths that can contribute to the overall success of organizations. Taken together, they represent a holistic approach to management—capable of taking full advantage of the entire spectrum of human talents.

By viewing feminine leadership as an effective complement to the traditional style of management favored more by men, one begins to see also how women's different style and perspectives can enhance managerial effectiveness and help organizations and our nation prosper and grow. After all, would society really be better off if a female manager behaved in exactly the same manner as her male counterparts? Or if a female justice brought exactly the same perspectives to the courtroom as her male colleagues? Or a female vice-presidential candidate campaigned with exactly the same vision as her masculine opponent? Once business and society become more familiar with the benefits of feminine leadership, I believe the answers to these questions will become more self-evident. But before this can happen, there must be a basic increase in awareness of feminine leadership as an alternate style of management.

In my own case, an awareness of this feminine leadership style began to develop in 1974 while I was working as an internal organization development consultant for the Bell Telephone System. Early that year, I was asked to create and manage an executive development program titled the Male-

Female Awareness Workshop. This program was designed to heighten awareness of sexism in the workplace and to aid in the integration of women into management and other nontraditional jobs. To my knowledge, the program was the first of its kind and, to this day, it remains the most ambitious effort of this sort ever undertaken.

For seven years, until the fall of 1981, the program attracted participants from across the nation. In time, it was opened up to participants from other corporations. Throughout those years, I had the opportunity to discuss firsthand the pressing issues that changing roles and relationships among men and women were creating within organizations. In all, I spoke with more than 4,000 managers who passed through the program. Split equally between both sexes, this group spanned all ages and races and came from every geographic region of the country. As a result of my discussions, I became acutely aware of the tremendous frustrations women managers were encountering as they tried to find their way and their place in male-dominated institutions. I also began to see an incongruity developing between the advice that was being offered to them and the actual problems they faced. It seemed to me that these solutions understated the complexity of the problems women faced and largely ignored the added value they brought to the managerial function.

During the summer of 1981, after leaving the Bell System to establish my own practice as a management consultant, I resolved to look closely at this developing issue in order to understand it more fully. What was preventing many competent women from succeeding within middle and upper management? Why were so few reaching senior levels in organizations? Why were so many frustrated in their jobs? As I reflected on my experiences working with women managers at all levels and the progress that affirmative action policies had brought for working women in the seventies, it seemed to me that efforts to promote equal opportunity had too often yielded bittersweet results.

While there were certainly more women executives than ever before, their impact on the way organizations functioned seemed to be minimal at best. Instead of humanizing the work environment, as many analysts of the late sixties had predicted they would do when their numbers increased, the majority of successful women had become clones of the traditional male executive. Right down to their pin-stripe suits and bow ties, these women were intent on competing with men and succeeding by beating them at their own game. But although this strategy was popular among many highly successful women in organizations, another consciousness was developing among some women managers that was quite different. This consciousness gave me my first real insight into the feminine leadership style they favored.

INITIAL QUESTIONS RAISED

In discussions with women executives at management development seminars and conferences across the country, it seemed that many were beginning to question the assumptions being made in organizations about how they should operate. Most of these questions were being asked by women who were still forging their careers and shaping their personal style of management. While they had difficulty describing what their preferred style would be, they had no trouble identifying their discomfort with the traditional managerial roles they were expected to play in order to succeed. What's more, they understood that these traditional roles prevented them from using their full range of abilities and forced them to behave in ways that limited their effectiveness as leaders.

7

After hearing them express concern about "losing their identities," "diminishing their competence," and "becoming male clones," a clear picture of the dilemma these women were facing began to emerge. It seemed to me that their concern was related to the model of effective management they were expected to follow. This model assumed that there was one "right" way to manage based largely on the behavior of those who had managed successfully in the past. In short, it represented the traditional approach to managing and leading. However, since few women had been part of the management picture until the late sixties, the model was based almost exclusively on experiences of successful men.

But was it reasonable to assume that women managers could and should operate along the exact same lines? By and large, most organizations thought so. What's more, most men and many women managers agreed with this assumption—although they often had very different reasons for supporting the idea. In talking with male managers, it was apparent that the majority saw the qualities of effective leadership as being the same for both sexes. Yet, their descriptions were usually based upon a paramilitary model of control and competitive behavior. On the other hand, women who supported the assumption frequently acknowledged that their natural inclinations were somewhat different from the traditional management model. Yet they insisted that they had to operate along traditional lines to prove they were as capable as men.

Nonetheless, my own observations about what was happening to women after a decade of climbing the managerial ladder led me to a very different conclusion. It seemed to me that the traditional management style was not effective for many women. Although some highly successful women functioned similarly to their male colleagues, and even a few were able to "out-macho" most of the men with whom they worked, the vast majority of women managers did not seem comfortable with the traditional leadership style used within most corporations. More important, this traditional style did not enhance their innate abilities or make the best use of their natural feminine skills and instincts. Instead, it forced many women to operate in a way that felt unnatural and rendered them less effective in their role as managers.

QUESTIONS ABOUT FEMININE LEADERSHIP

As I continued to talk informally with women about this idea of management style, a number of key questions began to emerge:

(1) What evidence already existed to support the idea that women might have a different, natural style of management than men?

(2) Why wasn't there greater support for the concept of feminine leadership among the small, elite group of women who had already made it into top management? Was their widespread acceptance of the traditional model a result of greater experience or were some other factors at work?

(3) Among women who rejected the traditional management approach (who were primarily in middle management), what did they find personally ineffective and confining about this approach? Did their discomfort pertain to certain tasks they were expected to perform or was there truly something about the overall approach that turned them off?

(4) If it were possible to identify the aspects of the traditional leadership model that some women felt caused them to be less effective, would it also

be possible to identify a different leadership style that more naturally suited women managers and also worked effectively in organizations?

(5) Assuming that the characteristics of this different style could be defined, did some women employ this nontraditional approach to management? If so, who were they and what were they like?

(6) Finally was the most critical and pragmatic question of all. If women did have a different and effective managerial style, specifically how could this nontraditional approach benefit organizations? Where was the added value for corporations?

REVIEW OF THE LITERATURE

My search for answers to these questions began with a review of much of the popular self-help literature for women managers. After studying some of the most popular texts on "how to succeed," I saw that the conventional wisdom being offered to women encouraged them to behave like men. Almost every piece of advice was designed to blur any differences that might exist between men and women. The experts urged women to be more strategic, assertive, and competitive and less emotional and sensitive. In addition, women were supposed to wear three-piece, navy skirt suits, play golf, and possess a thorough knowledge of professional sports. And they were never supposed to discuss their personal lives at the office.

Although I found occasional acknowledgment of the special insights women could bring to the role of managing, these comments were usually vague and offered no guidance or direction as to how their special qualities might be put to effective use. Instead, most of the advice focused on how women could develop typically masculine behaviors.

The paucity of information in these popular management texts led me to continue my search elsewhere. Reasoning that differences in style might well be related to differences in biology and socialization, I sought out the opinions of experts in both areas. In addition, I compared my own observations and impressions with those of other management consultants in the field. I was also able to examine normative data used by a major career counseling firm that did vocational testing of thousands of men and women managers each year. These data focused on a variety of basic management skills and vocational preferences.

The results of these efforts were quite remarkable. At the most fundamental levels, I uncovered much evidence of significant gender differences. What's more, my findings suggested that the impact of these differences would be noticeable in all aspects of life, including business. A growing body of empirical data from biology, psychology, and sociology convinced me that the premise that major differences in managerial style exist between men and women was not an interesting idea but a fact. However, I was still unable to articulate exactly how these differences would affect the behavior of male and female managers in a business setting. In what specific situations would men and women managers be likely to react differently? What would be the impact of their behavior on organizations?

DEVELOPING TWO MODELS OF LEADERSHIP

In order to expand on my observations and explore the basic idea in more detail, I conducted a series of in-depth interviews with men and women middle and senior managers in which I asked them to describe their style of management. I was interested in finding out exactly how they approached their role and what functions they thought an effective manager performed. From the results of these interviews, I compiled a list of several key variables that had been identified by the majority of respondents as important managerial functions. These included:

- the use of power
- managing work relationships
- problem-solving
- conflict management
- motivation of employees
- goal-setting
- decision-making
- teamwork.

Using these variables and other data collected in "expert" interviews, I then developed two leadership models that encompassed distinctly different approaches to each of the managerial functions identified above. In essence, one was a traditional model of management based upon accepted standards of masculine behavior and the second was a non-traditional model that relied on qualities considered to be more feminine, including the expression of feelings, the use of greater intuition in problem-solving, and an increased emphasis on personal relationship management.

Then it was time to find out what a larger cross section of men and women managers thought of these two distinctly different approaches as I had defined them. Did these man-

agement models reflect the real world? Did they truly describe the basic behavioral differences between men and
women? If so, what were the implications for the individual
and for the organization?

To test out my hypothesis, I chose two hundred women
and fifty men from a wide variety of organizations and entrepreneurial businesses to interview. The women were divided into two groups: those who had succeeded in their
chosen professions as senior executives in complex organizations or as entrepreneurs; and those who were still moving
up within management and developing their own leadership
style. The men were chosen using slightly different criteria.
They were managers who were described as enlightened by
their women colleagues. Each had given the idea of male-
female differences considerable thought and was willing to
talk openly about personal observations and experiences
pertaining to this issue.

FEMININE LEADERSHIP MODEL CONFIRMED

In the first week of the study, several of the highly successful women I contacted insisted that the differences I had
identified did not exist. Others, who acknowledged these
differences, refused to participate because of a fear of repri-
sal within their organizations. Then just as I was beginning
to become discouraged, I began locating women managers
who were interested in talking with me about the premise
and who had many opinions and experiences to share. Suddenly, the number of potential participants began to grow
as each woman I interviewed referred me to several others
with an interest in this topic.

The enthusiasm expressed by this group for the idea of
feminine leadership was enormous. It seemed I had tapped
into a source of energy and interest never explored before.

Most of these women were delighted to share their experiences as nontraditional managers and were eager to discuss the many differences they had observed in the generic management styles used by men and women. In addition, many were also able to identify benefits that they believed these differences offered individuals and organizations.

The response of the male managers to this idea was also interesting. While most had more difficulty articulating the impact of stylistic differences, they generally agreed that these did exist. Several men cited examples of differences they had observed in women colleagues and, generally, felt that these were of value to the organization. Only a small percentage of those I spoke with subscribed to the idea that women should behave like men, although they agreed that this was the prevailing sentiment within most organizations.

Three key findings resulted from these interviews. First, with some minor modifications, the two managerial models I had used to compare traditional masculine leadership with nontraditional feminine leadership held up. While everyone believed that many individual differences were unrelated to gender, there was general agreement regarding the idea of male-female differences in managerial style. Some managers were less aware of certain differences than others. However, there was support from a large number of men and women in every case.

Second, most of the men and women managers interviewed were in strong agreement that these two styles worked very effectively together. They described them as "complementary," "balanced," and "more responsive to changing business demands." Ideally, they believed that organizations which encouraged both styles would be most effective.

But despite a great deal of grass-roots support for using both styles, a third point of widespread agreement among both men and women was that organizations had not yet learned to recognize or encourage a feminine approach to managing. When pressed for examples, many were unable to come up with a single instance of this new leadership style receiving formal recognition and endorsement within a company. This finding was the most disconcerting and intriguing of all.

As an industrial society, we were facing an enormous productivity crisis. Throughout the 1970's and early 1980's, the quality of products and services produced by many of our nation's largest, most respected corporations was on a steady decline. At the same time, employee morale was slipping among both blue- and white-collar workers in many companies. Much of the blame for these serious declines was being directed at out-of-date management methods that were excessively numbers-oriented and impersonal. Yet, despite the apparent need for a change in leadership, it appeared that organizations had failed to recognize the vital role women managers could play in addressing these problems.

This underutilization of women's natural leadership skills seemed to be equally detrimental to the individual woman manager and to her organization. With nothing to be gained and much to be lost by functioning in this way, why were corporations unable or unwilling to change? What was preventing them from making the most of the talents and skills of their women leaders? Was it simply blatant sexism that kept them from recognizing the unique talents of women managers or were other, more subtle factors at work? It seemed that my search for answers was just beginning.

CORPORATE RESISTANCE TO FEMININE STYLE

Many pieces of the puzzle would need to be put in place before these answers became clear. The influx of women into managerial roles during the late 1960's and throughout the 1970's had created the untapped pool of feminine talent. Never before in the history of our society had so many women occupied visible leadership roles. Yet, this stronger feminine presence was having no ripple effect at all on the way businesses were being managed.

In the midst of this confusion, one fact remained clear. Within the management ranks of America's corporations, the leadership skills of literally tens of thousands of women who were not readily adapting to the traditional male leadership model were not being utilized fully. While these women were usually indistinguishable from other women, their natural approach to managing and leading was quite different, and their potential to improve organization effectiveness was enormous. But tapping this potential would first require an understanding of the forces operating within organizations to stifle and subvert feminine leadership.

Why had the mass entry of women into management done so little to affect the culture and operating style of organizations? The answer, I believe, has to do with a subtle but very powerful masculine bias that still permeates most companies. This bias transcends individuals and lingers as one of the fundamental assumptions that influence and shape the corporate culture.

A recent article in *Savvy* describes the results of a major study of women in banking, law, and architecture by psychologist Beth Milwid. The article discusses the barriers that many professional women encounter even after they have proved their competence to succeed at tough jobs. It states, "The testing period eventually passed. But the women then came face to face with more intransigent obstacles—the male-dominated company cultures. Men at the water cooler grew silent when a woman passed. Dinner conversations left her out. Decisions were being made in ways to which she had no access. The impenetrability of the old boy network was real. Although relationships with male peers were generally comfortable, those with older men, the men with real power, were not."[1]

Another recent article, in *Working Woman,* echoes the same theme, this time in the context of the high-powered investment banking industry. "But inherited prejudices die hard, and women's struggles are not over, especially in terms of advancement to the highest levels of business. . . . One woman who requested anonymity recalls her first couple of weeks on the job. . . . One of the firm's managing directors, a man, had gathered together the latest crop of trainees, half of them women, to meet the members of his department. 'He introduced all the men and completely neglected to introduce the women. He just didn't *see* them. I was so upset I didn't know what to do.' "[2]

Arlene Johnson is the vice president of corporate programs at Catalyst, a New York–based organization that works with individuals and corporations to develop career and family options. Discussing the effective utilization of women's talents, she remarked, "There are barriers to women's upward mobility. These barriers are very subtle and pervasive and have to do with false perceptions and mythologies. Raising awareness of these issues is the next step in the affirmative action process."

While Johnson is in favor of debunking outdated stereotypes about women's inability to be effective managers, she also believes that "stressing differences in the end creates adversarial relationships." Yet if the feminine leadership style is ever to gain recognition within corporations and contribute to growth and vitality, there appears to be no alternative but to acknowledge such differences directly. Only through the conscious efforts of managers to raise awareness of its benefits and to demonstrate the positive impact that this new, complementary approach to managing can have within organizations will this alternate style be accepted.

According to a Gallup survey reported by *The New York Times* in August 1982, "Sixty-eight percent of college-educated women . . . say their sex does not have equal job opportunities. . . . Moreover, when asked if a woman who has the same ability as a man has as good a chance to become the executive of a company, 71 percent of the women with a college education said that they did not."[3] From a very personal and pragmatic standpoint, women can no longer afford to ignore this issue if they hope to realize their full professional and earning potential.

The reluctance of most organizations to actively embrace feminine leadership has its origins in the history of the last two decades within our society. In order to better understand the bias against feminine leadership and the untapped potential of the feminine style itself, it is necessary to go back to the period of the late sixties and early seventies, when the initial mass entry of women into management occurred. The purpose of this foray into the past is not to criticize or to place blame but to understand the origins of the challenge currently before us.

Chapter Two

Masculinism in the Corporation

S cience fiction writer H. G. Wells once said, "We live in reference to past experience and not to future events, however inevitable." His wisdom is particularly relevant to understanding the position of women executives today, for their situation in contemporary organizations is still greatly influenced by the circumstances surrounding the initial large-scale entry of women into management in the late 1960's.

Through the early sixties, management was an exclusive male-dominated club—and most organizations would have been content to leave it that way. In this historical context, two key facts deserve special emphasis. First, our nation's economy was booming during the late 1960's, so the traditional male management style appeared to be continuing to work very well within industry. Second, Title VII of the 1964 Civil Rights Act made discrimination against women in education or employment illegal. Therefore, the mass movement of women into management at that time was largely the result of legal fiat. This single fact, that companies were forced to open their doors to women managers as a result of judicial mandate, has had lasting repercussions for women as a group both in terms of how corporations relate to them and how they themselves have had to behave within management in order to achieve any measure of success.

TITLE VII OF THE 1964 CIVIL RIGHTS ACT

As a result of Title VII, companies were no longer permitted to discriminate on the basis of sex. To add extra clout to this law, in 1967 the federal government issued Executive Order No. 11375, adding sex to other categories of discrimination prohibited by an earlier order that applied to government contractors. Wage discrimination and sex segregation were also addressed in the federal guidelines. What did this mean to organizations that did business with the federal government? In short, it meant that companies with contracts for more than $10,000 had to comply with this executive order or risk losing the government's business. Sex discrimination had now become an economic liability for many businesses. As a result, women would have to be moved into the mainstream of corporate life, even into management jobs.

Reading the handwriting on the wall was not difficult. Even those companies that did not do business with the government understood they had better begin to take women more seriously. By 1972, amendments to Title VII extended its provisions to all businesses with more than fourteen employees. The same standards of compliance applied to large and small employers alike. But while companies were now compelled to hire women into management, no law said they had to like it. Furthermore, most institutions had no interest in helping women make the transition into their new roles or in exploring the impact that their increased presence might begin to have on the organization culture. Instead, the prevailing sentiment was that women would simply have to adapt as best they could. An anecdote from the early days of women in the military academies serves to illustrate this point.

You may recall that the first women entered Annapolis, West Point, and the Air Force Academy as the result of a congressional ruling in 1975. Because of the strong male traditions characterizing these institutions, there was considerable public interest in tracking the progress of each woman cadet as she moved into the masculine world of the military. For many months, it seemed the newspapers were constantly carrying some story about the "young girls" who were training to become military officers.

Within each of the academies, great concern was expressed about how the presence of women might affect the norms, habits, and traditions of the institution. At one school, this question was raised at a meeting with the commandant. His reply was simple and to the point. "Nothing but the plumbing will change around here!" he exclaimed. Obviously, history has proved him wrong, but it is the resistance to change implied in his statement that is of interest here.

The story was much the same in the corporate world. To satisfy the government, organizations began to move women into managerial roles formerly reserved for men. And in order to assure the government that they were acting "affirmatively," elaborate mechanisms were set up in many organizations to track progress. It was the beginning of the affirmative action numbers game and organizations took it very seriously.

Within one large telecommunications company, for example, a unit was established to track affirmative action progress and monitor movement at all levels of the company. More than two hundred people were assigned full-time to aid in this statistical tracking and monitoring process. Unfortunately, far less attention was given to the formidable task of figuring out how to make the transition of women into management as smooth and painless as possible. As in the case of the military academies, the women were expected to adapt to the existing norms and standards of behavior.

WOMEN MUST ADAPT

From the late sixties on, adaptation has been a major requirement of women in nontraditional careers including management. In a sociological sense, women had invaded an alien culture when they entered the management ranks en masse. To prosper in this foreign environment, they had to understand and then act according to all its customs and accepted modes of behavior. The culture within a corporation is as real as the culture within any social group. The values of a corporate culture are shaped by those who control it, and these basic principles provide a common sense of direction for all employees. Values shape the basic belief system used to direct the activities of an organization, to set goals and determine appropriate standards of behavior.

The corporate culture that women managers encounter has been shaped entirely by men. Betty Friedan first described this male-centered culture and the ambiance it creates as masculinism. She used this term to depict the climate that women graduate students encountered at Harvard in the early 1980's.[1] It is also an apt descriptor of the culture with which women managers must learn to deal in the contemporary corporate world. While organizations do not exhibit all the qualities of masculinism to the same degree, its principal values are inherent in virtually every major U.S. company.

MASCULINISM

At the most basic level, the entire story of women in management—their successes, their failures, and their prospects for the future—can be understood within the context of masculinism. In order to understand this relationship more clearly, one must begin by taking a closer look at masculinism and its values, the corporate structures and climate it supports, and the types of behavior that it fosters.

At the heart of masculinism is the concept of competition. Within the world view of masculinism, all of business—and even life itself—is depicted in terms of an ongoing competitive struggle with clear-cut winners and losers. The primary, overriding goal is to win or triumph over your adversaries. In this respect, corporate masculinism resembles and was no doubt shaped by the values, goals, and even structure of the military. In her book *Games Mother Never Taught You,* author Betty Lehan Harragan discusses the similarities that exist between business and the military. She says, "If there's one place that most women have never been, and never hope to be, it's in the army. Therefore it may come as a shattering revelation to find out that collecting a regular salary from a business enterprise means that you are part and parcel of a classic military organization. Not some slapdash medieval legion where knights-errant occasionally jousted off to defend the honor of their lady fair, but a modern, mercenary, well-equipped, scientifically staffed military operation."[2]

The ethos of competitive sports is also alive and well within the corporate culture of masculinism. Sports analogies and metaphors pervade executive conversations. Expressions such as game plan, team player, end run, and scoring have become a permanent part of the business vernacular. In fact, the concept of business as a game is enjoying great popularity among many of the country's most successful executives.

In his book *The Gamesman,* psychologist Michael Maccoby describes the results of his study of executive behavior. He says, "The gamesman is the new man and, really, the leading character in this study. His main interest is in challenge, competitive activity where he can prove himself a winner. Impatient with others who are slower and more cautious, he likes to take risks and to motivate others to push themselves beyond their normal pace. He responds to work and life as a game."[3]

VALUES OF MASCULINISM

Since the culture of masculinism views business as a competitive struggle, it follows that certain values and patterns of behavior will be encouraged and reinforced—the values and behaviors judged to be consistent with the ultimate goal of victory.

First and foremost among these values is the need for tight control. The resultant behavior that supports this value is authoritarian management. Drawing heavily on the military model, the traditional organization is structured along rigid, hierarchical lines. The corporate pyramid is the metaphor used to describe the basic structure of most large organizations. At the bottom of this pyramid is the large mass of company employees; at the top, the company's chief executive officer. In between, on ever-shrinking, ascending tiers, are the various levels or ranks of corporate managers.

Successful movement up this pyramid or, for that matter, the ability to simply stay on it at all, requires absolute respect and deference to the individual on the level immediately above. Rank becomes the ultimate source of respect, although it is not always linked to ability or professional competence. Harragan describes this situation in another passage from her book: ". . . structurally speaking, your boss has life-and-death power over you. Your one-and-only immediate supervisor constitutes your sole connecting tie to the hierarchy. . . . There is no way you can leapfrog, bypass, overrule, ignore, challenge, disobey, or criticize your boss and not get penalized in the game."[4]

A second characteristic of masculinism is assertiveness or aggressive behavior. Just as absolute respect is required toward those in higher places in the organization, so assertive or domineering behavior is required toward those below. According to the traditional definition, a leader must direct and control the actions of those below him. It is expected that, as the boss, he will tell his subordinates what to do and that they, in turn, will carry out his instructions.

Likewise, competitive behavior is expected and reinforced in peer relationships within management. Since business is viewed as a competition with both internal and external competitors, peers must compete for a dwindling number of musical chairs at the next level of the pyramid. As one moves up, each promotion comes at the expense of fellow employees.

A third characteristic highly valued in masculine organizations is the ability to think analytically or strategically. In *The Gamesman,* Dr. Maccoby says this of the successful corporate executive: "He enjoys new ideas, new techniques, fresh approaches and shortcuts. His talk and his thinking are terse, dynamic, sometimes playful and come in quick flashes. His main goal in life is to be a winner, and talking about himself invariably leads to discussion of his tactics and strategy in the corporate contest."[5]

Within the value system of masculinism, control through careful organization and calculation is a critical virtue. In the past twenty years, the director of strategic planning has become a key staff position in most large organizations. Throughout many corporations and at all levels of management, the development of plans and strategies has now become one of the most time-consuming tasks.

In addition to these three qualities, the masculine corporate culture also places a high value on maintaining an objective, nonemotional attitude toward business. In a setting where the needs of individuals must often be subordinated and sometimes sacrificed to achieve the overall goals of the organization, emotional involvement with people is seen as unproductive. Instead of using employee satisfaction as a measure of managerial effectiveness, corporations often use financial results as the only leadership criterion.

MASCULINE LEADERSHIP MODEL

OPERATING STYLE:
Competitive

ORGANIZATIONAL STRUCTURE:
Hierarchy

BASIC OBJECTIVE:
Winning

PROBLEM-SOLVING STYLE:
Rational

KEY CHARACTERISTICS:
High Control
Strategic
Unemotional
Analytical

ALIEN CULTURE

The corporate world as it exists today is composed of values, traditions, structures, and behavioral norms linked to masculinism. Yet much of what masculinism promotes is by definition alien to the majority of women in our society. Neither nature nor social conditioning adequately prepares women for their first encounter with corporate masculinism. Dr. Harold Kellner, an organization consultant and clinical psychologist, devoted much of his career to studying the effects of masculinism on women managers. In describing the dilemma that the male corporate culture creates for women, he often used this analogy:

"Imagine yourself as a visitor to some remote part of the world where the language, the local customs and the day-to-day activities and communication patterns are altogether different from anything you have ever experienced before. From the moment you arrive, you feel somewhat awkward and out of place. People regard you with curiosity but remain distant. Your attempts to break the ice are all thwarted by your ignorance of the local customs. . . . As time goes by, you begin to feel more and more isolated. Since no one else shares your perceptions of what is happening, you start to doubt yourself. You lose confidence in your own judgment. After several months, you find yourself yearning for home. Nothing about this alien place seems to bring out the best in you. You're too busy trying to figure out the rules to relax or be yourself. What's more, no one even recognizes your frustration. People just seem to be impatient with you for taking so long to adjust to your new surroundings."

"HOW TO SUCCEED" IN THE MASCULINE CULTURE

During the past two decades, as we have already seen, most corporations and other institutions did little to help women adjust to the masculine culture. In fact, the prevailing sentiment within business was basically sink or swim. However, this did not stop other observers of the influx of women into management from offering them advice on "how to succeed." Throughout the 1970's there was an endless stream of books filled with suggestions, recommendations, warnings, and counsel written for women with an interest in career advancement. Although each new book laid claim to some unique strategy or insight, there was still a high degree of similarity among them regarding their basic assumptions about women. In essence, all of the advice was built around the assumption that women themselves would have to change if they wanted to move ahead.

With this idea as the cornerstone, women managers became the target of the most massive make-over in modern history. Those who wore dresses were advised by experts called wardrobe engineers to buy business suits. Those who were somewhat quiet and reflective during meetings were advised to enroll in assertiveness training classes. Since most women managers had never participated in team sports as little girls, it was obvious that they needed training in strategic thinking and sportsmanlike behavior to be truly effective. Then there was the issue of emotionality. What would happen to the professional image of these women if they were to let loose and cry at work? How could the men around them be expected to put up with tears and emotional scenes in the office? Something had to be done to solve this serious problem! Luckily, several experts on "how to manage your emotions at the office" were available to assist women with this sensitive and critical issue.

How did women react to all this unsolicited guidance? Very positively. Because they had a strong interest in career success, most took this advice very seriously. In fact, few women in management today did not consider the advice and counsel of a variety of "experts" on managerial success at some point in their careers. But despite a strong interest in this subject among most managerial women and even some men, none of the advice seems to have significantly enhanced the status of women managers in organizations. What's more, the need for accommodation expressed by most of the experts has been the single most important influence on the careers of women managers to date.

THE ACCOMMODATING ROLES

In business today, the concept of adaptation and accommodation by women has become so ingrained that the process can actually be broken down into identifiable stages. In the first stage, women are introduced to the masculine culture and encouraged to begin adapting to it. As time passes, and they succeed at "learning how to play the game," some women graduate to stage two and are granted conditional membership in the executive club. In time, a select few go on to the third stage and become isolated superstars, having learned to adapt to their environment by accommodating and not challenging the values of masculinism.

Although adaptation offers women managers the possibility of some measure of business success, it requires them to repress and essentially deny much of their natural identity and many of their most useful skills. Some are willing to pay this price; others are not.

During the past several years, the individual stages in this cycle of adaptation have been identified and analyzed by observers of the corporate scene. While not intended to be all-encompassing, the three stages described in this chapter represent the principal roles that have emerged for women managers in organizations during the last two decades. The impact of masculinism on women as a group becomes clearer as one examines each of these stages of gradual accommodation that women, as a group, are encouraged to move through during their careers. The three key stages of adaptation include:

Stage I: Fraternity Pledging

Stage II: Making the First String

Stage III: Splendid Isolationism

The case histories that follow depict the actual process of adaptation occurring during each stage. Although they have been written to protect the anonymity of the various women managers mentioned, they are based upon the experiences of real people. As such, they may not represent the actual experiences of every woman manager who has had to accommodate to masculinism, but they do describe many of the key issues with which most women must grapple as they climb the managerial ladder in corporations and continue to submerge their own identities.

Stage I: Fraternity Pledging

Rachel was determined to succeed. First she got an MBA, since people told her she couldn't go anywhere in a top organization without one. Then she got a totally new look including the "right" chalk-striped skirt suit and a briefcase from Mark Cross. Finally, after devouring every strategic book on corporate gamesmanship, power, assertiveness, etc., she got a job at one of the biggest consulting firms in Chicago.

She wasn't crazy about starting in the Research Department, since this meant she would have virtually no contact with the firm's clients. But everyone assured her it was a good place to learn the ropes. When her boss explained that some clients were uncomfortable around women, she was very understanding and agreed not to push too hard for greater exposure. She would let her boss decide when the time was right.

Meanwhile, Rachel continues to work on improving her "executive image." She has taken up golf, can talk football with the best trivia experts at the office, and has enrolled in a public speaking course at considerable personal expense to polish up her skills. Sometimes she still feels like a stranger when she's in a meeting with her male peers but understands that this is her problem. They just seem to do things differently and with more personal ease than she does. She thinks this is probably a signal that, as yet, she has failed to overcome her own fear of success.

She realizes that her way of doing things isn't "professional" enough. She has to stop being the nice guy with her subordinates and can't allow her emotions to take over. Most of all, she's got to continue working on her basic approach to dealing with her boss and her male colleagues. They seem to need things to be more concrete than she does. They also seem to avoid being direct about their own motivations and feelings on important issues. Maybe another strategy book can help her determine exactly how they do it!

Anxious to look the part of the successful executive, many women devour advice on "how to succeed" and willingly modify their appearance, their interests, and their behavior in an effort to fit the managerial mold. While such accommodation limits the negative impact that women managers may have on their peers in a new, untested environment, it

31

also restricts their ability to develop their natural instincts as feminine leaders. Instead of learning to trust their own feelings and use their perceptions to manage effectively, fraternity pledging causes women to gradually deny what they truly think and feel. Those who master the early lessons of pledging integrate many male characteristics into their style of management and begin to discard the natural qualities and skills that could be useful to them as feminine leaders. When they have proved to themselves and to others that this metamorphosis is complete, they are ready to move on to the next stage in the cycle of adaptation.

Stage II: Making the First String

In the Wall Street firm where she is an associate, Beth is considered to be a rising star. Her boss and her male colleagues describe her as sharp, logical, and aggressive. A few have even begun to talk about her as a potential firm partner.

In addition to her "remarkably competitive drive," she is also admired for her unemotional approach to problems and her ability to make men feel appreciated. The fact that some of the women in the firm refer to her as a real killer only reinforces her belief that she has finally succeeded in transforming herself into a woman with the right stuff to go all the way to the top.

Unlike the fraternity pledges who are still trying, Beth has succeeded in making the first cut and is now aiming for a slot on the executive varsity. To Beth, winning isn't everything; it has now become the only thing.

As for her earlier interest in staying connected to other women colleagues, Beth no longer feels a need for their support. She's managed to outdistance most of them and realizes that too much contact with other females could tarnish her image now. Besides, the only ones who interest her at this point are the few who still remain as potential competitors.

Beth fully understands her firm's situation. Because of the increasing number of women clients, there is mounting pressure to make a woman a partner and she is determined to be that woman. Since she understands that there is room for only *one* woman, Beth knows that it's critical for her to study the female competition and outmaneuver the others in order to win.

Although she is aware that there are several accomplished women in the firm, Beth never questions the assumption that there is room at the partner level for only one. Instead, she keeps her mind and her efforts focused on becoming that one woman and making the first string.

Until organizations view women as serious candidates for top management jobs and not just as tokens, every woman with an interest in advancement will be forced to confront the problem of how to compete fairly in a contest that is already rigged. Today, one popular method used by women to cope with this contradiction is adaptation. It involves taking on many of the aggressive behaviors that contribute to corporate masculinism and then killing off the female competition.

This strategy seems to be most strongly supported in companies where only a token commitment to equal opportunity exists. While the first stringer works to become more like men and to be *liked* by them, she also becomes a major obstacle to other women's achievement. By regarding other women as her only competition and embracing a masculine leadership style, the first stringer ignores the fact that many women possess the talent required to succeed. In addition, to demonstrate her loyalty to the values of masculinism, she may also feel obliged to cast the first stone when confronted with a woman executive who is working to develop her feminine leadership skills in lieu of accommodation.

Although many first stringers never realize their dream of becoming Number 1, some manage to knock out the competition and go all the way to the top. These women are sometimes referred to as queen bees because they tend to be protective of their special status. I think of them more as splendid isolationists, women who have felt obliged to ignore many issues related to the damaging effects of masculinism in order to earn their place in the sun.

Stage III: Splendid Isolationism

Margaret was the first woman in this Fortune 500 company to become a vice president. Eight years later, she is still the only woman at the top. Having lost contact with other women on her way up, she is now dependent on the men around her for support and counsel. Since many of them believe that Margaret was "damn lucky" to have gotten this far, they are universally unsympathetic to the problems and concerns she faces as the highly visible, lone woman at the top.

As the only woman officer, Margaret is frequently asked to deliver speeches to groups on the subject of women in management. She is also in demand as a board member for many other large organizations in need of a woman member. Although she is constantly encouraged by her company to play an active role in the business community, she still tries to stay as uninvolved as possible. She understands that all of this attention does not go over well with many of her peers and has found that, on occasion, they have been critical of even her most innocuous comments. As a result, Margaret refuses to give any informal interviews and speaks before audiences from a prepared text.

Realizing that she lacks a true support base at the office, Margaret has also learned to manage her situation alone.

Publicly, she denies that she has encountered any unique problems as the lone woman in senior management. Privately, when she is with her few trusted friends (none of whom work for the same company), she tells a very different story. But because she has had to endure the career tests and challenges alone, she is unsympathetic to the problems other women seem to be having within her company. In Margaret's view they have it easy.

Sometimes she feels burdened by the demands and requests other women make of her. She thinks the fuss that many are making about the need for role models and networks is ridiculous. She got to the top without any female role models and doesn't think other women need them.

As a splendid isolationist, Margaret has come to view her situation as the norm for any woman who wants to succeed. Although she knows it is different for many men who manage to easily combine career success with a satisfying family life and who are able to form closer bonds with each other, she doesn't dwell on these observations. Instead, she takes pride in knowing that she made it without any special help and believes that other women will have to do likewise.

There is little doubt that many women in senior management have gotten where they are today by playing accommodating roles and adapting to a masculine style of management. It is equally true that many of these women see nothing wrong with this process of adaptation. For just as fish spend their entire lives in water without ever knowing they are wet, so these splendid isolationists have spent their entire careers coping with masculinism without ever really knowing it existed. They learned to adapt and they succeeded. Why should it be any different for other women?

Until now, the desire for managerial success necessitated giving up one's feminine leadership style and adapting to masculine behavioral norms. Those women who were most able to do this had the greatest chance of succeeding as splendid isolationists. But while some women managers actually pass through each of these three stages during the course of their careers, others do not. Many become stuck in one of the earlier stages of accommodation. Others choose to abandon the cycle of adaptation and the corporate world altogether. To date, only a very small percentage of women who remain in large corporations have been able to develop and utilize their feminine leadership style in lieu of playing accommodating roles.

Today, twenty-one years after the passage of the Civil Rights Act, what has accommodating behavior achieved for women in business? On the surface, the statistics seem very impressive. According to a 1980 Census Bureau study, 30.5 percent of managers were women, compared with only 18.5 percent in 1970. What's more, in a number of fast-growing fields such as health care, journalism, and public administration, women managers had achieved, or were quickly approaching, majority positions.[6]

ROADBLOCKS TO TOP MANAGEMENT

But numbers such as these can be deceiving. For despite this incredible growth in the number of women professionals, top management still remains the exclusive domain of white men. Katharine Graham of the Washington Post Company continues to be the only woman chief executive officer within the Fortune 500.[7] Senior management today is still more than 95 percent male in major corporations across the United States. In addition, many analysts are predicting that the situation will remain essentially the same throughout the foreseeable future. As one *Fortune* writer observed recently, ". . . given that women have been on the ladder for ten years, . . . none currently seems to have a shot at the top rung. Executive recruiters, asked to identify women who might become presidents or chief executives of Fortune 500 companies, draw a blank. Even companies that have women in senior management privately concede that these women aren't going to occupy the chairman's office."[8]

In their struggle to move ahead in corporations, many women may have given up a lot more than they have received in return for adapting. If accommodation is what business expects of women, why hasn't this type of behavior reaped greater rewards for the many women who practice it? Why are most men at the top still reluctant to accept women as true colleagues?

In part, the answer may be related to what Dr. Natasha Josefowitz has described as "the clonal effect." In her book *Paths to Power,* she explains, "Just as individuals and families tend to replicate themselves, so do groups and organizations. The tendency is to replace lost members with people who have similar characteristics or to add people who would not change too much the dynamics of the usual communications patterns."[9]

Since the profile of the standard senior executive is still a white male, age fifty, with a wife who doesn't work, two children, and fairly traditional views on the roles that men and women should play in society, it's not surprising that more women aren't reaching the top. Consciously or unconsciously, business leaders are continuing to promote people with whom they are familiar and comfortable in working relationships.

THE FALLACY OF ADAPTATION

But "the clonal effect" isn't the only reason for women's failure to advance beyond the middle-management ranks.

The basic concept of women managers adapting to masculine norms contains its own Catch-22. When all is said and done, regardless of how adaptable some may be, women are still women. Even when they attempt to behave exactly like their male counterparts, they are still not perceived by others in the same light.

To capture the essence of this dilemma, a satiric comparison of businessmen and businesswomen became popular among executive women a few years ago and was widely circulated throughout many companies. Here is one version that made the rounds:

HOW TO TELL A BUSINESSMAN FROM A BUSINESSWOMAN

- A businessman is aggressive; a businesswoman is pushy.

- A businessman is good on details; she's picky.

- He loses his temper at times because he's so involved in his work; she's bitchy.

- He knows how to follow through; she doesn't know when to quit.

- He stands firm; she's hard.

- He is a man of the world; she's been around.

- He isn't afraid to say what he thinks; she's mouthy.

- He drinks martinis because of excessive job pressures; she's a lush.

- He exercises authority diligently; she's power mad.

- He's climbed the ladder of success; she's slept her way to the top.

- He's a stern taskmaster; she's hard to work for!

Today, the demands and inconsistencies being heaped upon women managers are creating a rising tide of disillusionment and frustration. Many are beginning to see their careers plateauing long before they had expected this to happen. In a recent survey, the majority of middle-management women interviewed stated that they believed they had already reached the highest level they would ever achieve within their organizations. In contrast, the majority of their male peers felt their prospects for further promotion were still excellent.[10]

Frustrated by what they see as the lack of opportunity within organizations and unwilling to make required accommodations in their natural leadership style, many of the best and the brightest women managers are opting to leave the corporate world altogether and strike out on their own as entrepreneurs. A 1982 article on women business owners reported, "In the last decade, while all eyes watched the explosion in the number of women who went to work outside the home—up 31 percent between 1972 and 1979—we overlooked this even bigger explosion: The number of women who decided to work for themselves rose by 43 percent. And self-employed women were increasing their ranks five times faster than self-employed men."[11]

Even if all were well in corporate America today, top management should be seriously concerned about this brain drain among some of its most talented middle managers. But anyone who has lived through the past few years knows that things are far from well in the American economy. Business has just emerged from a productivity and morale crisis unparalleled since the time of the Great Depression. Although the economic picture has begun to improve, there are still massive problems to be addressed, as evidenced by this country's ever-expanding, international trade deficit.

NEED FOR A NEW LEADERSHIP STYLE

If American business is to pass through this period successfully, new approaches and solutions will be required. Many of the country's leading companies have begun to recognize this fact and to take some of the steps necessary to address their problems. The crisis in corporate America is finally being recognized as real, but there is still a long way to go.

If it is encouraged and developed, feminine leadership can play a major role in the revitalization of American corporations. Yet, for the most part, corporate America has yet to embrace this nontraditional style, favoring instead a traditional, homogenized approach to managing and leading. But this approach seems to be less effective in the face of today's productivity and morale crisis. What's more, many corporate analysts now believe that these management methods, which worked so well in the past, are partially responsible for the serious problems business faces today.

Not only can't all those maladaptive women afford to go home again, organizations cannot afford to lose them. For within this emerging group of feminine leaders, business can find many of the managerial talents and skills desperately needed to resolve the current corporate crisis. All that is required is for organizations to take a closer look. But instead, while more than 30 percent of the nation's management resources remain severely underutilized, the crisis in American corporations continues.

Chapter Three
The Crisis in the Corporation

Something happened to American industry in the 1970's. Suddenly, the prices of American-made goods seemed to go up, while the quality of these same products went down. At the same time, the workmanship and value of many foreign-made products were improving rapidly. For the first time since the Industrial Revolution, the United States appeared to be losing its advantage to foreign competitors in many key industries.

And that wasn't the only problem. Without warning, the American work force seemed to be struck by a debilitating malaise. Morale in many large companies dropped and productivity fell off precipitously. From 1965 through 1973 productivity in the United States grew at an annual rate of 2.4 percent. From 1973 to 1978 it slowed to only 1.1 percent, and in 1979 productivity actually began to decline.[1]

For the first time in memory, the leadership position of American industry was being seriously threatened both at home and abroad. To the surprise of most Americans, the country seemed to be losing its competitive edge, something that had always seemed to be an inherent part of the national character. Business sputtered as the crisis in the corporation began to unfold.

After a decade of exhaustive analysis of this corporate crisis, two factors consistently emerge as the principal causes: (1) the changing nature of the world economy and (2) the changing nature of the American worker.

THE CHANGING WORLD ECONOMY

For most of this century, America prospered by concentrating on capital-intensive, high-volume industries that were based on the principles of standardized production. But as a result of deregulation and the tremendous growth in international trade, our performance began to fall off in the very industries in which we formerly excelled.

As symbolized by the assembly line, standardized production is based on the concept of breaking jobs down into their simplest functions in order to maximize efficiency and control. The compartmentalized jobs that abound within standardized production systems do not require the services of highly trained workers. Rather, semiskilled or even unskilled laborers can fill these job slots effectively. In a world economy, standardized production can be accomplished more efficiently in developing nations where workers with few skills are willing to work for substantially lower wages. This is precisely what happened in the expanding international market of the 1970's.

Harvard economist Robert Reich discusses this in his article "The Next American Frontier": "America's declining share of the world market has been particularly dramatic in capital-intensive, high-volume industries. Since 1963,

America's share of the world market has declined in a number of important areas: automobiles, by almost one-third; industrial machinery, by 33 percent; agricultural machinery, by 40 percent; telecommunications machinery, by 50 percent; metal-working machinery, by 55 percent. The globe is fast becoming a single marketplace. Goods are being made wherever they can be made the cheapest, regardless of national boundaries. And the most efficient places for much mass production are coming to be Third World countries."[2]

CHANGING WORKER ATTITUDES

The problems presented by cheap, international competition were compounded in the 1970's by radical changes in worker attitudes here at home. These workers, better educated than any of their predecessors, were also products of the post-Vietnam, post-Watergate, mass media era. In their minds, institutions of all types—business, government, and even religious—had lost most of their authority.

From this period to the present, survey after survey has shown this new-breed worker to have a substantially different attitude about work than his forebears. In "New Rules in American Life: Searching for Self-Fulfillment in a World Turned Upside Down," sociologist Daniel Yankelovich discusses these changes. He observes, "Not all workers are engaged in the search for self-fulfillment, but those who are retaliate for the lack of incentives by holding back their commitment, if not their labor. They resent sharp class distinctions between employees and employers. They do not automatically accept the authority of the boss. They want to participate in decisions that affect their work. They prefer variety to routine, informality to formalism. They want their work to be interesting as well as pay well."[3]

During the seventies, many of these new-breed workers

43

came to resent the authoritarian style of business management. Business leaders were perceived as wanting to run the entire show themselves with no input from their employees. In addition, these leaders were seen as striving to maximize their own short-term earnings with little regard for the welfare of the workers or the long-term health of their own organizations. Consequently, workers began to hold back in their efforts. In a recent survey, "only 23 percent of American workers say they are performing to full capacity, and 44 percent say they do not put extensive effort into their work beyond what is required."[4]

CONFIDENCE IN BUSINESS DECLINES

As the problems brought on by these two trends intensified, confidence in the executives running America's major companies dropped to the lowest levels on record. The trust that is essential for the health and vitality of all organizations suffered serious erosion. More and more, America's management leaders came to be viewed as an elite group, cut off from the majority of the work force and concerned almost exclusively with the advancement of their own careers and personal fortunes.

A recent article in *The New York Times* cites the results of an annual Lou Harris poll that measures our confidence in corporate executives. It states, "Only 18 percent of those surveyed last year placed 'great confidence' in American executives—down from 29 percent in 1973 and 55 percent in the mid-1960's." The article also refers to another poll from the Opinion Research Corporation that found "only 29 percent of Americans in 1983 rated corporate executives 'excellent or good' in ethical practices. That was down from 33 percent in 1981 and 36 percent in 1975."[5]

Distressingly, this disillusionment with American management is not restricted to just hourly workers or to the public at large. A rift has also begun to appear in the ranks of management itself. As a group, middle managers are also reporting a growing sense of alienation from their leaders at the top. A 1983 survey conducted by the American Management Association revealed a startling lack of confidence among this vital group in the people who were running their own corporations.

The AMA study reported that only 18 percent of the middle managers questioned had full confidence in their top management's ability to lead their organizations in the decade ahead. In their summary of findings, the survey's authors commented, "The unexpectedly low assessment middle managers give to the leadership abilities of their corporate heads signals a lack of faith and a pervasive disaffection that can mean only that, among middle managers— or at least among a significant segment—morale is low."[6]

How to address and solve the problems of declining worker morale and productivity and the growing pressure from international competition has become the central challenge of American business today. By now, most experts agree that there are no quick-fix solutions. Among those who have studied the current reality, there is the growing recognition that solutions to these difficult problems will require deep, fundamental changes in the nature and structure of U.S. corporations as well as in the attitudes and style of the managers who run them.

CHANGES REQUIRED IN U.S. INDUSTRY

As the production of simple, mass-produced goods shifts more and more to Third World countries with tremendous reservoirs of cheap labor, U.S. corporations must shift to more sophisticated industries that rely on the knowledge and skills of its better-educated work force. It is no accident that the businesses flourishing in the United States today are such knowledge industries as computer technology, electronics, pharmaceuticals, and telecommunications. In these areas, our nation holds, and should continue to hold, a tremendous competitive edge.

This does not mean that the United States should abandon such basic industries as automobiles, steel, or chemicals. But it does mean that the focus within these industries must change to the production of ever more sophisticated products. And undeniably, it also means that the overwhelming prominence that these industries once enjoyed in the American economy will continue to diminish.

But shifting America's industrial focus, although a tremendous undertaking, is not enough. As the experience of the last decade has already shown, other advanced nations, most notably Japan, are more than capable of competing in these same new industrial arenas. To compete effectively, basic changes are called for in the very structure of U.S. corporations and the manner in which they are run. These changes arise naturally from the character of the new, more sophisticated goods being produced.

CHANGES REQUIRED IN ORGANIZATION STRUCTURE

What new organizational structures are the prerequisites for renewed growth? Harvard economist Robert Reich provides a succinct and descriptive definition. In his view these new structures are more "flexible systems." According to Reich, flexible systems of production are called for when the ability to repeatedly solve new problems is more important than routinizing the solutions to old ones. Such systems are designed to maximize the sophisticated skills and knowledge of employees. Reich explains, "The tasks involved in flexible-system production are necessarily complex, since any work that can be rendered simple and routine is more efficiently done by low-wage labor overseas. Thus, no set of 'standard operating procedures' locks in routines or compartmentalizes job responsibilities."

He continues, "Skill-intensive processes cannot be programmed according to a fixed set of rules covering all possible contingencies. The work requires high-level skills precisely because the problems and opportunities cannot be anticipated. Producers of specialized semiconductor chips or multipurpose robots, for example, must be able to respond quickly to emerging potential markets. Delicate machines break down in complex ways. Technologies change in directions that cannot be foreseen. The more frequently the products or processes are altered or adapted, the harder it is to translate them into reliable routines. Again, if problems and opportunities could be anticipated and covered by preset rules and instructions, production could be moved abroad."[7]

In her book *The Change Masters: Innovation for Productivity in the American Corporation,* Dr. Rosabeth Moss Kanter also uses the term "flexible" to describe the character of organizations best equipped to succeed in today's competitive environment. She states, "The organizations now emerging as successful will be, above all, flexible; they will need to be able to bring particular resources together quickly, on the basis of short-term recognition of new requirements and the necessary capacities to deal with them. They will be organizations with more 'surface' exposed to the environment and with a whole host of sensing mechanisms for recognizing emerging changes and their implications. In such an organization, more people with greater skills than ever before will link the organization to its environment."[8]

The management structures required within flexible production companies are dramatically different from those found in traditional, standardized production companies. As the term "flexible" implies, this new kind of structure is designed to maximize adaptability or responsiveness to evolving technology and quickly changing competitive environments. Unlike the rigid, vertical management hierarchies of traditional organizations that compartmentalize job functions within separate departments, the management structure of flexible production companies tends to be much flatter or horizontal. These new structures foster a breakdown of distinctions between managers from different job areas and even tend to blur the lines between managers and the workers themselves. The basic management unit of flexible production companies is the team.

TEAM UNITS AND PARTICIPATIVE MANAGEMENT

The team unit has evolved because the problems and opportunities confronting companies today have simply become too complex and multifaceted to be dealt with successfully by a single chief executive or small group of top executives, no matter how brilliant. The team structure promotes free and open communications, which furthers the sharing of information essential to the solution of complicated problems across traditional departmental lines. In traditional hierarchical systems, the flow of information is restricted from top management down through the separate branches of the organization. The structure itself minimizes the possibility of communication across separate departments.

The team structure also works to downplay the awareness of rank among the managers involved. Good ideas and solutions to problems can come from any team member, regardless of status or level. This kind of team management has come to be known as participative management. Although pioneered in the United States, participative management is most strongly associated with Japan, because it is there that the team method of problem-solving has been most success-fully integrated into the permanent structure of many or-ganizations.

In his book *Theory Z: How American Business Can Meet the Japanese Challenge,* Dr. William Ouchi describes the process of participative management: "Typically, a small group of not more than eight or ten people will gather around a table, discuss the problem and suggest alternative solutions. . . . The group can be said to have achieved a consensus when it finally agrees upon a single alternative and each member of the group can honestly say to each other member three things: (1) I believe that you understand my point of view; (2) I believe that I understand your point of view; (3) whether or not I prefer this decision, I will support it, be-cause it was arrived at in an open and fair manner."[9]

In the opinion of many organizational analysts, participa-tive management provides the best solutions to complex problems because it maximizes the amount of knowledge and insight that can be brought to any situation. As the old saying goes, "None of us is smarter than all of us." This management style also promotes the fastest turnaround time because all of the key managers who will be involved in the implementation of decisions have actually had a role in making them. Finally, it helps ensure that important deci-sions will have the full commitment of key personnel, sim-ply because these same people have been an integral part of the management planning process. In this regard, the man-agement team approach goes a long way toward meeting the important needs of new-breed workers for greater involve-ment and a sense of personal accomplishment.

PARTICIPATIVE MANAGEMENT
SUCCESS STORIES

In the United States today, participative management through interdepartmental teams is more than an experimental concept. This new kind of management structure is being used with considerable effectiveness in a wide variety of American companies. An extensive list of success stories has already been compiled spanning both traditional and new high-technology industries.

One of the first major U.S. companies to implement the participative approach to management was Hewlett-Packard. As far back as the 1960's, this company began to utilize the team concept in planning and problem-solving. Today most of the company's fifty product divisions, each with 500 to 2,000 people, rely heavily on the team approach in managing. In fact, the team concept has become such a permanent part of the organization culture that it is explicitly described in the corporation's objectives. The statement reads, "Hewlett-Packard should not have a tight, military-type organization, but rather give people the freedom to work towards overall objectives in ways they determine best for their own areas of responsibility." Over the years, with the aid of the team approach, Hewlett-Packard has put together a tremendous record of success and has been repeatedly cited as one of America's best-run companies.

The Xerox Corporation is another sophisticated, high-technology company where participative problem-solving teams have been used with great success. According to Dr. Harold Tragash, director of organizational effectiveness and research, the concept of problem-solving teams was introduced broadly throughout the corporation in 1979. Since that time, the company has been extremely satisfied with the outcome of these efforts.

Xerox evaluates the success of its participative program on three different dimensions:

(1) hard results or the actual work improvements and cost savings generated;

(2) soft results that include such things as declines in employee absenteeism and tardiness, as well as improved job satisfaction;

(3) process satisfaction or the extent to which the process is positively embraced and institutionalized within the company.

On all three of these dimensions, the program has been rated a success.

Dr. Tragash recently conducted a spot check on ninety projects undertaken by participative groups throughout the organization. In this check he discovered that 50 percent of the improvements had to do with enhanced productivity, 25 percent with better safety or work practices, and 25 percent with quality control. Impressively, the direct cost savings from these programs alone were substantial. Tragash stated, "The impact on the bottom line from just these few projects was over $11 million."

But the success of participative management hasn't been restricted to high-tech companies like Xerox and Hewlett-Packard that manufacture sophisticated computers and electronic equipment. The team approach to managing has also been applied successfully in another much different industry—retailing. Retailing giant J. C. Penney began to establish problem-solving management teams in the 1970's.

In her book *The Change Masters,* Dr. Kanter talks about the success of the program there: "In 1981, for example, a terrible year for retailing, J. C. Penney stood out for its superior financial performance (an earnings rise of 44 percent on a mere 4.5 percent increase in sales). Success was attributed by top executives to 'a new management style involving teamwork' and 'creating developmental opportunities by helping people understand what happens at different levels of the organization' . . ."[10]

Even General Motors, for years the classic example of a successful standardized production company, has become an active innovator of participative management techniques in recent years. One of the earliest and most successful examples of how effective teamwork could improve quality occurred in the corporation's Inland Division, which produces such equipment as steering wheels and padded dashboards. Since the early seventies, when Inland's senior management began to de-emphasize vertical management and establish management teams, the division has consistently outperformed the corporation as a whole. In describing the product-team concept that has worked so successfully at Inland, the general manager who instituted this major structural change said, "In setting up these teams, we took it as an article of faith that intelligent people, with proper data and good analysis, will make good decisions. . . . The product-team concept strengthens management's ability to provide experience for each employee under such quality of work life dimensions as developing confidence in management, a sense of ownership, and employee commitment; building better relationships between employees and their supervisors, and among the work groups; and finally demonstrating respect for the individual and his opinions. We want each employee to know that he can influence decisions—but that he then also must be willing to share responsibility for performance."

Today, more than a decade after the product-team approach was pioneered at Inland, it continues to generate excellent quality and financial results. Along with many other major companies, GM has also carried the concept of participative management beyond middle management to first-line supervision and the assembly line workers. In most instances, the team units are known as quality circles. A typical circle is composed of up to a dozen workers and one supervisor who meet weekly to discuss ways of improving quality, raising output, and working more effectively together.

According to the International Association of Quality Circles, its 1984 membership included more than 2,000 American companies. Examples of savings and productivity improvements generated through these efforts are widespread. One typical success story, at Motorola, Inc., was reported in an article in *The Journal of Commerce.* Due largely to employee involvement efforts, the "cost of labor for one semi-conductor device fell to $14.40 a thousand in May, 1981 from $30.20 in 1976. . . . On another semi-conductor device, its labor cost fell to $2.43 a thousand from $2.80, and on still another it fell to $1.30 a thousand from $1.44."[11]

TEAM MANAGEMENT WITHIN SERVICE INDUSTRIES

Thus far, this discussion has centered on the need for American industry to shift to the production of more sophisticated goods, and on the increasing importance of a different, team-oriented management style to deal effectively with complex change in manufacturing organizations. What has yet to be addressed is the need for a similar shift in the style of management within the other vital sector of the American economy—the service sector. According to Labor Department statistics, more than half the labor force is currently employed in the service sector.[12] Included in these numbers are some of the country's most intelligent and talented professionals in occupations such as accounting, advertising, banking, financial services, insurance, and law.

Today, our service industries are heavily reliant on knowledge workers whose output is not hard goods or products but, instead, specialized forms of information. In these industries, which are so vital to the overall strength of our economy, traditional structures of hierarchical management seem to be extremely outmoded. Because they are heavily populated by information specialists—many of whom make up the new breed of knowledge workers—the team approach is often the most appropriate model for problem-solving and decision-making.

As we pass the middle of the decade, there is much encouraging evidence that America is responding successfully to the crisis in its corporations by altering the nature of its industrial output and by implementing corresponding changes in its management systems. However, the mere existence of management teams and quality circles within organizations is no guarantee that these relatively new systems will prosper and become permanent parts of the corporate structure. Even within organizations that have endorsed this approach, there is still much about the corporate culture which works against these new flexible structures. For participative management to succeed, there must be some fundamental changes in management attitudes and in the traditional definitions of what it means to be a leader.

NEW CONCEPT OF LEADERSHIP REQUIRED

Psychologist Michael Maccoby talked about these changes in a lecture he delivered called "Management and Leadership." In it he explained, "The most advanced corporations are the ones that recognize that they must manage people in a new way. In the past the definition of management has been controlling people and resources. Management means control and control systems. My most radical thesis is that the age of management is over. The most advanced corporations no longer need managers. . . . But we need leaders who help develop teams in which others share the functions of leadership."[13]

In his book *Leadership,* James MacGregor Burns labels this new management style "transforming leadership." He states: "The transforming leader taps the needs and raises the aspirations and helps shape the values—and hence mobilizes the potential of followers."[14] Instead of giving orders or directly controlling activities, these leaders set directions and let their followers carry them out in their own ways.

The characteristics of this new type of leader and the skills that are required to accomplish the task are substantially different from those of the traditional authoritarian prototype. Such new leaders must have a more egalitarian philosophy about the people they manage. Their skills must consist primarily of facilitating skills that bring out the best thinking within work groups, help to integrate different points of view, and encourage consensus problem-solving. Because these leaders rely less on the authority conferred by their hierarchical position, they must also build the trust and commitment of employees more through personal charisma and professional competence.

In his article "The Leader," Dr. Michael Maccoby comments, once again, on the need for a fundamental change in management. He refers to this "facilitative" approach when he says, "The best of all leaders is the one who helps people so that eventually, they don't need him. . . . When he is finished with his work, the people say, 'It happened naturally.' "[15]

Other researchers, with an interest in changing leadership needs, have also studied organizations and identified how the style of management used in the past may differ from the one required to successfully manage in the future. In a paper called "What Kind of Leaders Do We Need?" researchers Lynn Rosener and Peter Schwartz describe the differences they found between the more traditional Alpha style and the emerging Beta style of leadership this way: "The dominant Alpha style is based on analytical, rational, quantitative thinking. It relies on hierarchical relationships of authority. It tends to look for deterministic, engineered solutions to specific problems.

"The Beta leadership style is based on synthesizing, intuitive, qualitative thinking. It relies on adaptive relationships for support. It tends to look for integrated solutions to systemic problems."[16] While Rosener and Schwartz believe that the Alpha style remains appropriate in certain types of companies and situations and do not think this style will disappear in the future, they also believe that the Beta style of management can play a pivotal role in solving the types of productivity problems currently confronting American business.

THE ROLE OF FEMININE LEADERS

In addition, these authors also believe that the Beta style comes much more naturally to women managers than to most men. Consequently, in their view, women can make an invaluable contribution to resolving the present crisis in the corporation. In discussing this point they state, "The infusion of this style [Beta] into more traditional approaches represents the opportunity in the crisis—and women can

56

play an instrumental part in capitalizing on this opportunity.

"Although it is important to note that neither style is exhibited exclusively by one sex or the other, sex role expectations in Western culture have been found to polarize these behavior patterns between men and women in our society. Traditionally, most men act more in accordance with Alpha styles, and most women behave more in accordance with Beta styles."[17]

And so, as the evidence continues to accumulate in support of the need for fundamental changes in the nature and structure of American industry, new solutions have begun to emerge. But for these solutions to have their maximum impact, the senior managers who are currently running American businesses must demonstrate their commitment to and support for these new approaches and, in many cases, must alter their traditional management style. In addition, they must begin to accept the role that women managers can play in this important transition and encourage the different leadership style that women, as a group, bring to the workplace. Can America's top management embrace the changes required to turn the declines and failures of the recent past into tomorrow's successes? Although the answer is still unclear, one fact is already certain. Their ability or inability to fully accept these changing realities will have an even greater impact on our economy in the next decade than it has at any time in the past and will set the course for our long-term future as an industrial power as well. It is a challenge that will require vision, courage, humility, and, ultimately, the skills of both traditional managers and feminine leadership to resolve.

Chapter Four
The Case for Feminine Leadership

T hroughout American industry, there is more evidence than ever before of the need for change. In the midst of this mounting evidence, many analysts are pointing to the traditional leadership style that is used in the vast majority of American companies as a major obstacle to growth and improvement.

In the past most business leaders viewed participative management as unrealistic. Some even regarded it as a euphemism for abdication of leadership responsibility. But today there is growing support in many organizations for a more people-oriented approach. Commenting on this changing corporate ethic in *Megatrends,* John Naisbitt states emphatically, "The common law that governs employers and employees is still based on the master-servant relationship. . . . But it seems that change is on the way."[1] "Whether or not we agree with the notion or abide by it, participatory democracy has seeped into the core of our value system.

. . . All of the present impetus toward making corporations more open and more accountable . . . and the trend toward greater employee rights and worker participation originate in the new ethic of participatory democracy."[2]

Maybe the idea of participative management is nothing more than old wine in new bottles. Behavioral scientists have been touting it for more than thirty years. But until recently, few executives would listen and still fewer were willing to try it out. Now the situation has begun to change. It seems that changing values among new-breed employees and economic necessity have finally convinced many managers to take the idea seriously.

But participative management doesn't just automatically occur once executives decide to support the idea. As William Ouchi points out in *Theory Z: How American Business Can Meet the Japanese Challenge*, companies must first be willing to re-think their basic management philosophy and then begin rewarding managers for using a more participative style. According to Dr. Ouchi, one critical element of that style is interpersonal skill, a talent he believes is highly prized in successful Japanese companies but undervalued in most American businesses. It is also one he thinks can go a long way toward helping U.S. industry solve many productivity and morale problems.

As we have seen, the present call for a change in management style isn't just the result of difficult lessons learned from the Japanese in recent years. It is also based upon the successes of the few U.S. companies that have tried it. In their search for the best in American business, Tom Peters and Bob Waterman discovered that a genuine people orientation in managing is one of the defining characteristics of the "excellent companies" they visited.

Throughout their book *In Search of Excellence*, the authors cite many instances where participative management, increased employee involvement, and positive reinforcement have paid off in greater profitability for American companies. In addition, they go on to sing the praises of a more intuitive approach to managing—one that relies on gut instinct, flexibility, and the generating of excitement rather than on strict adherence to rational, analytical processes.

In the authors' opinion, American managers would do well to rely more on their own instincts in decision-making and not solely on rational data. They state, "The exclusively analytic approach run wild leads to an abstract, heartless philosophy. . . . The rationalist approach takes the living element out of situations that should, above all, be alive."[3]

So it would seem, from examining the evidence, that the art of managing is finally beginning to catch up in importance to the science. Today, even the basic definition of effective leadership is being reexamined in many companies as more and more executives begin to recognize that poor employee morale and declining productivity are largely problems of their own creation.

As one manager in a high-technology plant put it, "We have met the enemy and they are us . . . right down to the military analogies we use to describe almost everything that happens in our organizations. It's time we found a new metaphor for organization life. The military parallels of the past just don't apply anymore. The paramilitary leadership style that once worked so well simply doesn't cut it today."

Ironically, none of the writers and analysts who are talking about the need for change have made the connection between what they say will be required for corporate survival and the natural skills of women managers. Yet, in some respects, it seems that women managers may be better prepared to cope with the challenges of the future than many traditional male leaders who succeeded in the past.

For many of the characteristics being touted as critical for future success—concern for people, interpersonal skills, intuitive management, and creative problem-solving—are qualities that women as a group are encouraged to develop and rely on throughout their lives. As such, it seems the skills that women were encouraged to leave behind when they entered the world of management are finally being recognized as critical to their companies' long-term health and viability.

Despite the get-tough advice being offered to working women and the emphasis placed on rational decision-making models and masculine leadership styles in business schools today, there is growing recognition throughout industry of the need for more people-oriented skills—the same skills that most women are taught to value and utilize from the time they are little girls. These skills constitute a nontraditional, yet highly effective approach to managing, which I call feminine leadership.

FEMININE LEADERSHIP DEFINED

Unlike the traditional masculine style favored more by men, feminine leadership is a style of managing that utilizes the full range of women's natural talents and abilities as never before. It is an approach to leading that is linked to gender differences, early socialization, and the unique set of life experiences from early childhood on, which shape women's values, interests, and behavior as adults.

At its core, the feminine leadership style differs most dramatically from the traditional style of management in its reliance on emotional as well as rational data. Feminine leaders see the world through two different lenses concurrently and, as a result, respond to situations on both the thinking and the feeling levels.

By being in tune with the emotional cues and undercurrents that are a part of all human interaction, feminine leaders have additional data to consider when making decisions and are often more inclined to consider their own feelings and the feelings of others when seeking solutions to complex problems. As a result, they are likely to function somewhat differently from their more traditional counterparts in their roles as problem-solvers, decision-makers, and managers of relationships.

In short, feminine leaders are apt to be more concerned with maintaining close personal relationships with others. They are more likely to consider feelings as well as the basic facts in decision-making—to strive for solutions in which everyone is a winner and to avoid situations where someone must lose. They are also more inclined to subordinate short-term, personal advancement to improve the long-term health of the organization that they and their associates mutually depend upon.

Naturally, these qualities aren't equally pronounced in all women managers, nor are they totally absent in all male managers. However, a growing body of evidence suggests that, as a group, women compared to most men do indeed have a different natural style of management and are likely to function somewhat differently, yet effectively, in leadership roles.

As compared to the traditional approach to managing described in Chapter 2, the feminine leadership style is composed of many qualities and characteristics that are different from those used more by men. Yet, taken together, these qualities represent a leadership style that seems to work extremely well for many women—better, in fact, than the more traditional approach. Here is an outline of some of the key characteristics of this emerging style:

FEMININE LEADERSHIP MODEL

OPERATING STYLE:
Cooperative

ORGANIZATIONAL STRUCTURE:
Team

BASIC OBJECTIVE:
Quality Output

PROBLEM-SOLVING STYLE:
Intuitive/Rational

KEY CHARACTERISTICS:
Lower Control
Empathic
Collaborative
High Performance Standards

ORIGINS IN BIOLOGY

The origins of these differences are rooted in the basic facts of biology and physiology as well as in the fundamentally different ways in which boys and girls are raised and socialized within our culture. Not surprisingly, the precise nature of these differences and how they affect the aptitudes, attitudes, behavior, and even health of men and women is a subject of considerable interest to scientists and social researchers.

It has long been known that boys and girls display significant differences in basic aptitudes. In general, girls tend to be more proficient in verbal skills, while boys excel more in mathematics and visual-spatial abilities. In their book *The Psychology of Sex Differences,* researchers Carol Jacklin and Eleanor Maccoby describe these differences: "Tests of general intelligence do not show sex differences. . . . In subtests of special abilities, however, sex differences do emerge. In general, girls excel at verbal tasks and boys at mathematical and visual-spatial ones."[4]

Research psychologist Diane McGuinness is a colleague of Jacklin and Maccoby at Stanford University. In a recent interview in the book *Sex and the Brain,* she discusses differences in aptitudes between the sexes and the fact that many of these manifest themselves so early that they appear to be inborn. She says, "Some of these differences appear extremely early in life. And others are more obvious after puberty. But the fascinating thing is that they seem to be independent of culture—as true in Ghana, Scotland and New Zealand as they are in America. . . . Males are good at tasks that require visual-spatial skills, and females are good at tasks that require language ability. Males are better at maps, mazes and math; at rotating objects in their minds and locating three-dimensional objects in two-dimensional representations. . . . Females are much better at almost all skills that involve words: fluency, for example, verbal reasoning, written prose and reading. . . . Put in general terms, women are communicators and men are takers of action."[5]

In recent years, a number of scientists have speculated that differences in aptitude between the sexes may be due to basic differences in the structure of the male and female brain. These differences, they hypothesize, are the result of the different pressures that men and women have been subjected to over millions of years of evolutionary history. According to their theory, men in primitive societies were the hunters. To hunt successfully, nature selected males for such physical skills as eye acuity, gross motor control, and the ability to calculate distance and direction. Females, on the other hand, were selected for other qualities. As child-bear-ers and -rearers, it was necessary for them to develop finer language ability and emotional sensitivity.

From a commonsense standpoint, this theory may have validity. However, at the moment, there is inadequate empirical evidence to fully support this point of view. But while there may be some who would argue against the existence of brain differences between the sexes, none would dispute the dramatic impact of sex hormones on the everyday behavior of men and women. Dr. Estelle Ramey, professor of physiology and biophysics at Georgetown University, is a scientist with a strong interest in this subject. Much of her research has focused on hormonal differences between the sexes and their relationship to stress responses in adults.

According to her findings, women often have greater tolerance for stress because of their hormonal makeup. While Dr. Ramey holds that many elements of the male response to stress were extremely valuable in more primitive societies, she believes that they are less useful today. For example, a prompt clotting factor could have saved the life of an injured warrior or hunter in a primitive culture but can contribute to the risk of heart attack in modern man.

As she states, "In general, females have the advantage of added hormonal protection in managing life stress. Not only does this make them less likely to suffer from stress-related illness, it also means they are less apt to display aggressive behavior when placed in a threatening situation. Certainly, this suggests that women in business would also be likely to react differently to work-related stress than do many men."

ROLE OF SOCIALIZATION

But behavioral differences between the sexes aren't only a function of biology. Differences in socialization also play an important part in shaping our values, interests, and behavior during childhood and beyond. From the moment an infant is covered with the traditional blue or pink nursery blanket, adults begin to respond to the child based upon their own expectations of how little boys and girls are supposed to behave. Throughout the early years of life, parents and teachers continue to reinforce many behavioral differences in children based solely upon their sex.

In a typical study of the effects of socialization on male and female behavior, a group of elementary school teachers was asked to describe differences in behavior typical of boys and girls. They reported that boys tended to be more physically active, boastful, argumentative, and curious while girls were neater, more attentive, deferential to authority, and more verbal.

The degree to which such differences are the result of genetic makeup or socialization isn't easy to determine. Consequently, the nature versus nurture debate continues among scientists, educators, and many parents. What cannot be disputed, though, is the powerful impact that these differences have on us—regardless of their origins.

And what about in later life? Do gender differences disappear as we mature? Do we become more similar as adult men and women than we were as boys and girls? Although our interests may broaden to include activities and hobbies formerly thought of as the domain of the other sex, research indicates that basic value differences continue to exist between the sexes throughout adult life.

Unlike external behavior that can be erratic, basic values form the foundation of our character and personality. As such, they act as the guideposts for our decisions, our personal philosophies, our perceptions of the world, and our relationships. According to "The Study of Values," a survey that has been administered to thousands of college-age adults throughout the United States, men and women differ significantly in the priority they place on the six basic values measured. Interestingly, results show the average male profile to be the reverse of the average female profile.

According to the survey, men tend to be motivated more by the search for rational truth (the theoretical), the practicality and utility of things and ideas (the economic), and the desire for power and influence (the political).[6] As such, they place greater value on their ability to observe and reason objectively, to find useful purpose in their work and their lives, and to be influential and admired by others.

For women, there is a higher priority placed on form and harmony (the aesthetic), a concern for people (the social), and unity and spirituality (the religious).[7] As a group, women tend to show greater interest in and concern for beauty and creative expression, to be motivated by the desire to help and care for others, and to be guided by idealism.

"The Study of Values" has also been widely used in the field of executive career counseling. One firm that uses it to assess individual strengths and vocational interests is Caress, Gilhooly & Kestin, Inc., of New York. According to Edward Kuzukian, a spokesperson for the firm, trends among the thousands of male and female executives tested are consistent with those among the college population.

It should come as no surprise that differences in values tend to produce differences in perceptions, attitudes, and behaviors among managers. From examining the average profiles of men and women, it would seem that by working together, both groups can address a broader spectrum of organizational issues with greater awareness and balance than either group can address alone.

In her research on psychological differences between males and females, Harvard psychologist Carol Gilligan arrived at a similar conclusion. According to her findings, men tend to view the world impersonally, through "systems of logic and law." Women, on the other hand, view the world as comprised of relationships, "a world that coheres through human connection rather than through systems of rules." Dr. Gilligan's research goes on to suggest that a major challenge facing business leaders and educators in the future will be learning to recognize the "different voices" of men and women and how to put them to effective use.[8]

FEMININE LEADERSHIP MUST BE RECOGNIZED

If this feminine leadership style is a more effective alternative for many women than the traditional style favored by men, why isn't it recognized and encouraged in most organizations? Very simply, it isn't recognized because to do so requires acceptance of the idea that women, as a group, are different but equal to men. It requires a change in the way most business leaders, including many who consider themselves progressive, view the world.

Instead of recognizing the unique styles that men and women bring to their role as managers, what the vast majority of organizations have been doing for the past decade is trying to prove that men and women are exactly the same. In short, equality has been interpreted to mean that the exact same behavior based upon the same set of masculine standards must apply to all. The result is that women who succeed in management often do so by adapting to male norms, while those who stay themselves rarely receive the recognition or support they need to move ahead. Masculine bias, whether conscious or unconscious, continues to be the major obstacle facing most feminine leaders in corporations. Although these women perform competently, their style is often undervalued by male colleagues and bosses who are unaccustomed to working with this nontraditional approach.

A recent conversation with the vice president of marketing at a major health and beauty aids company helps to illustrate this problem. He stated, "A few years ago, I was very concerned about the need for increasing opportunities for women within my division. . . . But now, looking back, I'm not sure I made the right decision when I started pushing to hire more women. Because in spite of their educational credentials and their background, they don't seem to be doing as well as a group. A few have been promoted, but I can't honestly see any of these women moving up to senior management. Even though they do their jobs well, they just don't seem to stand out in the way that men do. They just don't seem to shine."

The problem of unconscious masculine bias, which defines performance standards in most companies, was also discussed by Betty Friedan in a 1983 article in *The New York Times Magazine.* In it, she describes the powerful impact of the masculine culture on women at Harvard University she observed while working as a research fellow at the Institute of Politics.

She states, "During my year there, I was asked to meet with the women at the law school, women medical students and interns, the women's group at the divinity and architecture schools. These women were awesome in their competence, but they made me uneasy. They seemed too neat, somehow, too controlled, constricted, almost subdued and slightly juiceless.

"A dean of one of the professional schools said: 'We take in the most brilliant women, of course. Their record of achievement is breathtaking, as are their scores on the admission tests. But for some reason, they don't do as well as they should when they get here. Can you explain it?'

" 'Not without interviewing them,' I said, 'but I have a hunch it's because your structures—your whole ambiance—

is so masculine; it alienates them somehow, though they might not be aware of it. Something around here must not elicit the best of female energy. But if that's so, you'd better find it out. Because it's also having an influence on the men that may not be conducive to the kind of leadership needed now.' "[9]

Although Friedan's comments describe the climate for women at Harvard, they could just as easily apply to the management culture of most of our nation's corporations. For the majority of women, it is still an alien culture where enormous trade-offs are required to achieve even moderate success. In order to maximize the contributions that both men and women can make in business, a new perspective is needed. The parameters of acceptable management performance must be expanded to include the total range of skills, both masculine and feminine.

The effects of masculinism and the pressures it exerts on women to conform may help explain the results of many recent studies that claim to have found no difference in the management styles of men and women. Since organizations have forced women to behave like men in order to succeed, it's not surprising that many successful women would identify with a more masculine management style in company-sponsored testing. In addition, the promotion process in most organizations has worked against women with a non-traditional style. Because many companies tend to unconsciously select women who fit the traditional mold for advancement, it follows that differences between the masculine and feminine leadership styles might become even less distinct at higher management levels within traditional organizations.

GROWING SUPPORT FOR FEMININE LEADERSHIP

Fortunately, there are signs of positive change in some organizations. As more and more women continue to move into management positions in companies across the nation, some are starting to question the assumption that success means having to become one of the boys. No longer convinced that they must prove their competence by conforming to the masculine style or by playing accommodating roles, these women recognize that another, more effective and more personally satisfying alternative is available to them.

During the past two years, as I traveled across the country and spoke with men and women about this idea, I've been encouraged by the amount of support for this feminine leadership style that seems to be developing throughout industry. Everywhere I go, I find people who seem to spark to the idea immediately. Not only does the concept of feminine leadership address many of the productivity problems that managers face today, but it also acknowledges the unspoken, yet obvious fact that men and women are different. In short, it affirms many of the experiences and observations of women managers that were difficult to understand or describe until now.

As one woman supervisor in the banking industry put it, "For the first time in a long time, I understand why I feel so uncomfortable in my job. I've been trying to change my whole approach . . . my style . . . to prove to my boss that I'm as smart and as competent as my male peers. I've been trying to do things the way other men do them . . . by being less emotional, tougher, and more analytical.

"It's a lot like trying to write with your left hand after you've been using the right one for thirty years. Instead of improving, you become less effective. You walk around asking yourself, 'What would a guy do in this situation?' and since you don't know, you try to guess. Meanwhile, you stop relying on your own instincts and stop trusting yourself."

For some women managers, there is nothing really new about the concept of feminine leadership. It is simply a new term that describes exactly what they have been doing throughout their careers. For others, there is the growing realization that they will never be comfortable or fully effective as traditional managers and, therefore, it is time to start letting their natural style emerge.

But whether they are recent converts or long-term supporters of the idea, these women share the conviction that they have something unique to offer their companies. By functioning as feminine leaders, they believe they are able to use more of their intuition, creativity, and interpersonal skill to solve managerial problems and to find greater personal satisfaction in their work. Regrettably, a few highly successful women I've spoken with have little interest in the idea since they themselves have succeeded by adopting the traditional masculine approach. But even in the rarefied atmosphere of upper management, increasing numbers of women operate as feminine leaders.

Dr. Yvonne Russell, physician and college dean at the University of Texas in Galveston, is one of these nontraditional superstars. At the time she was named director of Santa Clara Valley Hospital, Dr. Russell was the first woman in medicine to be appointed to the position. As such, she was aware of differences between her approach to managing and that of her male colleagues:

"As a nontraditional person, I knew that my own decision-making style was somewhat different from the one used by many of the men. Often it seemed that they wanted things to add up like the auditor's ledger while I relied more on my interpersonal relationships to complete the picture.

"In addition, I often saw men aggressively compete with each other without much concern for the long-term consequences of their actions on the relationship or the organization. It seemed to me that they had a very different definition of teamwork than I had.

"Some women in executive positions have also taken on that kind of win-lose behavior in recent years. But by and large, most women seem to be more concerned with everybody winning. Having greater sensitivity for the concerns of other people seems to be what helps us here.

"Where I think women managers have a special contribution to make is in the area of interpersonal skills. While we neither teach nor measure these skills, they are critically important in every business and profession. I think women have to do everything they can to use these skills in their work and to encourage their development in others. It's something special that we can and should be offering."

Lois Wyse, president of Wyse Advertising, is another highly successful woman who thinks women have something different to offer organizations. In her book *The Six-Figure Woman (and How to Be One)*, she advises the woman with a desire for corporate success to "follow your heart" and cites some of the qualities that the "female style" of managing can add to the corporate mix.[10]

These include:

- being able to shift and fix and manage the here and now;

- using maternal skills to manage effectively;

- using humor to reduce tension in meetings.

In a recent survey conducted by *Vogue* of twenty women at the top of their professions, the issue of differences between men and women was also addressed. While some of those interviewed insisted that there were absolutely none, others spoke about the ways in which they and other women professionals operate differently.

Muriel Fox, a nationally known spokeswoman on women's issues and executive vice president of the public relations firm of Carl Byoir & Associates, Inc., spoke about the differences she has observed: "Women lead in ways different from men's. Men, I think, have been programmed to give orders. Women have been programmed to motivate people, to educate them, to bring out the best in them. Ours is a less authoritarian leadership. I think women tend to play hardball less often. This is the trend of office politics anyway: the days of warring factions are over. We're talking now in terms of cooperation, and I think that is the game women play best. Working very hard is a given."

Jewel Jackson McCabe, management consultant and president of the National Coalition of 100 Black Women, also commented on what she thinks women can offer their organizations: "I would advise a woman starting out in any field to become comfortable with being a woman, to be comfortable with her body and her mind. Also, to be aware of the special sensitivity that women have, their ability to make things happen."[11]

Faye Wattleton, president of Planned Parenthood Federation of America, also echoed the theme that feminine leadership can add something extra to the organizational mix: "My sense is that women who try to be anything other than themselves are making a terrible mistake. Women bring unique qualities to leadership positions that should not only be recognized but exploited: our sensitivity, the way we relate to people are huge assets.

"But there's no question that we have to have confidence in our own point of view. Somehow women have this mystique about men in the workplace—that they have been anointed with wisdom and brilliance rarely afforded us. That just simply is not the case. Women can be as effective and as strong leaders as any among the men."[12]

One prominent woman described by many as a strong leader is Carol Bellamy, president of the New York City Council. As a manager, lawyer, and veteran of many years in politics, Bellamy understands the importance of balancing the rational and intuitive approaches to managing in organizations. She also thinks that together, men and women can use their styles to help each other be more effective.

"Although it's not as pronounced in all people, I think there's a difference in management style between men and women and I think you need that variety today. Men tend to operate according to a set of rules and to be very rational while women are not as structured and are more intuitive.

"In the past, male characteristics were thought to be good in business and female characteristics were considered bad. But I think people are starting to recognize that this was wrong. Today, as the job of managing continues to get more complex and managers realize that they have to be more inclusive of employees, women are gaining credibility. Because of socialization, I think women may have an advantage in this area. They've been taught to be more concerned with people matters.

"We've left the days of the aloof director or manager behind. Today we need to be more inclusive while we also continue to use a rational approach to managing. As men and women, we need to have a sense of our management styles and learn how to balance them and use them effectively in organizations."

Recognition of the need for greater balance between the

traditional masculine approach to managing and the feminine approach isn't an idea that appeals only to women. It is also one that rings true for some men and its appeal is growing among male managers. No longer convinced that sameness is equality, some men are discovering that women managers can be equally effective by being different. In a *SELF* magazine article titled "Emotions in a Woman's Briefcase," Michael Korda, editor in chief of Simon & Schuster, describes a shift in his own male consciousness regarding the notion of different but equal. Here are some of his thoughts:

"For years I've been arguing that men and women are pretty much alike. For example, a woman physicist doesn't approach a problem in physics from a special point of view —there isn't a 'woman's way' of thinking about physics or flying an airplane or programming a computer.

"These things are *true* and I make no apology for having said them. All the same, as the years have gone by, I've found myself wondering if this position wasn't perhaps a little . . . well, simplistic. I kept my mouth shut, but somewhere at the back of my mind I had my doubts that men and women do in fact think about things the same way (or even *do* things the same way, come to that)."

At this point, Korda goes on to offer some examples of differences that he has observed:

"Women are better team workers than men are. Women in organizations, however strong they are, tend to seek consensus, while men tend to distrust and fight it."

"Women in positions of corporate power tend to lead without a lot of bruising and unnecessary ego display."

"Women take the company's goals seriously, and are surprised to find, as is often the case, that men don't."

"Women on the other hand tend to operate with a more integrated thought process. They find it more difficult to separate their feelings from their work, which is to say they make decisions that involve their entire personality. . . . To put it bluntly, they remain more *human* than men do, precisely because they're not so divided in the way they think."[13]

While some may dispute a specific point of difference raised by Korda in his article, it would be difficult to ignore the strong case he makes for feminine leadership. More important, he isn't the only man making it today. The skills women offer and the organizational benefits that can result are becoming obvious to other men as well. In addition, more women are starting to challenge the dress-for-success, management-without-emotion stereotype that has been used to characterize the successful managerial woman of the past decade.

As one middle-management woman in the insurance industry explained: "Even though I like dresses more than tailored suits, have a hard time giving employees negative feedback, and have never played a team sport in my life, I'm still a darn good manager. When someone in the unit has a birthday, I sometimes bring in a cake. When people have personal problems, I'm usually there to listen. I know I operate differently than a lot of the men do but I have a very loyal and productive group just the same.

"In fact, the people who work for me tell me they're happier and more interested in their work now than they were before I became the manager. And I'm happy too. I like being the morale booster for the group and I also like getting excellent results!"

TWO STYLES: DIFFERENT BUT EQUAL

Today as never before, women are beginning to find their own style and their own voice as feminine leaders. Yet, while more are choosing this different but equally effective approach, they still recognize the benefits of the traditional masculine style as well. In interviews with more than two hundred fifty women and men in middle and senior management from the public and private sectors, from large and small organizations, and from every part of the United States, I found no major opposition to the traditional masculine approach to managing. Instead, there seemed to be enthusiastic support among these managers for an ideal organizational climate that recognizes and encourages *both* styles. And with productivity and morale in crisis in America, it seems the time is right for making this ideal a reality.

Just as differences in perception and experience of both men and women add scope and richness to family life, so these different views and approaches can enrich the quality of life at work as well. Basic differences in management style exist between men and women in a number of key dimensions. I will show you how these differences can be used in a complementary way to improve organizational effectiveness. The key dimensions we will examine include:

- The Use of Power

- Setting Performance Standards and Taking Risks

- Teamwork and Participative Management

- Interpersonal Effectiveness

- Conflict Management

- Intuition and Problem-Solving

- Managing Diversity, Stress, and Boundaries

- Pitching In and Professional Development.

In addition to my own observations, the experiences and reactions of many other feminine leaders will be used to clarify and illustrate each point. Although these comments were taken from interviews with individual women managers, I've chosen to include them because they are *typical* rather than atypical of the attitudes and behaviors of many feminine leaders and because they capture, in a personal way, the different style of leadership characteristic of this group.

Vive la différence!

PART
II

Chapter Five
The Use of Power

No issue is more central to a discussion of leadership than the subject of power. Within many companies, managers are assessed as effective or ineffective by colleagues and employees on the basis of how powerful they are. Getting more power is a goal frequently mentioned not only by managers who are just beginning to move up the organization ladder, but also by those who are close to the top.

Not surprisingly, the use of power is a skill that has been consistently singled out by critics as one in which many female managers are deficient. "She's not tough enough" or "She just doesn't know how to give orders" are complaints often leveled against female executives. In an effort to overcome these perceived deficiencies, women managers have been deluged with books on how to become more assertive and many have been sent for assertiveness training by their companies.

But this recent fascination with assertiveness is both unfair to the women managers who are bearing the brunt of the criticism and also misleading when it comes to a proper understanding of power—its sources and its uses within organizations. It is unfair because many women who have been criticized for their lack of assertiveness have been functioning in junior positions where blatantly assertive behavior would have been both inappropriate and ineffective. It is misleading because assertive behavior is only one of the ways that power can be effectively wielded in a corporate setting.

But when executives speak of being powerful, what do they truly mean? Are there any particular managerial qualities that make some people more influential than others? In 1980, as part of an assignment to develop an advanced management training program, I had the opportunity to explore the answer to this question. Several hundred male and female managers were asked to identify what issues they'd like to see addressed in an intensive seminar. Of the forty issues mentioned, power was at the top of their list. These managers said they wanted to learn to use their own power more effectively and to recognize the sources of their power more readily.

In response to this request, I devised a framework to help them define and identify sources of their executive power. The model was based upon a widely accepted definition of power as "the ability to influence others, to shape events, and to achieve personal goals." The framework presented in this chapter is the one I developed in 1980. Although more elaborate theories about executive power abound, I continue to find this generic model useful in working with managers. Of the several thousand who have seen it over the years, most believe that it clearly identifies the essential sources of their executive power. More important, it also helps to articulate key differences in the ways that male and female managers as groups tend to approach the use of power.

UNDERSTANDING POWER

Power is something people acquire and exercise through a combination of external resources and individual qualities. These resources and qualities are the currencies of power, which we use to pursue our goals and meet our individual needs. The sources from which we derive our power fall into two distinct categories: position power and personal power. Let us first consider position power.

POSITION POWER

Under position power, we find a variety of currencies that are external to the individual. Typically, these include the various authority roles and responsibilities that a person is assigned within an organization. The primary sources of position power are:

- allocating resources (including financial, human, and technical);

- controlling resources;

- hierarchical positioning (including organizational title, rank, contacts, and status).

Within organizations, each job carries some intrinsic power. Whether it's a first-line supervisory function or the CEO position in a major corporation, every job has some degree of position power. This power is nontransferable. When a manager moves out of a job, the position power associated with that job is utilized by the next manager who fills the vacancy. Therefore, such power is transitory. Its duration is unpredictable and often predicated on events that are beyond individual control.

Yet, precisely because it is a somewhat unstable and limited commodity in business, position power is also relentlessly sought by most executives. To understand the attraction that it holds for individuals, one needs only to observe the maneuvering and battling for position that takes place among senior executives during a major corporate takeover. Typically, there is a fierce competition for control of the business and when the dust settles, after the final maneuver has been made, there is both a winner and a loser at the very top.

What is at stake in such takeovers is the position power associated with managing and controlling the resources of the newly acquired corporation. In winner-take-all situations, the senior manager who assumes the role of chief executive is awarded all the position power associated with the job. The other contenders are often forced to relinquish all the status and authority vested in their positions. Most leave the business in search of new sources of position power in other organizations. Although transitory in nature, position power continues to be the strongest single motivator among many senior executives.

TRADITIONAL LEADERSHIP FAVORS POSITION POWER

Among traditional male leaders, position power tops the list of frequently used currencies. As one senior manager in the telecommunications industry explains, "It works fast; it's easy to use; and it stops an opponent dead in his tracks. There's a beautiful simplicity in position power that says,

'I'm the boss . . . and you're not.' " Yet, while it can be a relatively fast and easy way to attain one's goals, it is also temporal in nature. The phrase "you can't take it with you" very aptly describes the situation that managers face when they are forced to give up their organizational roles and all the position power that goes with the title on the door.

Because the traditional management model took much of its form and substance from the military, it is not surprising that formal authority is considered to be the major source of power within organizations today. Add to this the emphasis placed upon tight control within the masculine corporate culture, and one begins to see why position power continues to enjoy such popularity among managers. Both the corporate culture of masculinism and the paramilitary structure of organizations reinforce the value and utility of position power. Together, they suggest that organizations require a clearly defined chain of command to function effectively and that, primarily, managers need to understand the limits of their own position power to achieve their goals, motivate employees, and succeed.

PERSONAL POWER

Although decision-making authority and hierarchical position are sources of considerable executive power, personal power is a rich source of influence as well. Personal power comes from intrinsic qualities within an individual rather than from external roles. It is the influence that results from our individual skills, talents, and personal characteristics. Because it is directly tied to utilizing one's own natural resources, personal power is easier to maintain, modify, and enhance. As described by managers in the same 1980 study, personal power includes three basic components:

- Task Competence—which consists of the skills, knowledge, relevant experience, and educational background that one brings to bear in any situation.

- Interpersonal Competence—which is the ability to be socially skillful, to sense others' feelings, and to be personally persuasive.

- Charisma—which is made up of personal qualities that often appeal to the unconscious needs and fears in others. Physical appearance, enthusiasm, humor, animation, zeal, and presence are all potentially charismatic qualities that can have a powerful impact on events and people.

Personal power often takes less obvious forms than position power. It is power that others may choose to ignore in some short-term situations, but its impact can build and be sustained more easily over the long term. As it develops, personal power can also have a more positive impact on employee motivation and morale.

To appreciate how powerful task competence can be in shaping events and influencing decisions, one only needs to think of a manager with a high degree of expert knowledge in a given area. When corporate strategy is being shaped, technical expertise becomes a source of significant power. While generalists talk in generalities, the knowledge expert has specific data to draw on and can persuade others to support his or her position with facts drawn from actual work-related experience.

Intuition and sensitivity can also be powerful managerial tools in one-on-one situations and within decision-making groups. Understanding the emotional impact of one's behavior on others has obvious advantages. By being able to assess the unspoken reactions of colleagues and employees, managers get immediate feedback about how their ideas and behavior are perceived. With the help of this constant feedback, they can adapt an approach that maximizes their ability to be influential and decreases the possibility of alienating others. When selling an idea or assessing how appropriate the timing is for introducing new or controversial proposals, the ability to sense the prevailing mood or emotional tone within a group becomes a critical managerial skill. Although soothing others' feelings may not seem like a very powerful act, it is an example of how one's interpersonal competence can be used to reduce resistance and create a more positive climate for discussion and decision-making.

Charismatic qualities that enhance our personal power are as likely to be inborn as to be developed skills. While anatomy may not be destiny, there is little doubt that physical appearance and personal presence both have an impact on our ability to be influential. Although little can be done to alter these innate qualities, understanding how they can be used to emphasize visibility and persuade others increases the likelihood that such charismatic qualities will enhance rather than detract from our other sources of power.

Together task competence, interpersonal competence, and charisma form the basis of our personal power. While each one plays a unique and important role, they all share a common property. They are qualities and skills that are transferable to any job setting. Regardless of where we are in the organizational hierarchy or how often we change roles, our personal power remains constant, increasing our ability to deal effectively with change by supplying the ballast we require to manage it effectively.

FEMININE LEADERSHIP FAVORS PERSONAL POWER

At the very heart of managing and leading is the desire to influence people and events. All managers use their power to influence others and to achieve their goals. The frequency with which they choose to use each source of power is based largely on their own experience and personal comfort with each approach. Personal values also tend to influence this choice, as do the expectations of others in the organization. As managers try out various approaches to influencing, they begin to evolve a basic style that consists of the currencies of power which work best for them. Naturally, as they continue to achieve success with their preferred approach, they use some currencies with even greater frequency.

My own research has shown that, when given the choice, feminine leaders prefer to use personal power to influence organizational policies and practices and to motivate others. Although they recognize the importance of position power, they tend to use it more sparingly than traditional leaders do.

FACTORS INFLUENCING EACH STYLE

When it comes to using power, men and women start from a different experiential base. At the heart is the socialization process that sets out the parameters of acceptable behavior for each group. Coming out of the masculine tradition, one learns to take charge, to be visible, to strategize, and to see others as either supporters or opponents. On the other hand, the feminine tradition emphasizes the importance of building and maintaining productive relationships, of assessing accomplishments based on a set of internal standards, and of delivering service to others. The social scripts that both groups are expected to follow produce very different behaviors. Add to this the influence of biological differences on male and female behavior and you have the basis for the development of two distinct approaches to using power.

Distinctly different approaches to the use of power between men and women have been observed by many of the male and female managers I've talked to over the past few years. Rusty Renick, division manager of human resources at New York Telephone, spoke about the effects of socialization on the ways in which men and women managers use power. He said, "I subscribe to the notion that there are things women bring to management by nature of their socialization that are different from the kinds of things men have been taught regarding how to lead people, exercise power, delegate work or not delegate work as the case may be. If you're a guy, maybe one of your early tapes was that you should delegate in a military style, making very heavy checklists. In delegating work to subordinates, men tend not only to tell employees what to do but how to do it. Women take a different approach to power. They are much more used to what I call empowerment—talking to people and allowing them to decide. They'll say, 'Here's a job I want you to do,' and they'll set the guidelines, but that's it."

Noreen Haffner, a division manager with Southern New England Telephone Company, described the differences she has observed in the male and female approaches to power: "Men tend to be more role power oriented; I use both personal and position power. I think that I'm a good leader, one who makes the goals and objectives clear and who is also able to personally motivate people to work hard. I tend to use role power—that is, position power—less than many men around me, but have no reluctance to use it. If you really want people to respond to your leadership, you have to have a personal relationship with them. They need to know you're dependable and that you'll be there if they have a problem. That's personal power to me."

Randy MacDonald, director of employee relations at GTE, has also noticed differences in the overall approach to power between men and women: "The women managers that I have the most respect for are great consensus-builders. They do a great job of getting their ducks in a row before the decision takes place; then they help to facilitate the decision. Men often try to push things through. Women know where their allies are and when they are needed, they call them into place."

ASSUMPTIONS ABOUT THE USE OF POWER

With different approaches to power, traditional managers and feminine leaders make different assumptions about the willingness of others to support their goals. Whereas the traditional manager operates out of a belief that deference to authority is a given, feminine leaders do not presume that this is so. In addition, many women who choose personal power over position power see employee deference as a barrier to organization effectiveness.

One woman executive, the president of a publishing company, experienced the negative aspects of employee deference when she was named to her current position at the age of thirty. In reflecting on the early experiences she had as a publisher, she said, "I know that when I came here, a lot of people were apoplectic at the prospect of working for a young woman, but they were all running around like rabbits in a warren saying, 'Yes. Yes. Yes.' . . . It has taken me a long time to get most of my people to say 'No.' I saw how frightened they were of not pleasing me. . . . Many men take this kind of leadership opportunity to rule by fear. Women tend to manage by support and encouragement, by setting standards of excellence and example—they tend to do things themselves. Women have the patience to wait and to avoid exerting their role power until they understand what's going on."

Mary Kay Ash, founder and chairman of the board of Mary Kay Cosmetics, is another highly successful feminine leader who believes that maximum results are achieved when employees are dealt with as individuals rather than as subordinates who are expected to simply execute orders. She offered these comments on the topic: "I believe that there is no such thing as a subordinate. If the air-conditioning ceases to work in our building, then the repair technician becomes more important than the chairman of the board. We're all people working together toward a common objective.

"When I go to meetings, I make it a point to speak to every person, at every level. . . . When I'm out in the field, I try to make everyone I meet feel important. As a result, I am greeted personally by people I don't even know. I guess I think a man would have a very different viewpoint."

Another woman manager who shares this point of view is Michelle Martens, a human resources manager with Pitney Bowes. During a discussion of male-female managerial differences, she said, "My own experiences as a manager lead me to conclude that, as a woman, I'm more inclined to use personal power to guide and motivate others. I've worked with many men who seem to use their position power more often and who automatically assume that other people will do what they say because they're in charge. I think this is a rather fundamental difference between many men and women."

OUTCOMES

Another difference between the traditional and the feminine approach to power has to do with the outcome that each style is likely to produce. While the traditional approach tends to be faster—an easy means of avoiding stalemates and most effective when the support and cooperation of employees is a certainty—it does not encourage colleague-ship, shared accountability, or employee participation in problem-solving. Instead, it tends to focus the accountability for ideas and outcomes squarely on the shoulders of the manager.

The feminine approach often helps to create a more cooperative work climate by encouraging greater employee participation and shared accountability. It can be put to best use when a long-term approach to influencing events is required, when facts and expert information are critical to the effort, and where the quality of relationships within the work group is an important consideration. Its chief drawback is the time investment often required to shape events—without using position power and marching orders to accelerate the process.

Even in situations where they have significant position power, many feminine leaders still prefer to use their task competence and interpersonal competence to influence events and people. Some women executives state that they are cautious about using their position power because of the overreaction that it can sometimes create among employees. In attempting to anticipate the wishes of the boss, employees sometimes interpret a simple request for information to be a stronger, action-oriented directive. As Sandra Meyer, president of the American Express Communications Division and one of the top women managers in industry, points out, "I know the effect the stripes can have on others.

You speak with the authority of yourself as the person and also with the authority of the position. . . . The chairman of General Foods used to talk about how people would often translate his musing out loud to mean a direct order to do something. After hearing that story, I am now very careful, when I don't want to give an order but just want to ask a question, to preface that question with, 'This may sound stronger than I mean it to. . . .' "

Other women managers say that their interpersonal competence often allows them to be powerful without having to rely on their position power. Speaking at the Columbia Business School Club in New York, another well-known woman executive, Colombe Nicholas, president of Christian Dior, New York, stressed her reliance on interpersonal competence when she said, ". . . the ability to problem-solve is power. The ability to interact—to effect conciliation, compromise, team spirit . . . that is power. . . . My point is that you don't have to conform to some stereotype of a tough-minded executive in order to have and use power. In the final analysis you have to be yourself."

In general, the masculine and feminine approaches have several unique properties. First, the traditional masculine approach relies more heavily on the external organizational environment while the feminine approach draws more on internal personal resources. As such, the masculine approach to power is a more visible and assertive approach in which position power and charisma both play an important part. The feminine style relies most heavily on task and interpersonal competence and often requires more time to emerge and become truly effective. As is true in many other areas as well, each approach to power tends to complement the other. Each approach relies on a unique set of primary currencies that tend to be employed more often and in more situations.

In their research on leadership styles, Lynn Rosener and Peter Schwartz found several corresponding differences in the way men and women perceive power. According to their findings, the "direct power style," extrapolated from male perceptions, involves manipulation, rational analysis, and the desire to restructure. The "contextual power style," derived from female perceptions, focuses more on the sharing of internal resources and the establishment of interdependent relationships. While the more masculine style was described as "task-oriented, direct, aggressive and interactive with the environment," the feminine style was portrayed as being "indirect, interested in the subtleties of human interaction and in the more complex, more open and less defined aspects of reality."[1]

COMPLEMENTARY APPROACHES TO POWER

As a successful businessman with more than twenty-five years of experience in marketing and advertising, John Sheedy, president of Simon and Hilliard Advertising in New York City, is an executive who strongly supports the idea that, working together, men and women can cover the widest possible range of effective managerial behaviors. In this context, he offered some of his personal views about the contributions he thinks each group can make: "I have found women to be very easy to work with. . . . I don't think that women are intimidators and that is certainly one of the prevalent traits among many male managers. I simply haven't come across the female version of Type A, intimidating, authority figure behavior." In commenting on the strengths of traditional male managers, he went on to say, "The strengths of male managers are different. The best have vision, they're charismatic and they're strong. They can get organizations behind them to fulfill their ideas. They can 'rally the troops,' so to speak."

Rusty Renick at New York Telephone also sees the masculine and feminine styles as complementary. He states, "What we're ultimately trying to get to is what men and women can learn from each other that will maximize our respective repertoires of behavior. . . . Women are good at empowering and not having to know the right answers all the time. Men are good at using role power, and at being comfortable as authority figures."

CORPORATE IMPLICATIONS

American businesses are being challenged in myriad ways to become more responsive to change. One of the most significant challenges facing corporations today is winning the hearts and minds of many employees who have become disillusioned and demoralized about organizational life. Managing this new breed of workers, many of whom have the talents and creative ideas that businesses desperately need, will require new leadership strategies. On every managerial dimension, and especially along the dimension of executive power, basic changes will be required. As the need for change becomes more apparent, the direction of that evolution is also becoming clearer.

Although many traditional managers still disagree, the evidence strongly suggests that there is a growing need in organizations for managers who can use their internal resources to motivate and inspire others and who choose not to use their title and their role power to do so. Commenting on this change, Muriel Fox of Carl Byoir & Associates stated: "Many years ago a VP at one of the networks said, 'Women will never be leaders because they can't give orders.' Today, giving orders is no longer in style. . . . Women, including myself, have mainly been able to lead by inspiring and encouraging people to work on solutions—not by throwing their weight around. In this sense, we're really in step, as a group, with what's being demanded more of managers today."

But do these changes mean that managers will no longer be able to use position power to pursue their goals? Definitely not. What is indicated is the need for greater balance in the approaches used among managers to exercise power, the kind of balance that the traditional management style and feminine leadership can create when they are both developed and rewarded within organizations.

Unfortunately, most organizations are far from achieving this critical balance. Instead of making use of the talents of feminine leaders to improve morale and manage complex problems, the take-charge, action-oriented approach to power is still the only one that is widely recognized or rewarded.

Will it ever be so? In order to turn this problem around, organizations will need to take three major steps. First, they must become aware of how feminine leaders differ from more traditional managers on the dimension of power. What are the behavioral differences between a high visibility, high control style and a more participative, less directive approach? Second, the appropriateness of various currencies of power must be evaluated more in terms of long-range impact on the organization and less in terms of visibility and immediate results. In discussing this point, Dr. Estelle Ramey of Georgetown University states, "Our society and our organizations have learned to value masculine, 'quick-fix' traits in leaders. In a primitive society, a rural society, or even the industrial society of the early 1900's, quick fixes worked out all right. But they are less likely to work in a complex society. We need to look at long-range outcomes now. Service and patience are what can keep things running effectively today and women can contribute a lot in both of these areas."

Finally, organizations must look seriously at their executive development and succession programs with an eye toward encouraging a wider range of leadership styles among managers. Even the basic organizational perception of executive power must be enlarged to include interpersonal competence and task competence, as well as high visibility, aggressiveness, and control.

Initially, this shift in perspective will be difficult for many traditional managers to make. After decades of using military metaphors to describe managerial behavior, some won't find it easy to see the positive impact that a less visible, knowledge-based approach to power can have on people and issues. It's never easy to think about old ideas in new ways. But it is critical to the survival and continued success of corporate America.

Chapter Six

Setting Performance Standards and Taking Risks

At a mock graduation ceremony for twenty women in training to become service technicians, certificates of achievement were awarded to everyone who had completed the rigorous ten-week course. The inscription on the award read:

> *Whatever women do, they must do twice as well as men to be thought half as good.*
>
> *Fortunately, this is not difficult.*

A professional women's organization held its annual awards dinner to honor one member for outstanding achievement in business. When it was time to accept her award, the honoree walked to the dais and delivered a speech that brought the house down. It began, "The answer to both questions is 'yes.' Yes, I did work twice as hard to get this far; and, yes, I am twice as good as most of my male peers. Thank you for being the first people, other than my mother, to notice!"

WOMEN MUST WORK HARDER TO SUCCEED

If there is one fact of corporate life which women of all philosophical persuasions seem to agree on, it is that women must work harder as a group than men to succeed within management. Regardless of the stories one may hear about unqualified women who are allegedly promoted to satisfy quotas, most women managers still believe that, as a group, they are moving up the hard way—by working diligently to prove their competence again and again.

This sentiment was confirmed in a 1981 study, "Moving Up: Women in Managerial Careers," conducted by Anne Harlan and Carol Weiss for the Wellesley College Center for Research on Women. The study, conducted among male and female managers from two large retail companies, found, "Many women reported the pressure to perform was intense. . . . Greater pressures on women were noted by 42% of the men and 67% of the women in our sample."[1]

NEED TO OVERCOME NEGATIVE STEREOTYPES

What seems to drive women to put forth this extra effort? Judging from the responses of many successful women managers to this question, there appear to be several reasons. First is the persistent problem of negative attitudes toward women in leadership roles. Sensing that they are not welcomed within many organizations because they are women and that any failure on their part will not be tolerated, some women try to anticipate every potential problem in order to avoid costly mistakes. As a female lawyer in a major California firm put it, "Women not only have to prove themselves, they have to disprove negative stereotypes about women. You're going to have to be not 100% better than a man but 150%. An average woman isn't tolerated—you have to be exceptional."[2] Needless to say, keeping two steps ahead of every problem requires enormous amounts of extra work. Regardless of the time it may take, many women are willing to invest it in order to assure others that they are competent leaders.

The need for women managers to prove themselves in a sometimes hostile corporate environment also relates to their desire for explicit, objective standards by which their performance can be evaluated. This desire was reflected in the findings of a 1983 American Management Association survey. The study, conducted among more than 1,500 male and female managers, found that women gave "an effective performance appraisal system a much higher vote than men, rating it very important."[3] Employee relations specialist Randy MacDonald of GTE noted this same tendency: "Women know that they're trying to carve out their role and they also know that the willingness of a male manager to accept failure on their part may not be as great as that manager's willingness to accept failure from another male. Therefore, women must establish clear goals and standards against which to measure themselves in order to succeed."

VISIBLE ROLE MODELS

A second reason for this strong work ethic among women managers has to do with the visibility factor with which women must contend. Even though the number of women managers is greater today than ever before, they are still a minority within middle management and a rare species, indeed, at senior levels. Therefore, many women maintain that they are still an organizational curiosity as they move up the career ladder. This added visibility makes them more vulnerable to criticism, since their performance records tend to stand out more from those of male peers. As a result, they are extremely careful to avoid mistakes that would be likely to embarrass them or their organizations. In effect, they spend a great deal of their time trying to be perfect.

Because of their continued scarcity in middle and senior management, many women still think of themselves as pioneers working to increase opportunities for all women through their example. Even after two decades of expanding career options, it is not unusual to hear successful women talk about heightened visibility as a serious concern. One senior manager in the investment banking industry put it this way: "Being one of a handful of women in top management makes me an oddity in this institution. Even though I try not to focus on it, men and other women are always asking me how it feels to be here. There is no way you can forget the fact that you're different and that you are being watched closely by others. . . .

"Although I work hard to put it out of my mind, I realize that my unique position affects me. When I'm about to make a decision that has a serious element of risk or when I'm asked as a woman to speak out on an issue, I find myself thinking about what I intend to do in terms of how it will affect other women. Am I disappointing them? Am I damaging their chances for success? Am I supporting some negative stereotype through my actions?

"It's not something I need to remind myself to think about. At this stage, it's instinctive. It's a natural step that I take in decision-making. But despite what you might think, I don't find that this has hurt me. I think it's a factor that has enhanced my overall performance. I set the hurdle higher as a result of this."

Realizing what their success or failure can symbolically represent within organizations, many feminine leaders are apt to take extra time and care when making decisions. But unlike women managers who feel burdened by this extra pressure to "perform well for the sake of one's sisters" and who resist or deny this organizational fact of life, feminine leaders tend to see this more as an important responsibility and a factor that can have a positive impact on their performance.

In organizations where feminine leadership is encouraged, men as well as women are aware of differences in the way these managers approach setting personal performance standards. Gerald Tabaczyk is senior vice president and director of account management for Peter Rogers Associates in New York. As a highly successful "boutique" advertising agency, Peter Rogers has attracted many top professionals over the years. Included in this mix have been feminine leaders looking for a less bureaucratic, more supportive climate in which to work and grow. According to Tabaczyk, these women have brought many qualities to their work that have helped the agency maintain a high standard of client service.

In describing their particular strengths he said, "Generally, I think women managers are more likely to make sure they're right before they say something; and when they do suggest an idea, I have the strong impression that they've really done their homework. A man in the same position may use six arguments to emphasize his point, while a woman may only use half that number. But my experience has been that the woman will have thought out her ideas more thoroughly. She will want to be sure she's on firm ground before she takes a position, whereas he won't be as concerned about this."

Much of the advice given to women managers in the late sixties and early seventies focused on the negative impact of this need to be well prepared above all else. Throughout those years, women were criticized for being too invested in hard work and not concerned enough about political strategy. But today's crisis in corporations is creating a need to rethink this important issue. Are women worse off as a result of setting unusually high standards for their own performance? Does this cause them to function less effectively in their role as managers? Would organizations be better off if women were less driven by this need to maintain a high level of individual performance?

Within the context of declining productivity and morale in American business, the pursuit of performance excellence can only be viewed as more critical than ever before. While breaking new ground within management continues to produce a high degree of performance pressure among many feminine leaders, it is also generating a great deal of excitement and enthusiasm in situations where women believe they are being taken seriously. In such cases, there is a greater degree of optimism about the future and less cynicism regarding what really counts in moving ahead.

Dr. Sharon Connelly, assistant professor of public administration at the University of Southern California, has been researching factors that contribute to what she calls "work spirit," meaning the spark or vitality that is present when people love their work. In discussing her own view of women managers, she says, "Women still face the problem of having to work twice as hard as their male counterparts to be recognized. As they do this, they also have a capacity for energizing the situation and the people. It has to do with the quality of their energy—being upbeat, imaginative, and looking for other ways to get things done. Sometimes it's a lack of cynicism about what will work—trying something that others wouldn't."

IMMIGRANT WORK ETHIC

How is this orientation different from that of traditional managers? A growing body of evidence suggests that today's feminine leaders are similar in many ways to first-generation immigrants. As strangers in a strange land, they compensate for their ignorance of the local customs by focusing their energies on the things they do well. For the vast majority, hard work becomes the key to satisfaction and success. Because they are less politically aware, they are more likely to ignore politics in performing their work and to use one set of standards to measure performance, regardless of whether it is their own or someone else's. As the newest group to enter management, women tend to be less complacent about their success and their futures. Realizing from their own experiences that every step on the career ladder is fraught with potential problems, they take little or nothing for granted. Their response to almost every situation they encounter is the same. They continue to work harder.

Is this female work ethic really different from that of male managers? A study conducted by the American Management Association specifically addressed the subject of managerial values and revealed several interesting differences between a matched sample of men and women managers. According to the results, women managers placed greater emphasis on the importance of efficiency and high productivity than did men. In addition, women also rated ability, flexibility, cooperation, and skill as more admired personal qualities than their male counterparts. Although both groups placed considerable importance on every area, these differences proved to be statistically significant.[4]

The strong dedication that many women managers bring to their work was a key finding in still another study, the 1982 "Profile of Women Senior Executives" developed jointly by the University of California at Los Angeles and Korn/Ferry International, a prominent executive search firm. According to the results, 36 percent of the three hundred senior women executives surveyed stated that they put in more hours per week on their jobs than their male counterparts. In addition, among the more than thirty factors thought to be most important in bringing about their success, this group cited hard work and persistence as two of the top three.[5]

One successful woman who places a strong emphasis on high personal work standards for herself and for those around her is Dr. Donna Shalala, president of Hunter College. Before coming to Hunter in 1980, she held a number of responsible positions including assistant secretary of Housing and Urban Development (HUD). In speaking about her own style of management, she said, "I think the people who work for me would say that I'm obsessive about preparation. I'm very tough about the paper that goes out of my office. No one signs anything for me. On anything we send out, I'd rather do less and do it very, very well. I'm also someone who makes few public speeches but who works very hard to shape and refine any that I do give.

"At the same time, I'm very tolerant of mistakes. Senior people around here know that they can make mistakes, even terrible ones, as long as they work very hard and try very hard. I believe that there are some errors that simply can't be anticipated, but with those things that we can control, we need to do these very well."

Ironically, this commitment to high standards of performance has been viewed as a serious flaw in the way feminine leaders manage within some organizations. In such places, their belief in the importance of high standards and hard work is regarded as naïve and not in alignment with the "facts of corporate life"—namely, that political positioning is more important than managerial excellence. In places where this belief in politics above performance prevails, it is far more difficult for feminine leaders to succeed. Whereas most traditional managers can adjust to a highly politicized corporate climate by becoming more political, feminine leaders often find this adjustment difficult to make. Where there is a poor fit between their own values and those of highly politicized organizations, these women often feel obliged to move on and seek out other career opportunities where hard work and high performance standards are both rewarded. Sometimes, they are able to find such opportunities within complex organizations. Regrettably, many feminine leaders discover that their values are not widely shared in many organizations. Hence, they must look outside for a climate that is more supportive of their personal beliefs.

HIGH-PERFORMANCE ENTREPRENEURS

One of the principal reasons cited by many women entrepreneurs for starting their own businesses has to do with the declining work ethic and the increasing importance of politics in many organizations. It is a cause of serious concern for many. Dr. Janice Jones, president and founder of Chartwell & Company, a Los Angeles–based financial services organization, is one such case in point. In discussing the role that women can play within organizations she reflected on her own career experiences. "I have always had to excel in anything I ever did and it upsets me to see people who don't perform. Today, in many organizations, there is a tolerance for mediocrity. This unfortunate phenomenon has resulted in stagnated corporate growth and will continue, unless there is an increase throughout the business community in the demand for dedication, discipline, and excellence.

"I hope that the current spirit among women will make a

difference. The women I know who have risen to the top have succeeded on the basis of sheer hard work. In my view, they represent some of the finest managers I have seen to date.

"Among those who have survived in corporations and achieved, I think you will see a positive difference in attitude. There is a spirit of freedom and accomplishment within this group that you don't find among many men. I hope this spirit can fuel a new revolution in business."

WOMEN AS RISK-TAKERS

But what about risk-taking? How does the desire of women managers to live up to high standards and not make costly mistakes affect their willingness to take the calculated risks that are often essential to business success? Do women tend to take fewer risks than men in order to avoid error? One of the unfortunate stereotypes which developed in organizations at the time women first began to move into management was that women are "low risk-takers." According to research that focused on differences in early socialization, women are thought to be more risk-averse than men, more likely to view risk in negative terms, and less likely to seize opportunities with potentially positive rewards for themselves because of concern over the short-term risks that would be involved. The traditional social scripts laid out for boys and girls, together with a biology amenable to such conditioning, made a strong case. Girls and, later, women did seem to approach risks differently. But while gender differences could be identified, the explanations for these differences and, more important, their overall impact on organizations seemed to be tied to traditional masculine values and a belief in the pursuit of self-interest at almost any price.

Whereas women seem to bring a different orientation to risk-taking, one that carefully considers potentially negative consequences, it is not clear that this perspective is harmful to the woman herself or to her organization. Nor is it clear that this prevents women from taking reasonable risks. Sandra Meyer of American Express put it this way, "I'm a reasonable risk-taker but not a gambler. I tend to want to bet $2.00 on one of two horses to show." Gillian Martin Sorensen, the New York City commissioner for the United Nations and Consular Corps, expressed a similar willingness to take a reasonable gamble: "I suppose that from a distance I assess the risks and then follow through to a reasonable conclusion."

Nevertheless, in thinking about risk-taking behavior, one must allow that the exact same actions taken by a man and a woman manager are likely to elicit very different responses from colleagues and from the organization if they do not succeed. In most cases, the negative consequences are still far greater for women managers than they are for men. As public relations executive Muriel Fox put it, "Women cannot afford to make mistakes. If they did, they would hear 'I told you so.' Since they had to be more perfect, through the years, they took fewer risks."

In discussing the differences between men and women in the area of risk-taking, Jill Considine, president and CEO of The First Women's Bank in New York, offered this observation: "In general, men appear to be greater risk-takers than women managers but maybe this is because there is less for them to risk. For example, I think there is less risk for a man who decides he wants to be the chief engineer at a large automotive plant. For a woman to do this, there is a lot of risk. Considering the consequences of their actions, I think women achievers risk more every time they risk than men do. There is certainly a greater risk that they won't get what they want."

At the same time, the experience that women have gained within management over the last decade seems to have had a positive impact on their level of comfort with risk-taking. While they are still well aware of the potentially negative outcomes, today many women managers are more able to recognize the positives as well. Sister Colette Mahoney, president of Marymount College in Manhattan, believes that the image of women as low risk-takers is beginning to change. She says, "If people think that men are greater risk-takers I think it's only because women have not been in positions to exhibit that talent. As a female president, I have taken as many if not more risks than many of my male counterparts."

Carol Foreman is a feminine leader who knows a good deal about taking risks. Before founding her own public policy consulting firm in Washington, D.C., she served in government as assistant secretary of agriculture. During the fall of 1984, she was also the deputy cochair of the Mondale-Ferraro campaign. Based upon her observations and experience, she believes successful women managers are definitely risk-takers, maybe even greater risk-takers than men. She says, "I think women of a certain age had to come up through alternate routes and had to take risks where men didn't have to. Men got out of college and were recruited by IBM, or whatever, where the management structure said, 'Do not take a risk, just do what everybody says and you will succeed.' There were no comparable assurances for women."

There appears to be little doubt that as women have continued to succeed in breaking down the old barriers to career success, they are more predisposed toward taking risks. Past success has become a strong motivator for taking reasonable risks. Yet, at the present time, the focus of women managers' efforts continues to be on high-quality personal performance above all else.

BUSINESS NEEDS HIGH PERFORMERS

More than a decade ago, as women began to enter management in large numbers for the first time, many experts advised them not to bring their personal standards to the office. Several of the most popular books about women managers criticized women for being overly demanding of their own and others' performance; for expecting others to seek them out for rewards because of their diligence and hard work; and for refusing to view corporate life as a game that required risk-taking strategies formulated to advance their own self-interests.

Against the backdrop of economic prosperity in the late sixties and early seventies, it was generally thought that women would improve their chances for success by blending in rather than by magnifying their differences. The prevailing wisdom of those years was that women would never achieve equality or establish a strong presence within management unless they learned to play the game as men played it. Once they became part of the managerial infrastructure, they would then be free to change the rules.

But today, against the backdrop of the many challenges that exist in corporate America, it seems the time has come for women managers to press for change. Today, there is a need for a new kind of leadership; one that empowers and challenges people to find new solutions to old problems; one that encourages employees to set higher standards of quality for the services they perform and the goods they produce. Today's leaders must do more than judge the quality of others' performance. They must be willing to lead by example and demonstrate, through their own performance, that a quality effort really counts.

Since that initial entry into management almost twenty years ago, feminine leaders have been working hard to earn the respect and confidence of their colleagues and their organizations by delivering high-quality performance. While some others have used strategy and manipulation to succeed, these women have relied on their skills and their energy to overcome barriers to success. This commitment to quality can help revitalize the work ethic in many faltering organizations. Moreover, it can help to rebuild America's confidence in corporate leadership by placing performance excellence before political savvy.

Throughout corporations, much can be learned from the example being set by feminine leaders today. Particularly in the area of performance standards, their values are the ones that can help rebuild American industry and keep it competitive in the future. Instead of discouraging this attitude among women, it is time to start supporting their values and encouraging others to follow their lead.

Chapter Seven
Teamwork and Participative Management

In the early nineteenth century, the Duke of Wellington was said to have remarked that the Battle of Waterloo had been won "on the playing fields of Eton." Although the duke lived more than two hundred years ago, his outlook is still common among many business management experts. In their belief, because little girls have not been trained on the baseball fields of Boston or the football fields of Philadelphia, they are less equipped to function as members of management teams within business organizations.

This thinking goes as follows: Girls play competitive games in which they compete as individuals and boys tend to play more team sports. Thus, boys learn more about how to be good team players than girls do. Later on, as managers, they are more able to cooperate within their work teams even in situations where they have no rapport with coworkers; to accept differences in performance levels because they understand that you still need eleven to play the game; and to distance themselves from the emotional impact of failure by spreading accountability among all members of the team.

In their best-selling book *The Managerial Woman,* Drs. Margaret Hennig and Anne Jardim comment at length on this basic difference in the approach to teamwork taken by men and women. According to their findings, while boys tend to learn how to function effectively within a team setting, girls have a very different experience. Instead of focusing on winning, girls tend to think in terms of "doing the best they can." Later, as adults, women have greater difficulty distancing themselves from criticism. Because they have no sense of "a game being played," they are also less apt to employ strategies in pursuit of their own self-interests.[1]

Strategy, winning, and self-interest are the stuff successful managers are supposedly made of. At least, this seemed to be the managerial model held up as an example for women throughout the seventies. Now, however, with the business problems of the eighties in full view, one wonders if this highly competitive, strategic approach to managing, with its glorification of the pursuit of self-interest, was ever in the best interests of organizations, management, or anyone other than the individual himself.

But the problems of the eighties are raising even more fundamental questions about teamwork and its appropriate use in organizations. Today there are signs that a shift is occurring in many organizations away from hierarchical decision-making toward more emphasis on team decision-making. Although some managers claim this change is not a particularly significant one, others disagree. These men and women believe the basic nature of organizational teamwork is changing and that the kind of teamwork required for corporations to succeed, both now and in the future, is dramatically different from what has been effective in the past. Once again, the situation in organizations today seems to require a different perspective and a radically different approach.

These differences center around three important issues: the degree of structure and specialization in the roles of work group or team members, the function of the leader, and, finally, the assumptions that can be made about the environment in which the team functions. To understand these issues and their impact on the nature of teamwork, one must first understand the conventional approach to teamwork used widely throughout organizations and then contrast it with the approach needed today. How do most managers view teamwork? What do they define as their role in relation to the team?

TRADITIONAL DEFINITION OF TEAMWORK

In looking at the concept of teamwork, one cannot help noticing the influence of masculinism on the approach used within complex organizations. Among the most popular metaphors used to describe effective teamwork is the football analogy in which the group leader is compared with the quarterback who calls the plays and the members are organized into skill groups as blockers, kickers, and runners. Within the context of such a team, we see considerable role clarity, a high degree of specialization, centralized control, and a finite set of standardized responses or plays designed to overcome a variety of obstacles and to help the team reach its goal. It is a team in which the unifying goal is winning, presumably after having thought through all the strategic moves required to do just that.

If the sports analogy isn't to your liking, there is always the military metaphor. Once again, using this model, you have your lieutenant or general whose job is to keep the troops in line. Then there are the heavy artillery, the infantry, and the enlisted men. Finally, you have the enemy, the spoils when you win, and CYA for the times when you don't. To go along with this terminology, there are clearly defined limits of autonomy for every person at every level and an equally rigid organizational structure in which officers don't talk directly to enlisted men.

What both of these team-related metaphors share is a rather specific set of roles for every player, the belief in the importance of a single powerful leader, and a highly detailed, rigid set of procedures designed to keep the work of the group functioning smoothly and effectively during times of peace as well as while under fire.

"OK, I get the point," you say. "But are these images that widely used within organizations today?" If you want to get the answer firsthand, all you need do is listen to the discussions that take place as a routine part of any executive meeting. The use of sports talk and military language is rampant throughout organizations, and the belief in the concepts that these symbols represent is also widespread. As Betty Lehan Harragan states in *Games Mother Never Taught You*, "The military influence on business is morphologic. . . . The combination of military structure with team sport operation is a natural one from management's viewpoint."[2]

But how do these notions of team play fit within the dynamic corporate environment of the eighties? How well are they holding up under the pressures created by increasing competition in the world marketplace? The answer is that they are not holding up well at all. Despite enthusiastic attempts by many traditional managers to apply them, dramatic changes in the operating environment due to social and economic forces have created a strong need for a redefinition of teamwork, with new roles for all the team members and a more flexible set of operating rules. Within this changing environment, feminine leaders possess the basic skills and the vision required to respond to this need, for they function more as contemporary leaders need to function and less like traditional managers.

FEMININE CONCEPT OF TEAMWORK

Where traditional managers believe in the importance of controlling or managing the efforts of their subordinates, feminine leaders take a totally different view of their role. They see themselves primarily as empowerers, the individuals responsible for encouraging greater autonomy among group members and, thereby, improved quality in the team's output. In many respects, the differences between the traditional masculine approach to team management and the approach taken by feminine leaders are similar to differences often observed in the general male and female attitudes toward child-rearing. While many fathers want to be more controlling with their children and are comfortable in the role of disciplinarian, mothers often want to encourage self-sufficiency and seem to know intuitively that children need leeway to grow and develop in order to realize their full potential as adults.

Feminine leaders understand that controlling others' behavior does not produce the quality results that encouraging them can. How do they know? Many say they discovered this from their own negative experiences as subordinates. Others will tell you that it is just instinctive with them. In both cases, it appears that socialization and biology have equipped feminine leaders with important insights required for effective leadership today and a natural, more participative style of management. Together, they have helped to create a group of human beings who believe that positive, satisfying personal relationships are the bedrock of all productive human interactions and who are convinced that winning is the result of personal achievement and of empowering others to do the best they can rather than good strategy and expecting others to follow orders.

In her recent, highly publicized studies of gender differences, psychologist Carol Gilligan has explored the many ways in which women's psychological perspectives differ from those of men. Discussing the greater importance women tend to place on building a network or web of relationships, Gilligan points out that "the images of hierarchy and web, drawn from the text of men's and women's fantasies and thoughts, convey different ways of structuring relationships. . . . The reinterpretation of women's experience in terms of their own imagery of relationships thus clarifies that experience and also provides a nonhierarchical vision of human connection. Since relationships, when cast in the image of hierarchy, appear inherently unstable and morally problematic, their transposition into the image of web changes an order of inequality into a structure of interconnection."[3]

Connectedness and building networks in which one is at the center rather than hierarchies in which one is on top are both critical elements in effective feminine leadership. As such, they represent a unique view of the leader's role, one that seems less naïve and far more pragmatic than ever before. In discussing their personal philosophies of effective leadership, I asked several hundred successful women executives to share their views. How did they see their own role as team leaders? How did they define effective teamwork? What did they expect from the members of their work teams? What constituted good team play?

Although their specific examples were related to each woman's work setting, there was remarkable agreement among this group about the nature of teamwork. One response that typifies the view of many women regarding teamwork was offered by Martha Stewart. As a former stockbroker, successful author, lecturer, and founder of the largest fancy catering business in Connecticut, she understands the importance of good teamwork from her own experiences in developing and managing many diverse entrepreneurial businesses. In reflecting on those experiences she said, "I think women work better as a team. Men have a peculiar competition going almost all the time and it can turn into something very unpleasant. On Wall Street I saw men who worked as a team—but a team of total individuals who really didn't complement each other. I think women tend to rely on each other more and are more effective in teams. In comparison to men, they are able to subordinate their individual needs in favor of what's good for the team."

Another woman who has applied her own approach to teamwork in building a very successful business is Deborah Fields, the founder of Mrs. Fields's Cookies. Starting out in California in 1977, she has now expanded her operation to one hundred sixty stores in the United States and abroad. During a recent discussion she too had several points to make about the meaning of teamwork: "I think women in general are good at dealing with people and taking individual needs into consideration. I think it would be great for business if more managers would work to make their teams feel special, needed, and capable of doing anything."

COOPERATION VERSUS COMPETITION

Cooperation and empowerment, or the ability to make people feel they are capable of doing the best work possible, were the points raised again and again in interviews with women managers. But what of the old adage that men have a leg up in organizations because of their experiences playing competitive sports during childhood? If women tend to place greater emphasis on cooperation and positive relation-ships, what do boys learn playing team sports that they can then apply as team managers in organization settings?

According to one senior male executive in a multinational pharmaceutical firm, the lessons learned by many boys have less to do with teamwork than they do with competing and with winning. In this sense, many men have a very different view of teamwork but not necessarily a more effective ap-proach to managing teams. Here's what one man who has given this subject some serious thought has to say about teamwork: "I think that much has been made of the male's ability to be an effective team player because of socialization and team sports training. But when you say 'effective team play,' what are you really talking about? If, by effective, you mean aggressive, competitive, and driven to win, then I would agree that many boys learn these lessons playing football, basketball, and such.

"However, if what you mean is a willingness to work cooperatively with others and to share credit for accom-plishments with others, I don't necessarily agree that these are the lessons learned by boys when they compete. Nor do I think they're the values reinforced by many parents. If you've ever watched the way parents carry on at a Little League game watching their children playing ball, you know what I mean. The last thing they are interested in is coopera-tion. They want their kid to get all the breaks and walk all over the others.

"I think one of the strongest learnings men get from play-ing sports is the importance of being the star, not of sharing the success. Beating out the other guy and making the win-ning touchdown, that's what team sports teach little boys to value. Frankly, these seem to be the values that drive a lot of men throughout their entire adult lives, too."

Winning and competing for the top spot are two of the

principal rules of competitive team play. While they both can be useful strategies for succeeding within organizations, they tend to undervalue the need for positive, cooperative team relationships in which all members can grow and prosper. In reflecting on the values taught in competitive sports, Barbara Fiorito, a vice president with Chemical Bank, had this to say: "Personally, I believe the team sport/fraternity ethic is misunderstood by many people. For example, while it's true that boys know they need eleven players for a team, the two 'losers' picked to fill the last remaining positions are likely to get no real support and will probably never move up.

"Although this is used as an example of the way men work effectively in teams, this practice really has nothing to do with good teamwork. It's inside out and backwards. Unskilled players stand little or no chance of improving or succeeding in this environment. They are only chosen to fill the roster.

"On the other hand, girls are more apt to believe that how one plays the game is more important than winning. Doing your 'personal best' is what counts more with girls. Generally, I don't think that men's sports teach these same positive human values."

THE WILDERNESS SURVIVAL PROBLEM

While interviews about teamwork can illustrate philosophical differences between traditional management and feminine leadership, it is easier to see these differences at work in an actual group decision-making activity. One activity that I have often used in management development seminars to illustrate various approaches to teamwork is a wilderness survival problem. In this exercise, managers are told they have just crash-landed in a remote location and that they must organize themselves to preserve their limited resources (food, water, etc.) and to maximize their chances of being rescued. The group is given a list of available resources (an inventory of items salvaged from the plane wreckage) and asked to reach consensus on how to proceed. With limited information, they must work together to develop a plan of action taking into account the few items that they have among them (typically, these would include a compass, jackknife, flight plan, limited amounts of canned food, etc.) which might prolong their chances of survival.

Throughout this activity, which can last anywhere from sixty to ninety minutes, members of the group struggle to reach agreement on how to proceed. Should they remain at the site of the crash or should they move on? How can they protect themselves from overexposure to the hostile elements? What must they do to survive in this alien place?

Very often, in mixed groups of men and women managers the differences in approach used to solve this problem can be quite dramatic. For example, it is not unusual for the majority of the men in the group to assume that the women members have no knowledge or experience applicable to the problem. Hence, at the outset, the women are more often the members of the group with less influence. In addition, at least one or two male members usually attempt to take control of the group and, thereby, manage the discussion in a way that supports their personal views and opinions. Sometimes one may succeed in getting the other members to follow a set of procedures suggested to maintain order during the discussion. Very often, these procedures include calling for a vote at critical points in the discussion. Not surprisingly, this call for a vote often comes at moments when the leader's opinion seems to be carrying the group. Sometimes, this direct attempt by male members to assume the role of the traditional leader is thwarted by others who resist being managed or controlled in this way.

CONTROL VERSUS CONSENSUS-BUILDING

While some male members compete for control, female members are more likely to aim for compromise or consensus-building. They are more often the members who poll the group for ideas, who support the right of all members to express their opinions, and who are more willing to modify their own views based upon the evidence presented during the discussion. While males tend to control and maneuver within the group in order to satisfy their own self-interests, females demonstrate less vested interest in proving that they are right and more interest in maximizing the chances for an outcome that is satisfying to everyone within the group. But does this focus on meeting people's needs detract from the quality of the decisions that are reached in groups where women members have considerable influence? Generally, do the groups with strong traditional leaders make higher-quality decisions because of the direction and guidance that these leaders offer? As you may have already guessed, the answer to both of these questions is an emphatic no.

Time and time again I have watched groups of between twelve and twenty managers struggle with these problems. Sometimes they reach decisions with the help of a formal male leader. (In the hundred or so seminars where I have used this activity, I have never seen a woman become the formal group leader.) In other groups, the influence of the female members tends to distribute the leadership function more evenly within the group. At various points in the exercise, different members make procedural suggestions to help guide the group's discussion or contribute ideas in an effort to influence the final decision, but no one member becomes the formal leader for the duration of the exercise. While this latter approach looks less orderly and more fragmented at times, it does help to establish a less competitive and more cooperative climate for discussion in which the win-lose element of voting is minimized and the energy of the group is directed at reaching decisions that every member can support.

DIFFERENT APPROACHES PRODUCE DIFFERENT OUTCOMES

The differences in approach already outlined tend to produce different group outcomes. While these will vary in intensity within individual groups, the most common difference that can be seen across groups has to do with ownership in the final decision. In more traditional groups, where competition for leadership, minority-majority voting, and manipulation in the pursuit of self-interest have a stronger influence, the final decision is likely to be supported with less enthusiasm by the general membership. Although it may be the right decision from the standpoint of its technical merit, it will not be one that all members played a substantial role in shaping. Hence, there will be a wide range of feelings, from very positive to quite negative, about the way in which the group worked and about the final decision itself.

In groups where the influence of feminine leaders is strong, ownership in the final decision is usually higher. Because most members had an opportunity to influence the group's decisions, even if their original ideas were not all accepted, members tend to have more positive feelings about the results. As far as technical merit goes, there is no reason to believe that this consensus process produces decisions of lower technical quality. In fact, the latter seems to be true.

Human Synergistics, a firm that has developed several group decision-making exercises used widely in management development programs, has published some interesting results about the wilderness survival decisions reached in female manager groups, male manager groups, and mixed groups. In forty-eight teams studied, segregated female groups were found to reach the best technical decisions (in comparing their results to the opinions of wilderness survival experts), with some mixed groups in which men and women were represented about equally following close behind. The teams that scored lowest, in terms of the overall quality of their decisions, were those in which males were in the majority.[4]

Results such as these suggest that basic differences exist in the approach to teamwork taken by women and men. However, it is important to note that they also suggest men and women can reach decisions of higher technical quality by integrating their approaches to teamwork rather than by using the traditional approach alone. Balance and integration of masculine and feminine styles can produce better quality and greater ownership in team decisions than the traditional approach does on its own.

INCREASED EMPLOYEE PARTICIPATION

Teamwork is just one element of participative management that feminine leaders define and approach quite differently from traditional managers. Whether they are working in a team with peers or managing a work group, feminine leaders tend to behave in very similar ways: putting cooperation ahead of competition and seeking input and support from all members of the group. To them, participative management, from fostering open communication and soliciting employee input to establishing mutually agreed upon goals and encouraging creativity and increased autonomy among team members, is more than a set of techniques. It is a basic operating philosophy that guides their every action. Because participative management is an integral part of the way feminine leaders operate, it is not viewed as a threat to their authority nor is it something that they are reluctant to support. Dealing with problems by facilitating the development of solutions within the group is a natural part of their management style.

In contrast, many traditional managers see increased employee participation in decision-making as an erosion of their influence and, in some cases, a threat to stability and the organization structure itself. In organizations where fear and distrust of participative processes prevail, attempts to increase employee involvement and to move decision-making authority down to lower levels are frequently met with strong resistance. Descriptions like rebellion and anarchy are used to describe this process, and people line up on each side of this issue according to how tough or soft they are as managers. Needless to say, being labeled soft is nothing short of an insult in some organizations. But feminine leaders are willing to risk this because of the value they believe the team approach can add. Sometimes, women point to the traditional managers they have worked for as their inspiration for developing a more participative style. Stephanie Solien, executive director of the Women's Campaign Fund, heads a national fund-raising organization that raises money for women political candidates. The success of her effort greatly depends on the cooperative efforts of her entire staff. Consequently, she is a strong believer in the importance of teamwork and participation. In reflecting on how she developed her own participative style she said, "One of the practices that I have instituted, as a result of observing many men who did not do this, is holding regular staff meetings. I think employee involvement and two-way communications are critical to the effectiveness of this organization."

As defined by many feminine leaders, participative management includes sharing critical information with employees to enable them to function more effectively. This is a significantly different approach from that of many traditional managers. Whereas traditional managers often regard knowledge as a source of power, particularly when that source is somewhat limited, feminine leaders view it as a source of empowerment. Hence, it is less likely that one will find secrecy and a reluctance to share information within a feminine leader's work group. This emphasis on shared knowledge is also related to the role of knowledge worker that many feminine leaders play within their own work groups.

THE PROBLEMS WITH PROFESSIONAL MANAGERS

One recent development within many organizations has been the emergence of the professional managers, or people who see their sole function as overseers and supervisors of the output of others. Generally, these managers do not regard themselves as knowledge workers or producers. Instead, they see themselves as coordinators who rely on the members of their staffs for ideas, information, and the outputs required to satisfy customer needs. Indeed, many of these management generalists never write their own correspondence or deliver a speech that they themselves have written because their technical knowledge of the businesses they run is so limited. Having operated in a knowledge vacuum throughout much of their careers, they do not regard a basic knowledge of their organization's business as important to their functioning. Instead, they rely on the specialists within their organizations to write their letters and speeches and to respond to any requests they receive for technical information. The only thing that their employees are never expected to do is receive credit for such shadow assistance. As the managers, they must sign the letters and give the speeches. After all, that's what they're getting paid for.

But is this truly what today's managers are getting paid for? If so, it seems a gross misuse of their time and energies. As participative managers, many women realize that they must be more than supervisors. In addition to encouraging others, they must also be able to contribute ideas and information that move the work of the group ahead. In essence, they must be models of what a high-performing employee should act like right down to contributing their own ideas to the group's decision-making efforts. Participative managers must, indeed, participate!

LIP SERVICE NOT ENOUGH

Unfortunately, some traditional managers have little understanding of what participative management is or how to implement it but still feel obliged to give it lip service support. Despite their professed belief in its benefits, their actions continue to be those of the authoritarian leader. Where managers seem unable or unwilling to walk like they talk, their superficial commitment to participative management can do even more damage to employee morale than authoritarian management methods have done in the past. For the philosophy of participative management carries with it the implicit promise of greater dignity, recognition, and shared values, as well as increased trust and cooperation among all members of the organization. These are ambitious goals for any manager to work toward—and impossible ones to achieve without a sincere and lasting commitment.

Since American business leaders first saw the positive results of participative management methods used by many Japanese competitors, there has been enormous effort expended throughout the United States to copy this approach but with far less positive results. The names of U.S. companies that have attempted to implement participative management methods without building senior management commitment could probably fill a small telephone book. Countless examples exist in which employees have been encouraged to offer their input to solve company problems only to discover that management is not at all committed to taking their ideas seriously. Because of the increased tensions and additional morale problems that have often resulted where participative management has been poorly implemented, many companies are beginning to view it as a process too dangerous to implement.

As an example, let's take the president of a leading manufacturing company, who is considered by many to be an enlightened manager and innovator. At a recent human resources conference, he was invited to talk about the role that participative management might play in the future. Speaking extemporaneously, he began by admitting that he knew little about participative management and employee involvement and then went on to describe them both as "loaded pistols." Needless to say, his audience was stunned by these comments and, as the group responsible for implementing employee involvement throughout their own organizations, they were also extremely discouraged.

But to expect that traditional managers can easily change their style, priorities, and basic approach to leading and become participative is naïve and unrealistic. Even under the most supportive and favorable circumstances, where the necessary corporate commitment, incentives, and structures are in place, such changes are evolutionary rather than dramatic. As Rosabeth Moss Kanter points out in *The Change Masters,* "participators are made not born."[5]

Yet, there are those who seem to take to this style of management easily, like fish to water. Instead of danger, they see opportunity. Instead of fearing a loss of control, they are excited by the prospects of renewed energy, creativity, and the increased freedom that participative management can produce. As participative leaders, they have a lifetime of training to draw on and the natural instincts to help guide their day-to-day actions.

In talks with feminine leaders, this interest in teamwork and participative management stands out immediately. It is clear, seeing them in work groups, that their actions are guided by a strong belief in the value of consensus-building and cooperation. While they understand the need for honesty and direct feedback, they see no inherent conflict between these and the need for cooperation and trust within their groups. In fact, they are quick to tell you that both are necessary elements in effective teamwork.

Amy Levin, editor in chief of *Mademoiselle* magazine, spoke about this need for honesty, direct feedback, and cooperation in work teams. In describing the way in which her work team deals with these complex needs she said, "I don't know what group could work together more effectively than the women who work here. They have meetings where many different points of view must be woven into consensus and they all work very hard at reaching this goal. I often function just in the capacity of saying, 'That's good, that's not, let's stop.' If I were to be too authoritarian, this group wouldn't be nearly as effective.

"And I don't mean that we don't talk openly about our differences. I think everyone feels free to say, 'No. I hate that idea,' without upsetting everyone else. We have that much respect and trust among us. I don't know any men who work together as well as the women in this group."

Although there is a need for a more participative style of management throughout organizations, it is not realistic to expect such a change to occur rapidly. People change slowly. More important, most will never alter their basic values and beliefs. It simply isn't possible in every case to change what has taken a lifetime to build. While this holds true for traditional managers who have spent their careers competing, controlling, and strategizing in order to succeed, it is equally true for feminine leaders. Forcing one group to adopt the behaviors and values of the other won't work. Using the strengths and the talents of both will.

Chapter Eight

Interpersonal Effectiveness

If there is one aspect of management where stylistic differences between men and women are most evident, it is in the area of interpersonal effectiveness—that is, managing relationships and managing one's own feelings as well. Here, one can easily see vivid contrasts between the approach used by feminine leaders to manage work relationships and the approach used by most traditional managers. While interpersonal competence is a recognized source of power for all managers, it is much more than this to feminine leaders, for establishing and maintaining effective relationships is the cornerstone on which their entire approach to managing and leading is built. Instead of regarding relationships as the necessary means to further one's ends, feminine leaders regard quality in relationships as a worthy end unto itself. The result is a very different approach to dealing with people, an approach that depends on a unique set of highly developed people management skills.

"And just what are these skills?" you ask. They are actually rather simple and straightforward functions like listening carefully and giving clear, direct feedback. The uniqueness lies in the attention feminine leaders give to the subtleties of human interactions, the proficiency with which they use their interpersonal skills, and the results that their approach produces within organizations.

Imagine, for a moment, the difference one would notice between a complex piece of baroque music played by a classically trained musician and that same piece of music played by a student with little formal training. Both the experienced musician and the amateur may, indeed, play the exact same notes, but the overall results of their efforts are likely to be very different. Where the first would be smooth and flowing with a natural ease and lilting grace, the second would be hesitant and choppy. Where the skilled musician would be able to uncover and enhance the nuances and complexities of the piece, the amateur would be forced to focus less on these in order to concentrate on hitting the right notes. As one listened and compared these two players, the professional's depth of experience and the amateur's limited interpretive skills would be difficult to ignore.

KEY INTERPERSONAL SKILLS

In the realm of interpersonal effectiveness, feminine leaders have much in common with skilled musicians, for they bring a wealth of life experience to help them manage relationships effectively and possess a finely honed set of skills required to achieve this goal. Unlike traditional leaders, who may hit the right notes but miss the richness and complexity of the music, feminine leaders see the intricacies in human relationships and believe that, like every other set of issues, these must be managed rather than ignored. To accomplish this goal, several key interpersonal skills are required. The following is a listing of those interpersonal skills frequently identified as more finely developed in feminine leaders:

- *Sensing Skills:* The ability to pick up on nonverbal cues; to place oneself in another's position, either literally or figuratively, and to understand his or her feelings and reactions.

- *Listening Skills:* Paying close attention to what is being said by others and how it is being stated. Using nonverbal cues to encourage open discussion. Letting people finish their thoughts without interrupting.

- *Management of Feelings:* Being attuned to one's feelings and to environmental conditions that trigger various feelings. Using one's own feeling reactions as an emotional barometer within group settings. Expressing feelings as a method of enhancing communications and asking for feeling reactions from others. Reacting spontaneously to situations. Considering feelings when making decisions.

- *Intimacy/Authenticity:* Developing a personal rapport with others. Sharing personal data about oneself and encouraging others to do this. Focusing on the whole individual, not just the employee.

- *The Use of Feedback:* Giving clear, direct performance feedback that focuses on actions. Soliciting feedback from colleagues and employees. Using feedback to modify one's behavior.

- *Assessing Personal Impact:* Understanding the impact of one's behavior on others. Recognizing how one is being perceived and the consequences of one's actions on relationship-building.

SENSING SKILLS

In their popular book on corporate excellence, Tom Peters and Bob Waterman emphasize the importance of "management by wandering around."[1] Meeting with people on their turf, seeing employees at work in their natural habitat, and encouraging candid, informal exchanges are techniques that are part of this managerial approach. Another popular concept used to illustrate the same principle is "deep sensing." As described in an article titled "The Visible Manager," this technique is largely the result of using one's common sense. The idea is that, if managers really want to know how something is working within their companies, they need to get out and talk to employees.[2]

To find out where the problems and the opportunities really are, managers must experience what is really happening within the organization rather than sit in their offices and wait for the reports to be sent in. Some traditional managers understand the importance of such informal contacts. They believe that the quality of their own decisions can be enhanced by getting information directly from those employees who are implementing the actual change. As one chief operating officer of a prominent company put it, "If we install a new system in the Buffalo branch office, by the time the progress reports get from Buffalo to me in New York, they've lost most of their punch. It's a little like sewer water, by the time it gets filtered a dozen or more times, it looks like spring water when it finally arrives here. But while it may look good, it doesn't tell me what I need to know."

Finding out what's on the minds and in the hearts of employees has recently begun to be viewed as a useful and necessary step in the overall management process within many companies. Although it is talked about as something new and different, many feminine leaders argue that "management by wandering around" is an aspect of the way they have always operated. One highly successful woman manager who believes that this is so is Ellen Sulzberger Straus, president and general manager of WMCA Radio. As an executive with a great variety of experience in broadcasting, journalism, and politics, she thinks there is something to the idea of stylistic differences between men and women. In discussing feminine leadership she had this observation to offer: "Generally, women do understand the dynamics of human relations and are more interested in them than are most men. They have better sensing skills and, as a result, employees often feel a kind of caring on the part of a woman manager."

Looking beneath the surface to find out what's really on someone's mind is a talent that requires careful attention and an ability to empathize with people. Dr. Sharon Connelly of USC calls this characteristic "the ability to pay delicate attention." She believes that most women, as well as those men who have developed more feminine traits, are able to pay closer attention to their surroundings, to pick up on more verbal and nonverbal cues, and to empathize with the feelings and reactions of others.

In reflecting on her own career, Mary Kay Ash recently wrote about some of her early experiences working for many traditional managers who lacked this ability to empathize. In her view, "Their shortcomings were due to a lack of empathy for their associates. They failed to ask themselves that all-important question: *'What would I do if I were the other person?'* "[3]

LISTENING SKILLS

For many feminine leaders, empathy for the positions of others is required for good decision-making. One skill that makes gathering such data easier is the ability to listen carefully to what others are saying. Listening is one area in which women have received considerable training. Despite the negative stereotypes associated with girls' socialization as good listeners, this ability to listen well is a useful and increasingly important managerial skill in today's corporate environment, for accurate sensing can result only from careful listening. One interesting outgrowth of early socialization is the nonverbal behavior that women tend to exhibit when they are listening. According to the research, women nod their heads more during discussions and maintain more continuous eye contact as well.[4] What these active listening responses tend to do is signal the person who is talking to continue. They encourage the other person by indicating that the listener is tracking with each thought. In contrast, research conducted during the last decade indicates that men tend to use fewer nonverbal cues when they are listening. In addition, they tend to talk more in mixed groups, taking almost twice the airtime that women do, and also interrupt the flow of conversation more frequently.[5]

One of the many ways in which feminine leaders use their finely developed sensing and listening skills is to hear and to decipher what's not being said by others as well as what is. By being aware of the feelings of others, which often remain unspoken, women managers can develop a more complete picture of what is occurring within their work groups. How are people feeling about their jobs? the work climate created by the organizational structure and senior management? their relationships with coworkers? What do they really think of the organizations they work for, and more important, how do they view the role they are expected to play in order to achieve corporate goals? Tuning in to emotional tones and nonverbal cues can often help in finding the answers to these questions.

In many innovative corporations, the perceptions and feelings of employees are beginning to get some serious attention from senior management. In some companies, elaborate surveys are now being used in which employees are polled regularly for their reactions on critical issues. What these surveys provide is a general profile of the organizational climate and the problems and issues as seen through the eyes of workers. Unfortunately, in some places such surveys are used to compensate for a lack of sensing skills within management.

While they can help to sharpen management's focus, employee attitude surveys cannot replace direct contact between managers and their work groups. They cannot capture what is below the surface—the thoughts and feelings that employees have about themselves, their colleagues, and their work that they are reluctant to express. Very often, these feelings provide invaluable data about the organization itself and can serve as a powerful catalyst for change if they are recognized and understood by managers.

MANAGEMENT OF FEELINGS

While sensing skills and listening skills are key ingredients, the ability to manage feelings is an equally important aspect of interpersonal effectiveness. Although some traditional managers still believe there is no room for emotions at the office, the fact is that everyone has feelings whether we choose to acknowledge them or not. Unlike thoughts, our feelings can usually be stated in simple terms: We feel good or bad, happy or sad, fearful or courageous. When it comes to feelings, just a few descriptive words are required.

Yet, for many men and fewer women, acknowledging one's own feelings is one of the most difficult tasks. While each of us has a need to express our true feelings, we often confuse the way we feel with what we think. From early childhood, we are taught to value rational thought and to discount our emotional reactions to situations. Over time, we learn to mask our feelings from others and to ignore them ourselves.

To varying degrees, this is what socialization does, especially to little boys. By encouraging boys to ignore their own feelings, society tends to blunt their ability to respond emotionally to other people. Later as adults, many men are able to rationalize their reactions to most situations without ever examining how they feel. Eventually, after years of careful neglect, they lose touch with their inner emotional life. Even in cases where they want to feel and to express their feelings to others, they are unable to do so.

Losing touch with one's own feelings is a rather sad but real part of growing up male. While there are signs that this pattern of socialization may be changing somewhat, this change does not appear to be having much impact on organization life. In most corporations, expressing emotion is still considered "unprofessional," and having sympathy for the feelings of employees is often viewed as a waste of time. Yet, for feminine leaders, monitoring feelings is as important for effective management as a road map is in a strange city. Feelings are the guideposts required to understand all human interaction. Without them, one can only begin to speculate about the quality of a relationship or an interaction. With them, there is a much greater certainty of accurately perceiving others—both where they stand and how they feel.

POWERS OF EMPATHY

Recognizing the feelings of others isn't easy. It requires an ability to empathize and to project oneself into another person's situation. "How might I feel under similar circumstances?" is a question commonly asked by feminine leaders when assessing the emotional tone of a situation. To answer it, they must have a high degree of awareness of their own emotional makeup. As the people largely responsible for the maintenance of relationships within the family and, later, within organizations, women stay in regular touch with their own emotions and use their own feelings to gauge the emotional tone of one-on-one and group interactions.

One aspect of early socialization that has a direct effect on the behavior of feminine leaders is the social permission they receive to express their feelings. Since, as young girls there was nothing inappropriate about showing emotions, feminine leaders see emotions as a natural part of human interactions. Even in the work setting, where traditional leaders avoid any emotional display (other than anger) and discourage these interactions with employees, feminine leaders do not. In fact, many speak of the discomfort they have felt working in companies where the feelings of employees were ignored. As one woman journalist with a Chicago newspaper said, "Around here the only feeling that's OK to express is anger. No one ever talks about being scared, hurt, or happy. It's as though any admission of such things somehow diminishes one's stature. So instead people act tough or else they react like robots . . . with no emotion at all. Coming from a totally different kind of environment, where I felt free to share my feelings with my friends and my colleagues, I sometimes now feel as though I've landed on the moon. People, including many of the women, think they have to behave like macho newspapermen all the time instead of human beings."

To feminine leaders, managing feelings does not mean suppressing them or discouraging others from displaying their emotions. Instead, it means providing opportunities for the healthy venting of strong feelings as a means of working them through. One key difference between their approach to the issue of emotionalism and the approach of traditional leaders is this provision of an outlet for the expression of strong feelings that they themselves require and that they also provide for others. In the view of feminine leaders, productive human interaction involves the exchange and expression of both thoughts and feelings. Because they see emotions as playing a significant role in human communication, feminine leaders believe that feelings deserve acknowledgment just as thoughts and ideas are acknowledged. When they are not dealt with openly, negative feelings tend to become exaggerated, like a sore that festers. On the other hand, if positive feelings are consistently ignored, they begin to lose their luster like a flowering plant that receives too little sun.

Because feminine leaders have learned to communicate with their feelings as well as with their thoughts, their view of human interaction takes into account the dialogue that is constantly occurring at both the emotional and intellectual levels. They pay close attention to what is being said and the emotional tone associated with every statement or action. As such, they are trained to be keen observers of both the content of interactions and the process or method used to communicate.

As process observers, women tend to pay closer attention to how people interact as well as to what they have to say. In one-on-one interactions, they study nonverbal cues such as facial expressions, posture, and degree of eye contact, as well as verbal cues like vocal inflections, the timing of interruptions, and the general level of interest or excitement conveyed in the other person's voice. Women's heightened sensitivity to nonverbal cues was confirmed by the results of an extensive study published in 1979 under the title *Sensitivity to Nonverbal Communication: The Pons Test.*

Developed and refined by a team of five researchers from Harvard, Johns Hopkins, and the University of California, the Pons Test measures the ability to decipher nonverbal cues transmitted by facial expressions, body movements, and tones of voice.

The research described in the study was conducted among carefully controlled samples of more than 4,500 males and females of varying ages. The data showed "females to excel over males collapsing (examined collectively) over all age groups" in all areas of nonverbal communications.[6] The report continued: "Because the sex effect shows up so early, we would have to assume that differential learning of nonverbal skills occurs very early . . . . More research relating non-verbal sensitivity to sex-role socialization is necessary before we can begin to understand the origins of the sex differences we have observed."[7]

PROCESS AND FACILITATION SKILLS

In addition to heightened sensitivity to nonverbal cues, women also have a more fully developed set of process skills. They are both skillful observers and facilitators. In group situations, women look for and discover patterns of communication. They notice who talks to whom, who initiates topic changes, where the unspoken alliances are within the group, where the potential conflicts are, and the group's general level of receptivity to various ideas and proposals. While they are equally interested in the content of discussions, their process observation skills help them fill in the gaps between what people say and what they truly think and feel.

With the benefit of this additional data, feminine leaders are often in a better position to facilitate improved group interaction and discussion. Within their own work settings, they are able to help coworkers interact more effectively by acknowledging their feelings and by guiding or facilitating group discussions to create a supportive climate for the open exchange of ideas.

Process skills give feminine leaders a three-dimensional view of human interaction. They are able to see and understand the thoughts, feelings, and behaviors of other people and to use these data to formulate more appropriate responses. While traditional male managers judge most interactions solely on the basis of the rational facts that they see before them (be they ideas or actions), most women also look at the emotional undercurrents that lie beneath the surface of every human exchange. Instead of separating out feelings from thoughts and behaviors, they integrate all three sources of data and react accordingly.

SENSITIVITIES BIOLOGICALLY BASED

Although the impact of biological differences between the sexes is not, as yet, fully clear, a growing number of scientists are beginning to speculate about how behavioral differences in the area of interpersonal sensitivity might be linked to biologic ones. In *Sex and the Brain*, Jerry Levy, a biopsychologist at the University of Chicago, speculates about the possible connection between hemispheral differences in male and female brains and interpersonal skills. Here are some of her speculations:

"The evidence, you see, is that the hemispheres of male brains are specialists—they speak different languages, verbal and visual-spatial. And it may be that they can communicate with each other only in a formal way, after encoding into abstract representations. The hemispheres of female brains, on the other hand, don't seem to be such specialists. And they may be able to communicate in a less formal, less structured and more rapid way. If this is so, then it's entirely possible that females are much better than males at integrating verbal and non-verbal information—at reading the emotional content of tones of voice and intensities of facial expression, for example; at interpreting social cues such as posture and gesture; at quickly fitting all sorts of peripheral information—information in different modes—into a complete picture. This may be at the root of what we call female intuition, the ability of women, which men think illogical, . . . to produce a complete character analysis, later often proved right, of someone they've met for only ten minutes."[8]

Some traditional managers who recognize the different perspective that feminine leaders bring to group situations have learned to make use of these skills within their organizations. These managers make it a point to ask for feedback from feminine leaders at the end of meetings in order to get their process observations about how the group seemed to be working. Although it would undoubtedly be more beneficial if all managers were able to use their own observation skills to assess the emotional tone within group meetings, it is far more difficult for many men to do this.

A prerequisite to becoming a skillful process observer is an awareness of one's own feelings. For the many men who have lost touch with their own emotional reactions over the years, this is a difficult if not impossible task. However, as the need for these skills becomes greater within organizations and society at large, an increasing number of traditional men are becoming more interested in developing their own interpersonal effectiveness through enhanced group process skills. For such men, the process insights of feminine leaders can be particularly useful in learning to see what really lies beneath the surface of group interactions.

In his best-selling book about Theory Z management, William Ouchi emphasizes the importance of group process skills for today's successful manager. He also states his belief that many of these skills can be acquired by those with an interest in learning this different style of leadership. "Just as one can learn in medical school to interpret an X ray meaningless to the untrained eye, so one can learn to 'see' group interaction in quite a different way than that of the layperson. Learning to see when a group moves too quickly to a solution in order to avoid discussing the real problem, learning to observe how some members interfere in subtle ways with an open discussion, learning to note when the group drifts off course—all of these are acquired skills."[9]

HEAD AND HEART

While traditional managers are working to acquire the techniques used naturally by feminine leaders, some are also realizing that there are other reasons for encouraging women to be more themselves in the workplace. Feminine leaders bring an openness and depth of feeling for other people with whom they work that can only be described in terms of having "heart."

In his book *The Gamesman,* Michael Maccoby discusses the lack of heart among successful executives in the corporate world. His research indicated that, by and large, corporations reward executives for using the head to relate rationally to their work, solve problems, and develop ideas. In his view, the qualities of the heart are missing from organizations and are underdeveloped in the executives who run them. In describing the dichotomy that seems to exist between the head and the heart in organizational settings, Dr. Maccoby shared these eloquent thoughts:

"People think of qualities of the heart as opposite to those

146

of the head. They think heart means softness, feeling, and generosity, while head means tough-minded, realistic thought. But this contrast is itself symptomatic of a schizoid culture, in which the head is detached from the rest of the body. In pre-Cartesian traditional thought, the heart was considered the true seat of intelligence and the brain the instrument of thinking. It is more precise to say that some kinds of knowledge require both the head and the heart. The head alone can decipher codes, solve technical problems, and keep accounts, but no amount of technical knowledge can resolve emotional doubt about what is true or what is beautiful. No amount of technique can produce courage. The head alone cannot give emotional and spiritual weight to knowledge in terms of its human values. The head can be smart but not wise."

Later in his book, Maccoby goes on to say, ". . . the development of the heart determines not only compassion and generosity, but also one's perception-experience, the quality of knowledge, capacity for affirmation . . . and the will to action. . . .

"The quality of perception depends on our openness to experience. We can 'see' that another person is sad or happy, but if our hearts are open to him, we also experience with him. Empathy and compassion . . . are activities of an open, listening heart."[10]

Michael Maccoby's work is based on research of a largely male sample of managers. Of those interviewed, only 4 percent were women. Given the accommodating roles that many successful women have felt obliged to play in the past, it is likely that few if any of those in this sample used a feminine leadership style to manage, for despite the evidence that points to the need for greater heart within management, women have been advised continuously to suppress their emotional nature on the job.

147

WOMEN ADVISED TO SUPPRESS EMOTIONS

Even in *The Managerial Woman*, one of the most widely read books about how to succeed in business, this is the advice offered to women executives regarding the expression of emotions in an office setting: "Women grow up in an environment which allows them and often encourages them to express emotion freely and openly. It is entirely acceptable for girls to cry. Men grow up learning that it is unmanly to cry, that only sissies show emotions that are not aggressive and hence 'masculine.' Most men learn early in life to build defenses against expressing those feelings or emotions they have learned to see as 'feminine.'

". . . What we do want to do—placing no value judgments whatsoever—is to consider the impact on individual women of the stereotype many men hold about women at work: that under pressure, when criticized, when attacked, women will get so upset, be so unable to manage their feelings, that they will break down and cry.

"There is truth in this stereotype. Women tend to express feelings far more directly and in doing so they often make men extremely uncomfortable."[11] Here again, the advice to women who wanted success is: Manage your feelings so as not to make men uncomfortable. During the mid-seventies, with the vast majority of working women still outside the managerial ranks in corporations, this expedient advice seemed to make sense.

Ironically, despite the dramatic changes that have taken place throughout American industry since that time and the enormous need for a new approach to leadership today, accommodating advice continues to be offered to women managers. In a recent article written for The Conference Board's monthly publication *Across the Board*, readers were told, "Life and human nature being what they are, different-but-equal is a wishful myth" for women managers. Consequently, women were advised to learn to control their communication style (that is, the way they talk) because, "For many corporate women . . . significant differences from men's communication styles can . . . become a subtle but powerful career liability."[12]

A far less subtle liability can be seen in organizations where managers lack the heart and wisdom required to see the inherent benefits in feminine leadership. For if maintaining their feminine style presents problems for female leaders, changing it to conform to masculine norms creates far greater difficulties for both the women and their organizations. Today, organizations need the interpersonal perspectives, the people orientation that women provide. They have to appeal to their employees' needs for human recognition, dignity, and fair treatment as well as to their desire for challenging work. Today, organizations must begin to develop more authentic, intimate relationships among employees at all levels and the first step toward greater cooperation, intimacy, and trust must be taken by middle and senior management.

INTIMACY AND AUTHENTICITY

This need for greater intimacy within organizations is an idea that most American business leaders have yet to accept. In the opinion of many, the idea is antithetical to the way professional business relationships have been developed and managed in the past. While this is absolutely true, it is also true that the strictly business approach to management used in the past is far less effective today. Instead of maintaining social distance at work, today's managers must be able to demonstrate caring, support, and concern for people. They must be relationship-builders first and supervisors second. But this change has been slow in coming.

149

FEMININE LEADERSHIP

In analyzing the reasons behind this reluctance to change, Dr. William Ouchi has contrasted Japanese organizations, which recognize the need for intimacy, with American businesses, where intimacy is regarded as inappropriate to the work environment. Commenting on the way in which American business leaders approach this idea he wrote, "In the contemporary American mind, there is apparently the idea that intimacy should only be supplied from certain sources. The church, the family, and other traditional institutions are the only legitimate sources of intimacy. We resist the idea that there can or should be a close familiarity with people in the workplace. 'Personal feelings have no place at work,' is the common feeling. Yet we are faced with an anomaly. . . . The Japanese example forces us to reconsider our deeply held beliefs about the proper sources of intimacy in society."[13]

The value of intimacy in the workplace is something most feminine leaders do not talk about. They recognize that the subject would be deemed inappropriate by many of their colleagues. Nonetheless, it is a quality they strive to build and maintain within their work groups. Some describe it as "getting to know the people as people . . . instead of as employees." Others talk in terms of "being supportive of people, being available if there is a personal problem." In each case, their emphasis is on reaching past the surface of professionalism in order to touch people and relate to individuals.

June Gottlieb, a former account supervisor with Ted Bates Advertising who now heads her own marketing consulting firm in New York, commented on this feminine leadership quality: "Generally, women are more interested in personal viewpoints. Where men may see this personal focus as irrelevant, women do not. I think women are less apt to use a 'strictly business' approach to management and this style serves many of us very well."

Donna Ecton, a graduate of the Harvard Business School and past president of MBA Resources, an executive placement firm, also talked about her own approach to relationship-building and intimacy in a recent magazine article: "Women have an advantage in business if they realize that they don't have to act like men. When I was managing 650 people, I was very unorthodox. I baked cookies for people and hugged them when they did well. People need to feel valued and cared about."[14]

USE OF FEEDBACK

Maintaining an organizational climate in which people feel valued and cared about requires ongoing attention from management, the kind of attention that women exhibit naturally as feminine leaders. One important element of good maintenance is regular feedback. As Ken Blanchard emphasizes in *The One Minute Manager,* people need to know where they stand and ongoing performance feedback is the best way to let them know.

Perhaps being outside the informal communication network used by many male managers causes many feminine leaders to place a high priority on regular feedback. As a woman executive recruiter stated, "The most powerful positions in this country are held by men. And there is sufficient discomfort with bringing women into the 'off the record' kind of meetings that I think it will be a long while before you'll have a woman as part of the inner circle."

As members of the outer circle, women managers have had limited access to informal feedback about where they stand in organizations and have had to rely on formal organizational processes such as periodic work reviews and annual appraisals to gauge their perceived effectiveness. Because these formal processes have been the primary source of feedback and reinforcement for many women, female managers tend to see such mechanisms as more important tools than do many traditional managers. One recent survey conducted by the American Management Association points up this difference in the way men and women view the formal organization. Results show women executives place a higher value on the importance of organizational stability than their male peers.[15] To many women, a stable environment, in which the parameters of acceptable performance are clear, is still the only environment in which they believe they will be treated fairly.

Fairness is still a major issue for most women managers today. As such, letting employees know where they stand continues to be of prime importance to feminine leaders. Looking at the backgrounds and experiences of many feminine leaders, it is easy to see how the treatment they received as employees has played a key role in establishing their priorities and shaping their managerial values. As the recipients of less than equal treatment in the past, many feminine leaders feel a great sense of commitment to treating employees differently—with the respect, support, and concern that they themselves seldom received. This empathy for employees, growing out of prior experience as an employee, often guides the judgments and actions of feminine leaders, for the concerns of employees are a high priority within this group. Interestingly, the same AMA survey also reported that women managers ranked employees much higher than male managers did in terms of their organizational importance.[16]

ASSESSING PERSONAL IMPACT

Not only is regular feedback a high priority among feminine leaders, but the quality of that feedback is also extremely important to this group. While the impact of direct feedback on someone's feelings may be of little concern to some traditional managers, it is of high concern to feminine leaders. These managers believe that feedback, both positive and negative, can be of value only if it is accompanied by respect for the individual and a high degree of trust.

Where many traditional managers ignore the emotional impact that negative feedback has on employees, feminine leaders use a different approach in order to encourage rather than attack. As Amy Levin of *Mademoiselle* states, "Women's social skills are more finely honed and these skills come into play more than most people realize in managing. In terms of feedback, women know how to state the negatives in positive terms. Nonetheless, they are able to let people know when something is unacceptable. But they do this without hurting or destroying relationships."

In building her cosmetics company, Mary Kay Ash developed some unique guidelines for feedback which reflect the concerns that many feminine leaders have about maintaining positive relationships. Here are her thoughts on feedback:

"I think women use more diplomacy, more tact, more of their own feelings than men do in managing. Many men seem to think they can go directly to the point and that it doesn't matter who they hurt in order to do it. I think it matters a great deal. Human society is very delicate. Direct criticism can injure people even if they pretend not to be injured. Nobody likes it.

"One of my favorite sayings is that in this company we stack every bit of criticism between two heavy layers of praise. I think this is a more diplomatic, concerned approach."

Unlike traditional managers, feminine leaders see nothing antithetical in maintaining positive work relationships and giving clear, direct feedback. In fact, many say that as work relationships improve, so does the level of honesty within the organization. Why can this group accomplish what traditional managers often maintain cannot be done? It is a simple matter of interpersonal effectiveness: of sensing, of listening, of managing feelings, of knowing when to confront and when to support, and of conveying sincerity, caring, and respect to other people. It is a simple matter, but it is not easy.

Yet, in observing these women as they meet with employees, manage their work groups, make decisions, and deal with difficult issues, one begins to think that interpersonal effectiveness is easy to develop. Watching these women use their skills is a bit like watching an Olympic athlete in training. What you observe looks simple and effortless, so much so that you may begin to think you can do just as well yourself. This is the real measure of the feminine leader's ability. She performs so well, it looks easy. Just as sensing, listening, expressing feelings, and sharing honest feedback are all important ingredients in successful personal relationships, there is increasing recognition that they are equally important in healthy work relationships. But, traditionally, organizations have placed a low priority on these skills and, as a result, have encouraged and rewarded a managerial style that can be characterized as both impersonal and distant.

Although most managers have been reinforced for being task-oriented at the expense of employee concerns, even authoritarian organizations have placed limits on the level of impersonality deemed acceptable. In some companies, executives who overstep the boundaries of acceptable behavior are sent to charm schools to tone down their managerial style. Occasionally, at the suggestion of their organizations, these managers may attend sensitivity training sessions in which they are encouraged to examine the impact of their interpersonal style on others in a less threatening, anonymous environment.

BENEFITS OF SENSITIVITY TRAINING

When they are used to enhance sensitivity rather than to punish the insensitive, awareness seminars can help managers develop insights into the impact of their behavior on others and can give them the clear, direct feedback required to modify their style. However, these sessions are not intended to be used as remedial training for managers who need to be "fixed." Because they have been misused in this way by many organizations, such developmental experiences have acquired a negative reputation that is largely undeserved.

The history of the T-group, or sensitivity training group, underscores the shortage of interpersonal effectiveness that has existed within management for several decades. When it was first used in the late forties and early fifties, the T-group was designed to develop the emotionally flat side of traditional male leaders by helping them develop a greater awareness of their personal impact on others and the interpersonal dynamics that affect work relationships. Through participation in small, unstructured groups, managers were encouraged to share their feelings and to give and receive feedback regarding the effectiveness of their interpersonal styles. Over time, as interpersonal and group process skills remained low priorities within organizations, T-groups became passé. In the last few years, as these skills have increased in importance within organizations, sensitivity training has begun to build momentum again.

What is most interesting about T-groups today is the qualitative difference in the interactions of such groups because of the increase in the number of women managers who participate. Based upon my own experiences in T-groups, I believe that the presence of a critical mass of women has added immeasurably to the value of the learning for all group members. As practitioners of a different managerial style, women are more able to share their personal insights, experiences, and sensitivities within these groups and, as a result, are often instrumental in helping male colleagues appreciate and understand many complex interpersonal issues.

Feminine leaders also display remarkable skill in deciphering their impact on others. Within the context of the T-group, where greater awareness of one's impact is a major goal, women often demonstrate that increased awareness of personal impact is a direct result of paying delicate attention through sensing and active listening as well as through the honest expression of ideas and feelings. Whereas many men fail to see how their intended impact differs from the actual effect that their ideas and actions have on others, most women are able to gauge their real impact with a remarkable degree of accuracy.

While some behavioral scientists contend that women managers should avoid these experiences and, instead, concentrate on becoming desensitized in order to reduce their vulnerability in organizations, others, like myself, disagree. We think the T-group offers women managers an opportunity to use all their interpersonal skills in a mixed setting and to discover the powerful impact that these skills can have on team effectiveness and other individuals. In this sense, experience in a T-group is often a source of positive reinforcement for feminine leaders who can use it to refine their natural skills and insights in a supportive setting. In addition, the value of the T-group in developing awareness among men and women of stylistic differences can be enormous, provided all participants attend voluntarily.

HOLISTIC MANAGEMENT

Throughout the contemporary research on U.S. companies, there are numerous examples of the need for a more integrated approach to management, an approach that balances the importance of profit against the concern for people. Whether one calls these qualities of the head and heart holistic management, Theory Z, awareness, or sensitivity, the emphasis is largely the same. Today's competent manager must not only possess the talents and insights required to improve the bottom line, but must also possess the interpersonal skills required to empower others. But while recent research points to the need for a more balanced approach to managing, it has not gone far enough in identifying the chief source of this balanced style. Once again, feminine leadership, as an antidote to today's organizational problems, has been largely overlooked by the experts as well as by organizations.

It is time for the blinders to come off. What made American industry grow and prosper in the past was its ability to capitalize on new ideas and move in new directions. To regain our prominence in the world marketplace, new ideas and new approaches to leading and managing are needed once again. Given the high demand that exists today for interpersonal skills, it seems obvious that feminine leadership is precisely the kind of new approach that can help American business manage change more effectively and prosper once again. The resources required to implement this approach already exist. Thousands of women managers are at the ready. All that is required now is for organizations to let them manage with their heads *and* with their hearts.

Chapter Nine
Conflict
Management

Within complex organizations, where rapid change has become the only predictable constant, the ability to manage conflict productively is an increasingly important part of every manager's role. Skills for productive conflict were not as critical in more stable organizational environments of the past, but they are extremely useful to managers in today's more dynamic and complex organizations. Every change—whether the result of shifting environmental conditions, changing strategic direction, new organizational structures, procedures, or personnel—creates some degree of turmoil and conflict. To deal effectively with change, managers must recognize the conflicts that it often creates and work to resolve them.

WHAT IS CONFLICT?

Conflict is the tension that results from forces acting in opposition to each other. It is the simultaneous occurrence of incompatible activities. One way to think about conflict is in terms of a traditional tug-of-war. Here we can readily see the forces in opposition, as each team attempts to pull the rope and the other team over to its side. All conflicts, whether they occur within us, between individuals, or between groups, contain this quality of tension. Sometimes, we experience the tension as forces pulling in opposite directions, such as when we cannot decide between two appealing or unappealing alternatives. At other times, the conflicts we engage in may seem more like arm wrestling. We are pushing in one direction and being opposed by someone or something that is pushing back. Although most organizational conflicts are not as visible as an arm wrestling contest, they often occur in much the same way. A procedural dispute develops between two work groups and, as a result, both groups try to overcome the objections and resistance of the other and push the solution that best serves their needs. In other cases, where a group may believe that its functional boundaries and authority are being endangered by some corporate change, such as an organizational restructuring, a counterforce may be put into place as a delaying strategy to preserve the status quo. With every change comes new opportunities and new conflicts.

Typically, the sources of organizational conflict fall into four categories:

(1) *Multiple-Role Conflict:* An example of a role conflict would be a situation in which a manager is pressured to take sides in an organizational dispute involving colleagues and employees. In such a

case, one may be forced to choose between loyalty to peers and loyalty to the work group.

(2) *Scarce Resources:* Within all organizations there is a finite amount of time, money, and human resources available to achieve personal and organizational goals. A major source of conflict occurs whenever the demand for these resources among managers and work groups outstrips their availability.

(3) *Differing Values and Priorities:* Often the most difficult organizational conflicts to resolve are those involving value differences. Because they are the foundation of an individual's basic approach to life, values are unlikely to change over time. Hence, disputes over the relative importance of basic values between individuals or groups are unlikely to produce much movement or change in position on either side.

(4) *Differing Perceptions of the Problem:* Although organizational members may be in general agreement that a problem exists, there is often little or no agreement regarding anything else. Differing perceptions regarding the causes of organizational problems, their impact, and appropriate solutions can often create defensive behavior and conflict among individuals and work groups within the same business.

Because of the rapid rate of complex change within today's organizations, managers must deal regularly with two types of conflict that occur at the group and the individual levels. The first, intergroup conflict, is often related to changes in policies, practices, and corporate structure that place work units from the same business in opposition to each other. As corporate goals and strategic direction change, it is quite common to find subsets of the same organization opposing each other on how to achieve the desired results.

The other type of conflict that all managers must deal with regularly is interpersonal conflict. Unlike intergroup conflict, interpersonal conflict occurs at the individual level. It is the tension that develops between individuals in an organization due to philosophical differences and differing perceptions of the way work should be done, as well as to personal goals that are in opposition. While there are other types of conflict, both within the individual and at the organizational level, those that occur between individuals and between work units tend to be two prevalent types within modern organizations requiring ongoing attention from management.

Increasing and rapid corporate change tends to produce more conflicts now that require the attention of management than ever before. In addition, because of the growing need for cooperation and collaboration within work groups, managers must exercise greater caution in arbitrarily resolving intergroup conflict and involve employees more in the resolution process. The growing need for interdependence between people and work groups within organizations translates into a need for increased managerial competence to handle conflicts effectively. Today, managers must be negotiators, mediators, and facilitators. They can no longer afford to be simply decision-makers.

Managers must be able to accept conflict as an inevitable part of organizational life. For just as the process of change is becoming a given throughout industry, so the conflicts that inevitably result from change are also becoming a way of life in most organizations. It's not easy for many managers to accept the inevitability of conflict. For those who still yearn for simpler times, when organizations were more stable and the boss was the final arbiter of the occasional conflict that erupted, this change is particularly difficult to accept and support. But it is one that more and more managers recognize as necessary for survival. Once conflict is seen as an inevitable by-product of change rather than as something either positive or negative, it is easier to approach, understand, and resolve effectively.

MALE-FEMALE APPROACHES TO CONFLICT

As is true in other areas, socialization plays a key role in shaping the conflict management styles of men and women. Typically, the range of acceptable behaviors for boys and girls in handling conflict has been quite different. While most boys have been encouraged to exhibit anger openly and to occasionally use physical force in resolving conflicts, girls have been discouraged from displaying these behaviors. Instead, they have been taught to take a more conciliatory role in conflict situations, to relieve tensions that exist between individuals and groups rather than to escalate them. While this does not mean that girls never engage in fistfights or that boys resolve conflicts only with physical violence, social conditioning does tend to reinforce different behaviors for males and females in conflict situations.

In reflecting on her own experiences as a young girl and adult in many conflict situations, Gillian Martin Sorensen, New York City commissioner for the United Nations, offered these thoughts: "I have never liked fights. I can remember being a mediator in arguments between my brother and sister from the age of six. Whether this is a feminine trait is hard to say. But I use this ability daily and I can trace the instinct back to instances in the family and back to childhood where I was the peacemaker. I was the one who got the kids in the playground back in their right corners in the sandbox. . . . Today, this is an ability that I often bring to bear in my work. I find that my current job draws on many of the capacities that I have always had. It is rewarding to be able to bring all of these abilities into play."

While research has proved that socialization has a powerful impact on adult behavior, it alone does not account for the observable differences in conflict management styles favored by men and women. Only when you consider the impact of societal conditioning and basic biological differences between the sexes can the preferred styles of managing conflict exhibited by each sex begin to be understood.

MALE-FEMALE RESPONSES TO STRESS

Dr. Estelle Ramey of Georgetown University believes that differences in the male and female responses to stress, which often accompanies conflict, are the result of hormonal differences as well as societal conditioning. In discussing the impact of biological differences on male and female behavior, she states, "Unlike men, women don't get as fired up with adrenaline because they don't have as much testosterone. They don't get the blood pressure elevation that men get. They don't react to conflicts in terms of rage. It's not that women aren't aggressive. They handle their aggression in a different way. If you look at other animal species, it's apparent that the female can be extraordinarily aggressive. But she picks the areas that she will defend. She's less likely than the male to respond aggressively to every provocation. This is true among men and women as well."

She continues, "Obviously, as Samuel Johnson said in

reply to the question 'Which is more intelligent, man or woman?' it depends on which man and which woman. You have great differences among women and among men. But you also have these biologic differences between the two groups that account for behavioral differences. It's not just societal influence that accounts for these gender differences, although society plays an enormous part."

In the area of conflict management, men and women executives do exhibit different behaviors and tend to employ different behavioral styles. While the origins of these differences are complex, the behaviors that typify masculine and feminine styles of conflict management are frequently easier to identify. Let's examine some of the most apparent distinctions now, recognizing that these differences are more prevalent in the behavioral styles of some men and women than in others.

FIVE MODES OF CONFLICT MANAGEMENT

Throughout the last three years, as part of an ongoing effort to gather support material for this book, more than three hundred men and women managers have been surveyed using the "Thomas-Kilmann Conflict Mode Instrument."[1] This questionnaire identifies five basic modes of behavior used to manage conflict situations and asks respondents to assess the frequency with which they use each mode. While the validation study for this instrument, completed in 1978, shows no significant differences in preferences based upon gender, my own data show a marked difference in the styles or modes preferred by the 171 men and 145 women managers who completed the questionnaire. The sample consisted primarily of middle-level managers from a variety of industries, including the health care, financial services, telecommunications, high-tech, and petroleum industries, as well as the federal government. Although most of those surveyed were participants in management development seminars that I was conducting at the time, very few were aware of the purpose behind my collecting this survey instrument data. Hence, the group was not particularly biased in favor of such stylistic differences before completing the questionnaire. Nonetheless, the results of this data collection show a marked difference in the modes of conflict management behavior favored more by men and those favored more by women.

THE COMPETITIVE RESPONSE

According to my survey findings, which have been supported by anecdotal material collected in interviews with men and women managers as well as by other research, male managers show a strong preference for two behavioral responses in conflict situations. The first (using the same "Thomas-Kilmann Conflict Mode Instrument" categories) is a competitive response to conflict, frequently referred to as a win-lose approach to conflict resolution. In using this mode of behavior, a manager will compete to overcome any opposing forces in order to assure that his/her position prevails. The underlying assumption is that conflict is a contest which someone will win and someone else must lose. The goal is to be victorious.

In observing this mode of conflict management in operation, we again see primary emphasis placed on winning and on satisfying one's personal agendas. Just as these themes play an important part in shaping the masculine corporate culture, they also influence the primary style of conflict management used by many male managers. Aside from the personal satisfaction one may derive from winning, the organizational advantage of this competitive approach is its usefulness in situations in which time is short and immediate action is required. A potential disadvantage is the tension that may build between the winners and the losers as a result.

In discussing conflict management, Julie Heidt, a district manager with Michigan Telephone, had this observation regarding differences in male and female styles: "As far as conflict management goes, I see men tending to 'rant and rave' or directly confront rather than negotiate. For many, conflicts appear to be 'winner take all' propositions. As a woman manager, I think I am more likely to acknowledge another's feelings and to try and change the environment to a more productive one . . . without reaching an explosive level."

A similar observation was made by Judy Godwin, a sales engineer with the Inland Division of General Motors and the highest-ranking woman at the plant. While cautious of generalizations, she does believe that men and women manage conflict differently. She said, "Women tend to bring a win-win perspective to management and to teamwork. Men tend to have more of a win-lose perspective which does not necessarily provide the best answers in problem situations. Win-win is not a secretive approach but a communicative approach. It creates the best situation and makes things happen."

THE AVOIDANCE RESPONSE

The second mode of behavior favored by many men in managing conflict is avoidance. Although such behavior may seem inconsistent with the competitive style just discussed, a closer examination points up the compatibility of these two approaches. As a strategy for managing conflict, avoidance is really the opposite side of the same competitive coin. Faced with a conflict situation where winning is simply not possible, what can a competitive manager do? He can avoid the conflict completely, thereby avoiding any potential loss, in the hope that his odds of winning will improve the next time. In this case, the same underlying assumption that conflict is a contest applies. However, the goal here is to avoid losing. The benefits of this strategy were succinctly described by one manager who quoted the old adage, "He who fights and runs away lives to fight another day."

COMPROMISE

In addition to competing and avoiding, which were the primary conflict management modes favored by male managers in my study, compromising was often identified by this group as a secondary or backup mode. In cases where neither of the primary modes could be used effectively, male managers indicated that they would then look for some reasonable compromise in order to resolve a dispute. Such compromises always require some degree of negotiation and generally wind up being trade-offs in which both parties make some concessions and maintain part of their original positions.

In examining all three modes of behavior just described, I am struck by the action-oriented, short-term, solution-seeking quality that characterizes each. When faced with a conflict situation, many men seem to prefer decisive action over long-term negotiation or a short-term strategy that puts the conflict temporarily on hold. In situations where neither of these is workable, some compromise, which appeases both parties, seems to be the next best approach. In each mode a relatively high value is placed on competing and a lower priority is given to the maintenance of positive relationships. In this sense, the immediate gains achieved through "winning" tend to be viewed as more important than the longer-term negative consequences that "losing" may produce in one's opponent.

Is this action-oriented, short-term, solution-seeking approach that men favor supported by biological research? Dr. Estelle Ramey believes so. She states, "In terms of behavior, men are designed, physiologically, for shorter, action-oriented lives. They are more directed towards immediate solutions, using big muscles. Women are designed for the long, chronic stress of childbearing and nursing."

Many women managers are also aware of contrasts between the conflict management style they use and the style preferred by their male peers. Elaine Wolan-Martin, a human resources manager with Ohio Bell Telephone Company, stated, "In my view, women tend to be less confrontive in conflict situations than men. I think men are more likely to just go in and deal with the conflict without a lot of prior analysis. Whereas, I would be more inclined to analyze the situation in depth before acting."

Christine McCoy, division chief for the National Park Service in Philadelphia, is another feminine leader who is aware of differences in the styles favored by men she has worked with and her own style of managing conflict. She puts it this way: "Let me contrast my own style with the style of a former male boss that I worked for at a previous place of employment. I would say he was more inclined to make rapid decisions and to be product- and task-oriented. In contrast, I am more inclined to gather information and examine a conflict from many different angles. I think my approach is more product- and process-oriented.

"In addition, I have found many men more willing than I am to ignore some situations—difficult situations to resolve. I think I am more of a 'pulse-taker' than some of my male counterparts."

COLLABORATION

In contrast to the short-term, action-oriented style favored by male managers, feminine leaders approach conflicts from a very different perspective. Theirs is a style that incorporates a strong and constant concern for the quality of relationships, regardless of the source of the conflict. In examining the same survey data, we see women managers showing a strong preference for two different modes of conflict management behavior. The first, collaboration, is an approach to conflict management that seeks to find different, more satisfying solutions to complex problems than those proposed by either side. This win-win approach is based upon a consensus-building strategy for resolving differences rather than a competitive one. It assumes that a satisfying solution, which all parties can support, is achievable and that such a solution can be developed through discussion, sharing of personal viewpoints, and creative problem-solving.

In describing her own style of managing conflict, Dr. Donna Shalala of Hunter College emphasized the importance collaboration plays when she said, "I think collaborative skills and the ability to get diverse groups of people behind a decision are qualities of a good politician and a first-class leader. In my current position, I often describe myself as a tugboat captain—pulling this big institution along. Change is more likely to stick if lots of people participate in the decision-making and have a real stake in the change. The more collaboration the better and the better people feel about the decision."

Noreen Haffner of Southern New England Telephone also offered comments on the importance collaboration plays in the approach used by many women managers to resolve conflicts. She stated, "Another dimension to the style of management more often used by women has to do with their ability to conceive of and, therefore, actualize a 'win-win.' Women are not as inclined to get stuck in the mode of 'I know I've won if you've lost.' Women look for a win for everyone. Not that this attitude is always explicit, they just seem to work longer and harder for the resolution of an issue which is best for everyone. As a result, there is often more synergy in solving the problem."

Unlike the competitive approach discussed earlier, which has the advantage of being quick and direct, a collaborative approach to conflict resolution requires time and ongoing attention. For this reason, it is frequently an approach that is viewed as less pragmatic in many organizations. However, its key advantage, as a strategy for building individual and group "ownership" in decisions, is becoming more important within many companies where major changes now require careful attention and implementation support from employees.

ACCOMMODATION

The other behavioral mode favored more by women managers surveyed was accommodation. Although this mode did not receive as high a rating as collaboration, many women managers indicated it was their second choice as a method for managing conflict. Here, again, we see the strong emphasis placed on the importance of preserving relationships, even at the expense of achieving one's goals, for accommodation involves subordinating one's own self-interests to those of another person. It means backing off from a previously held position and honoring the wishes of others. The accommodating mode assumes that the nature of the relationship between the parties in conflict is more important than the outcome. It is a style many women seem to favor in situations where their own stake in a particular outcome is low and their investment in preserving a positive rapport is higher.

While collaboration and accommodation are the behavioral modes women managers chose most frequently, they also indicated that compromising is their preferred backup style for managing conflicts. As was true with the male managers, women generally saw this as the style they would use when their other, preferred approaches had no chance of succeeding. In examining the overall approach to conflict management preferred by these women managers, we see a familiar thread woven throughout. Generally, the focus is less action-oriented and more people-oriented while the time perspective seems to be longer-term than that of many male managers.

EMPHASIS ON MAINTAINING RELATIONSHIPS

Although women like to resolve conflicts in a way that satisfies their own goals, they seem to balance this against the importance of their relationships with coworkers. To feminine leaders, winning isn't the only thing. The way one works with others or the process that is used to resolve differences also counts. Again, Dr. Ramey offers these observations about the long-term people orientation that many women seem to favor in resolving conflicts: "Both physiologically, because of their response to stress, and psychologically, because of training, women tend to be oriented to seeing matters over a much longer period of time. You don't throw the baby out and get yourself a new one because he dirtied his pants today. Women recognize that the baby is just the beginning and that this relationship is going to go on for years and years.

"Men are more inclined to think in terms of immediate resolution. This has to do a great deal with social conditioning and the unfortunate fact that, today, many companies tend to reward immediate results and encourage managers never to look past the quarterly earnings report. But if what we want to move towards is an industrial society built on delivering excellent service rather than on the 'quick-fix' solution, it is women who are trained to stay in it for the long-haul."

Another successful woman executive who shares some of the same views is Lynne O'Shea, director of communications and public relations for Arthur Andersen & Company in Chicago. Before joining Arthur Andersen, O'Shea was vice president of communications at International Harvester and the youngest corporate officer in the company's 150-year history. In reflecting on the differences in conflict management styles that she has observed between men and women she said, "I think one area of real difference has to do with the amount of time allotted to resolving conflicts. I believe women will allot a larger block of time to handle a given conflict.

"Also, their pacing is often quite different. They may not solve a problem in just one meeting, where I think the man goes for resolution more quickly. Women put the pacing of an encounter on a longer time horizon than the male does. Much has been written about these long- and short-term horizons. Because we women live longer, spend more time with children and watch them grow up and so forth, we believe that there is more time to go for a permanent solve. Things don't have to be solved within the next five minutes. We go for a permanent solve, rather than a temporary one."

Another prominent woman manager who believes her own approach to handling conflict is somewhat different from that used by many men is Sister Colette Mahoney, president of Marymount College in Manhattan. Here is what she has to say about the contrasts she has observed: "In handling conflicts, I will first speak to the individuals involved and then try to bring all the parties together. . . . I suspect that a woman in either the academic or the corporate community is more persuasive in handling conflicts than men. I have a tendency to try to reconcile the parties in conflict, whether with me or another administrator. I suspect that men are more likely to make the decision themselves, without weighing in with the people involved."

In 1983, I was asked to give a presentation on "skills for productive conflict" to a gathering of the presidents of the thirty largest Junior Leagues across the country. As the chief executive officers of community service organizations with thousands of volunteer members and millions of dollars in operating revenues, this group had a strong interest in the topic. After completing the survey questionnaire and discussing the five modes of conflict management, a member of the group asked me how their overall profile might compare with that of a similar group of senior male executives. As we talked about the differences that would be likely to emerge in such a comparison (within this group collaboration was the primary style), I was struck by the realization that, as two groups, men and women seem to have almost polar opposite approaches to dealing with conflict. While this does not mean that there is never any crossover between the two groups, it does suggest that successful conflict resolution entails a very different approach in each case. In addition, these opposite approaches also indicate that there is more than one effective way to resolve many conflicts.

MANAGING CONFLICT REQUIRES A RANGE OF BEHAVIORS

The preference for some modes of behavior over others indicates that neither group tends to use the widest range of behaviors available for managing conflicts. Instead, men and women each tend to rely on a narrow range of different approaches that overlap in the compromise area. Whereas men are most comfortable competing or avoiding, women are least likely to use these two approaches to manage conflicts. At the same time, the two approaches that women favor more, collaborating and accommodating, are the modes favored least by many men.

What do these differences in style suggest from the standpoint of organizational effectiveness? First, they suggest that both men and women managers may sometimes rely too much on their preferred modes of conflict management and utilize too little the approaches preferred by the other group. In situations that demand a totally different, less predictable style of resolution, this overreliance can become a liability. Instead of choosing the most appropriate style, men and women may sometimes opt for the approaches with which they are most comfortable and most skillful in managing. The net effect is similar to what happens when one uses a screwdriver in place of a wrench. While it may work sometimes, the fit and the end result will not always be as good.

A second organizational implication related to these differing styles of conflict management has to do with the range of behaviors available to both men and women. The five modes of behavior described in the "Thomas-Kilmann Conflict Mode Instrument"—competing, avoiding, compromising, collaborating, and accommodating—represent the widest spectrum of approaches available to managers for productive conflict resolution. Each can be an effective means of handling some conflicts, while no one approach can be effective in every case. By working together and learning to utilize their preferred approaches to complement each other, men and women in management can increase their individual effectiveness and the ability of their organizations to resolve conflicts productively. Again, we see the benefits that both men and women can derive from learning to recognize and work with their differences in managing conflict. Again, we see the enormous benefits that can accrue in organizations where both the masculine-competitive approach and the feminine-collaborative approach are understood, valued, and encouraged.

One of the most vivid examples of the impact conflict management styles of men and women can have on a team's ability to work effectively together and solve problems occurred at a management development seminar sponsored by NTL Institute in Snowmass, Colorado. The incident, which occurred during the middle of a week-long program, was not only rich with examples of the advantages and disadvantages of using each style, it also served to point out in a rather unique way how the styles often preferred by men and women can work effectively when used together. Here is a brief account of what happened.

THE "EGG-CATCHING CONTEST"

During the conference, which was developed to help managers increase their ability to resolve conflicts productively, twenty-one men and women middle managers were divided into three groups: a mixed group of men and women, an all-female group, and an all-male group, each one of approximately the same size. The three groups were told they would each be participating in an "egg-catching contest"* and were presented with an odd assortment of items including cigars, multicolored construction paper, safety pins, twine, bubble bath, an empty wine carafe, and

---

*Although many seminar leaders have adapted this creative design, credit for the original idea goes to Dr. Kenneth Sole, an organization consultant based in Durham, New Hampshire.

other nonessentials. After all the materials had been carefully meted out to ensure that each group had received essentially the same "tools," the managers were brought into a large conference room, completely unfurnished except for several dozen raw eggs that were dangling precariously from the ten-foot ceiling on tiny strings. In order to win the contest, the seminar leaders explained, each group had to construct a device using the materials they had just received in which to catch one of the eggs. The only rules of the contest were: (1) that the egg had to "free fall" into the "catcher" without being touched directly by any team member and (2) that it had to come to rest no more than a half inch above the floor without breaking.

The teams were given a maximum of one hour to design and construct their catchers but could stop the action any time they determined they were ready to test their device. Throughout the exercise, a portable video camera was used to tape portions of the action in each group. The management of interpersonal and intergroup conflict was the key issue highlighted in the taped sequences.

At the start of the exercise, each group gathered in a different corner of the conference room to begin its work. Almost immediately, differences in the approach taken by each to solve the problem began to emerge. In the women's group, the focus of discussion was on how the group would make decisions. Throughout the exercise, this group attempted to use a consensus approach to decision-making. Interestingly, after a few early expressions of concern and speculation that, unlike the other two groups which had male members, no one in this group "knew anything about principles of engineering or physics," the women did not seem very aware of the other groups' presence. Their focus remained on the task and their relationships with each other.

Within the all-male group, there was a great deal of joking

over the way the groups had been composed. Several members said they were glad to see a group of all women because they knew that this would ensure "who came in third." At least three design ideas were offered by group members early on but none got past the proposal stage. Twenty minutes into the exercise, having reached no agreement on which idea to develop, the men decided to send out an industrial spy to find out more about what was happening in the other groups. As the spy made his way around the room, the rest of the group split up into several small subunits and began to work on different ideas.

Meanwhile, in the mixed group, several interpersonal conflicts had erupted early on among the male members. One man attempted to seize control of the decision-making process while several of the others immediately resisted. Initially, an intergroup conflict began to develop as the men argued among themselves, virtually ignoring the input of the women members. Finally, as the men became somewhat frustrated, one of the women moved into the discussion and acted as a mediator in the conflict. As the tension began to dissipate, the group started to discuss how it would work together and polled each member for ideas about how to proceed.

Throughout the exercise, the mixed group continued to be focused about equally on the task and the decision-making process, with the men offering more of the design ideas and the women focusing more on the group's methods for working together. Occasionally, there was some crossover between the roles that each subgroup played. Throughout the exercise, members seemed comfortable with each other and contributed their thoughts with enthusiasm. There was a sense of ownership in the product being developed among all the members. In addition, there was an ongoing awareness of the presence of the other two groups, and this helped to keep the group focused on its task and moving ahead.

Although it should come as no surprise, the mixed group was the first to solve the problem and successfully tested their egg catcher in front of the two other groups. Once they were finished, tension seemed to escalate between the all-male and all-female teams, with the men teasing the women and joking about the "hopelessness" of their design. Throughout the exercise, the women continued to make decisions using a consensus process and spent a considerable amount of their time testing for agreement. Their design, which consisted largely of a paper cup filled with bubble bath and cotton, was not the most aesthetically appealing in the contest. However, shortly after the first group finished, the women tried their design out and, to the astonishment of everyone, it worked. (After the egg was caught, the male group demanded to examine it to be certain there were no surface cracks!)

Now only a short amount of time was left for the men to try out their catcher. It had taken the group almost forty-five minutes to agree on one design and, in fact, some members were still working on an alternative approach as the hour ran out. The design work continued for another twenty minutes as the group constructed an intricate web of twine, resembling a basketball net, around the legs of a chair. When it was completed, it was, by far, the most interesting and elaborate of the three designs. However, since only a few of the members had taken part in developing the design, it did not seem to be something that every team member felt "ownership" in developing.

While the mixed group had clearly won the contest, throughout the remainder of the week members of the all-male group continued to point out that their design was still the "best." Although these comments were always said in a playful manner, they served to highlight the disappointment several of the men had experienced in not winning the contest. Interestingly, by the close of the seminar three days later, the men who had participated in the all-male group were referring back to the episode as though they had won the contest while the other two groups had ceased mentioning it at all.

Even though no great significance was attached to "egg catching," many of the men in the same-sex group assigned considerable importance to winning. Whereas the women had measured their success in terms of their ability to work together and to solve the problem, the male group was more concerned with the intergroup competition. Hence, although neither group finished first, the women seemed satisfied with their group's performance while many members of the all-male group felt obliged to defend and rationalize the outcome.

Although many experts continue to suggest that competitive team sports help young boys develop the skills required for effective teamwork in organizations, this activity dramatized the other lessons often learned by many males in team competition: that there is little joy in solving a problem or reaching a goal if someone else has gotten there first; and that "winning" always means being better than someone else rather than being the best that you can be.

But if differences in the male and female styles of conflict management are this apparent, why are they not more obvious within organizations? In some settings, where feminine leaders are not expected to conform completely to the same set of behavioral norms as male managers, these differences are in evidence. In these cases, both men and women managers can readily observe how effective the two styles are when used to balance and complement each other. However, the homogenized style supported in most organizations, with its emphasis on traditionally masculine behavior, inhibits these differences from surfacing and discourages most women from exercising their natural skills.

Within the context of executive development seminars, where emphasis is placed on developing a wider range of approaches to managing difficult issues, women managers often have greater opportunities to demonstrate their effectiveness than they do in their regular work environment. The talents and competence they display when they are encouraged to experiment with a wider range of behaviors are not aberrations. It is the behavior many women managers are compelled to use at work that does not reflect their true abilities.

MANAGING CHANGE REQUIRES A FULL RANGE OF CONFLICT SKILLS

Throughout most of our nation's organizations a dichotomy continues to exist between the style of leadership required to manage in an increasingly complex world and the style currently in use within management. Nowhere is this dichotomy more evident than in relation to the management of conflict. Not only is the present need for women's conflict management skills enormous, but the underutilization of these skills is also having a serious impact on economic and social conditions throughout our nation and the world. Today we live in a world where competition for scarce resources has become a struggle for survival among individuals, organizations, and nations; where winning and losing can have profound consequences; where competition must be balanced by an increased emphasis on collaboration.

More than ever before, we need the collaborative skills that feminine leaders offer within our organizations. Not only are these conflict management skills important to re-building our faltering economy and our businesses, they are critical to building a better, safer world as well. For today's leaders, both male and female, this is the most important task of all.

Chapter Ten
Intuition and Problem-Solving

Intuition, or the ability to take a quantum leap and accurately judge a situation on the basis of limited conscious data, was for much of the postwar era considered to be the exclusive domain of women. Up through the late sixties, "women's intuition" was a popular term used to describe the quick insights and nonrational approach women seemed to favor more than men in attempting to psych out situations and people as well as to make decisions and solve problems. Although no one questioned that women did seem particularly able to make quick, insightful judgments about situations and people, neither did anyone see this as a skill that might have some application within the world of management. Like other qualities associated more with women, intuition in problem-solving was not regarded as a skill to be taken very seriously by organizations. In fact, evidence suggests that because of its association with women, intuition was undervalued, misunderstood, and regarded as virtually useless in many businesses.

Over time, as many valuable feminine qualities were confused with negative stereotypes about women, intuition became a topic that even women managers refused to discuss or take seriously. With the heavy emphasis placed on rational, quantitative management throughout organizations and the desire on the part of both men and women to avoid sexist stereotypes, feminine intuition became something of an embarrassment. Being told that you had it was akin to being told you were the victim of some dread disease. At the very least, it was not considered to be a proper, professional approach to problem solving.

Throughout this period of denial, which coincided with the rising popularity of masculinism in most organizations, there was also some discussion among researchers about the linkage between intuition and many significant accomplishments. Albert Einstein reportedly said that he discovered the theory of relativity using an intuitive problem-solving approach. A computer analysis "proved" that the intricate music of J. S. Bach was too complex to have been composed through a rational, deliberative process and therefore was judged to be the product of intuitive thinking. Yet examples such as these notwithstanding, intuition suffered from negative press in our society. Initially, it was viewed as nonserious because it was thought of as a feminine trait. Later, it became a stereotype considered to be overly conventional and formulaic.

The negative consequences of prejudice and an overly simplistic approach to integrating women into management both contributed to the devaluation of intuition as an important managerial skill. As an attempt was made to upgrade the status of working women, many of their unique talents, such as sensing and intuitive ability, were mistakenly dismissed as negative stereotypes. Instead of recognizing these as skills that women could use to enhance effectiveness in the business world, corporations focused entirely on teaching women analytical skills. As a result, intuition as a feminine trait came to be considered a wives' tale and a myth left over from medieval, unenlightened times.

RENEWED INTEREST IN INTUITION

Then in the late seventies, just after intuition was finally laid to rest as a non-issue, something remarkable happened. In analyzing the reasons their businesses were doing so well, some Japanese managers started mentioning their reliance on intuition. They seemed to believe that intuition enhanced their ability to solve problems and improved the overall effectiveness of many of the management methods they had borrowed from the industrialized West. As Shigen Okada, a successful Japanese industrialist, stated, his large retail store chain had benefited from ". . . adoption of the West's pragmatic management combined with the spiritual, intuitive aspects of the East."[1]

Slowly, with the attention of many U.S. industrial giants focused on Japan's competitive success, interest in intuitive problem-solving began to increase within American businesses. In addition, the traditional rational approach to problem-solving and decision-making, which had long been the benchmark for effective management in the United States, seemed to be faltering. Quantitative analyses and deductive reasoning no longer seemed to be as efficient or effective in solving many complex organizational problems. While American businesses collected more data to support their competitive strategies, conditions in the world marketplace shifted dramatically, leading to the obsolescence of ideas before they left the drawing boards. Many large American companies that had prospered in the past by using a highly structured, rational approach to problem-solving found themselves being left in the dust by smaller, more flexibly organized and managed competitors.

OVERRELIANCE ON RATIONAL THINKING

Finally, after decades of total reliance on the rational approach to managing, it was becoming apparent that in some situations, a quantitative, analytical approach was not an appropriate method for problem-solving. In their book *In Search of Excellence,* Tom Peters and Bob Waterman discuss the inherent problems that can result from an overreliance on quantitative analysis. They make their point rather emphatically when they say, "What we are against is wrong-headed analysis, analysis that is too complex to be useful and too unwieldy to be flexible, analysis that strives to be precise (especially at the wrong times) about the inherently unknowable—such as detailed market forecasts when end use of a new product is still hazy. . . . We are also against situations in which action stops while planning takes over, the all-too-frequently observed 'paralysis through analysis' syndrome. . . . Above all, we deplore the unfortunate abuse of the term 'rational.' "[2]

In seeking solutions to complex problems, corporations that had developed and grown prosperous during the post–World War II industrial boom had come to believe that all variables were somewhat predictable, that absolute right answers did exist. Just as a tight, hierarchical pyramid came to characterize the organizational structure of most successful businesses, so a tight, step-by-step approach to quantitative data collection and analysis became the management model for effective problem-solving and decision-making.

But as conditions in the marketplace began to change during the late sixties and early seventies, due to the impact of technology and increasing international competition, many managers recognized a developing need for a different, more flexible and efficient problem-solving process. The dawn of the intuitive age had finally come.

BENEFITS OF THE INTUITIVE APPROACH

Although many businesses still overrely on traditional, quantitative measures to identify solutions to complex problems, intuitive processes are becoming an integral part of the approach used to analyze and solve problems in many companies. This rise in popularity can be attributed to three key factors. First, the intuitive approach, which relies more on inductive reasoning, allows one to manage complexity with less quantitative data, not that these data cease to be important. They are still necessary for effective problem-solving; however, they become one leg of a three-legged stool that forms the basis of intuitive problem-solving. In addition to quantitative data, the other two factors consist of prior experience (and the generalizations one can make about the present based upon the past) and gut feeling based upon hunches and nonrational data.

Secondly, the intuitive approach is often a more direct route to innovation, a fact that has enhanced its value in today's competitive marketplace. Instead of relying solely on observable facts and known quantities, intuition frees the human mind to speculate, to follow hunches, and to discover potential and creative approaches to problem-solving. In effect, the intuitive approach looks at problems through a different lens and makes use of emotional as well as rational data in formulating solutions. The result is often a novel solution that may seem to defy conventional wisdom while, at the same time, prove to be quite workable.

In recognizing that the whole is often greater than the sum of its parts, intuitive problem-solvers rely on their instincts and feelings as well as on hard data to make decisions.

Although they recognize the importance of considering hard data, they also see the inherent trap in overrelying on quantitative methods to develop innovative solutions to complex problems. As J. W. Marriott, president of the Marriott Corporation, reportedly said, "Too many American companies have developed into bureaucracies. Too many decisions are made at the top, and action has been overwhelmed by reports and board meetings. Problems are overanalyzed to death in too many businesses."[3]

The third reason that intuition is becoming increasingly valued in organizations has to do with effective people management. Not only is intuition an effective approach to dealing with difficult problems, it also can be enormously helpful in managing complex interpersonal relationships. Sensing and intuiting work together to supply managers with useful data about employee perceptions and attitudes. They make it possible for a manager to stay tuned in to employees, to hear what remains unspoken, and to see what is not visible in the organizational climate. As such, intuition is critical to understanding people, their needs, and their real concerns.

Throughout U.S. industry, as managing complexity, increased innovation, and interpersonal competencies continue to grow in importance, intuitive skills in problem-solving and people management become more necessary. Within rapidly expanding knowledge businesses, where employee involvement and flexible management approaches are key, the intuitive approach to problem-solving is playing a particularly important role. Yet most traditional managers know little about intuition, how it works or where it comes from, and even less about how to develop their own ability to use intuition effectively. For a few moments now, let's examine the origins of intuitive thinking.

RIGHT HEMISPHERE SKILL

According to scientific research into the functioning of the human brain, the right and left hemispheres seem to be used for distinctly different tasks. The left hemisphere is the center of language skills, verbal communication, sequential reasoning, and logic. The right hemisphere seems to be largely responsible for visual-spatial skills, the processing of emotional data, and abstract patterning. While the left side utilizes language to process information and to communicate, the right uses nonverbal symbols. Because intuitive thinking involves a nonrational approach to problem-solving, one that generates solutions based largely upon feelings and nonrational data, the right brain is believed to play an important part in this process. It is thought to be the hemisphere that is primarily responsible for the flashes of insight associated with intuition. The left brain attempts to find meaning in situations based upon a sequential analysis of the rational facts, and the right brain scans for patterns, associations, relationships, and symbolic metaphors that help us to make sense of the present. These associations take the form of emotional reactions and hunches based on factors that often cannot be verbalized. Despite the imprecise quality of such reactions, there is overwhelming evidence that this intuitive process works. In fact, it appears to be the most effective method of problem-solving available for some managers.

WOMEN: INTUITIVE PROBLEM-SOLVERS

Not surprisingly, many women managers favor the intuitive approach to problem-solving over the more traditional rational model. Some state that they find intuitive thinking to be a better fit with the way they process information and make sense of the world. Others believe that it is a less deliberate, more innate process for problem-solving—one that comes more naturally to them as women.

According to Dr. Donna Shalala, throughout her very successful career in government and higher education, intuition has come to play an increasingly important part in the way she solves many problems. In describing her own approach, she offered this observation: "Sometimes I'll trust my gut more than my head. Logical information might lead me in one direction and my feelings in another. Whereas I would have followed my head ten years ago, now I'm as likely or more likely to go with my gut feeling. It's ironic—you'd think the opposite would be true as you move to the top but it's not.

"I think men are less likely to have fine-tuned their intuitive skills because many of them do not trust their own feelings. Yet, many of those who succeed and who are truly talented leaders use a combination of rational and intuitive problem-solving skills. Felix Rohatyn [chairman of New York City's Municipal Assistance Corporation and a partner of the leading investment banking firm Lazard Frères and Co.] is a good example of a very successful man who uses his intuition very well. In the mergers and acquisitions field, he is highly skilled at sizing up the competition."

In his book *Intuitive Management,* Dr. Weston Agor reports on his own study of the management style similarities and differences between men and women. While testing more than two thousand managers throughout the public and private sectors to determine the degree to which they relied on intuitive and rational approaches to managing, Dr. Agor found a significant difference in the styles preferred by men and women. His findings, which indicate that women show a consistently stronger preference for the intuitive style of managing over men, support the premise that women rely more on intuition in solving problems and tend to use this approach as an integral part of their management style.

Dr. Agor's findings also revealed an interesting similarity in the styles of women managers and of men in top management positions. Although men as a group tended to rely less on intuition, results showed that their use of intuitive thinking increased as their position within the organizational hierarchy increased. Hence, the men who indicated that they relied more heavily on intuition were those in top management positions. In their approach to problem-solving, women managers and top male executives have much in common.[4] Yet, the majority of men tested did not seem to share this characteristic. Their preferred style focused more on the traditional rational approach.

THE ROLE OF SOCIALIZATION

What accounts for this difference in the styles preferred by most men and women? There is no doubt that social conditioning has played an extremely important part. For most women growing up before the late sixties, female intuition was considered to be an acceptable, albeit incomprehensible facet of the way they were expected to approach problems, analyze situations, and make decisions. On the other hand, the social script for males emphasized the importance of rational, logical thinking and of remaining cool and unemotional when making decisions. With the enormous societal pressures placed on girls and boys in the past to conform to these two very dissimilar approaches to problem-solving, is it any wonder that today men and women in management use different styles? Perhaps in time, as the impact of socialization changes due to society's changing expectations for both sexes, we will see a decrease in these differences but this is not the case today. Nor is it likely to be the case in the foreseeable future.

In reflecting on the impact of socialization on the use of intuition among men and women, Walter Blass, director of strategic planning at AT&T, stated, "Some managers, and I think they tend to be more women than men, rely on that intuitive part of themselves in making decisions. These are the people who will say, 'I don't know why it is but I just feel that something is so.' I think the reason men don't trust their own intuition is due largely to the way they are socialized, although biology may also play some part."

THE ROLE OF BIOLOGY

Today a growing body of scientific evidence suggests that biological differences are also responsible for some of the dissimilarities in the way males and females process information and relate to their environment. Not only do hormonal differences have an impact on male and female behavior, it now also appears that innate differences in the structure and functioning of the male and female brains may also account for some gender-related behavioral differences never before understood.

For instance, while it has been a long-established fact that women have a better recovery rate after strokes than men and are not as likely to suffer permanent brain damage, there is finally some evidence available that may in time explain why this is so. Thus far, this evidence demonstrates that the connective fibers carrying information between the two hemispheres in the human brain are almost 40 percent greater in the female brain than in the male brain. Along with the results of many other neurological studies, this information suggests that the female brain may be less lateralized than the male brain. In other words, each hemisphere may not be as specialized in its functioning and, as a result, the female brain may be more able to integrate the functions of language and visual-spatial analysis. This could account, in part, for those intuitive abilities that seem to be more developed in women as a group than in men and also more often preferred by them as a method for problem-solving.

According to the results of tests done on thousands of men and women nationally by the Johnson O'Connor Research Foundation, Inc., women demonstrate superiority in several natural aptitudes that relate to effective management.[5] Four of these, "ideaphoria" (the rate of the flow of ideas in verbal discussion), "silograms" (the ability to form associations between known and unknown words), "observation" (the ability to perceive small changes in physical details), and "abstract visualization" (the ability to deal with abstract problems, ideas, and principles), add support to the idea that some of women's intuitive skills may be the result of natural, inborn differences. If the feminine preference for intuitive thinking is based on biological differences as well as societal ones, this might help to explain why some male managers have difficulty understanding this nonrational approach to problem-solving.

While there seems to be a strong case building within many organizations for a more balanced approach to problem-solving, one that relies on both rational and intuitive data, there is still considerable skepticism among some traditional managers regarding the value of intuitive thinking. Because many have come to rely solely on their ability to solve problems using a logical, rational process and have not developed their individual capacities to think intuitively, they fail to understand what intuitive thinking can do or how it can be put to effective use within management. Yet, the need for this nontraditional approach to problem-solving continues to increase as complexity and the demand for innovation increase within businesses.

INTUITION AT WORK

In describing her own style of management and the balance that she seems to strike between the intuitive and rational approaches to problem-solving, Sandra Meyer of American Express said, "I think of myself as a creative person. My reputation is that I'm very analytic, but in my view I combine being analytic with being creative. I've been working since 1957, so a lot of what may look intuitive is based more on my having done it nine times before—and knowing how it's going to work out."

In some companies, seminars in innovation and creative problem solving are being offered to develop awareness and reawaken creative problem-solving abilities among managers. But the process is a slow one. In other corporate settings, the talents of feminine leaders as intuitive problem-solvers have begun to gain recognition and are being used to help organizations move more rapidly into the intuitive age. Throughout many organizations, the impact of this feminine leadership style is being felt more strongly, and the complementary nature of the approaches used by men and women to solve problems is becoming more evident.

At J. Walter Thompson, one of the nation's largest advertising agencies, Ruth Downing Karp, a senior vice president and creative director, observed, "Men tend to give direction and expect others to respond. However, individuals have their own emotional dynamics and may react negatively to this approach. A woman, on the other hand, is often able to instinctively intuit the type of person she is dealing with. The result is that she is more able to motivate that person. Many good creative people in this business, who may have some personality quirk or an inability to relate to others, often bloom when working for a woman. I can think of several specific cases where women managers were very tolerant and more able to create a positive creative environment for their subordinates, who in turn became far more successful."

Unlike feminine traits that seem to be less developed in most men, intuition is an ability some male managers have also learned to use effectively. Although it isn't often discussed publicly, some male executives seem to rely quite heavily on their intuitive abilities. Interestingly, this phenomenon is one on which many feminine leaders comment. Dr. Janice Jones of Chartwell & Company in Los Angeles said: "I think men use a lot more intuition in business than they let on. Many of my male employees will talk about a 'sense' they have of something or a 'feeling.' I know I use intuition when making deals. I've put my money behind projects because I felt they'd be successful and they were, whereas some deals I thought about long and hard didn't work out as well. A lot of men I know use intuition to make decisions. Some of the most powerful businessmen I know approach business with a gut feeling and some even consult the stars and use psychics. But they won't talk about this. It's the last thing they would want anyone to know."

The image of the successful American business executive has long been one that emphasized thinking rationally, remaining cool in times of crisis, and making decisions on the basis of facts rather than feelings. Now it seems that this image is not only out of sync with today's needs, it may also be somewhat misleading about the way many successful male leaders really operate. For while it seems that more women managers at every level feel freer to use their intuitive abilities to solve problems, some top male executives apparently have been operating this way all along. In other words, intuition as a key success factor for managers may not be very new at all, although there may be more explicit discussion about it today.

Jill Considine of The First Women's Bank spoke about her

own use of intuition in making key management decisions. In comparing her style to that of many male executives she has worked with she said, "I think I am highly intuitive. In my experience, I have found that some men approach problems this way while others operate very differently. In general, the men I have worked with have had less faith in their intuitive ability. I'm not saying theirs wasn't as good or better than mine, but they had less confidence in this ability in general. Instead, they seemed to like to see that one plus two equals three and then prove it again and again. Perhaps that's why some men seem to have an easier time with math —because it's something you can prove. Intuitiveness seems to have more of a homey, comfortable feeling to women."

Deborah Fields is another feminine leader who sees differences in the approach she uses to solve problems and the one preferred by many male managers. As she observed, "Many men, like my husband, Randy, use a very different approach to problem-solving. What works for me is rather unconventional. I use my intuition and my emotion because I believe in using the things that are a part of me. I think men are emotional, too, but they don't use their emotions to solve problems. While most men agree that emotions and intuition are good, they have been taught throughout their lives to rely on other things. In business schools, they are taught to be analytical—a very different style of management than the one I use."

A SOURCE OF CREATIVE SOLUTIONS

As the demand for innovation continues to expand in direct proportion to competitive pressures from abroad, American managers will be increasingly challenged to think in nontraditional ways in order to develop creative solutions to many problems. In some cases, as the pace of change accelerates, an intuitive approach to problem-solving will be absolutely critical. Within the financial services industry, where recent government deregulation has led to major strategic change, the need for intuitive problem-solving is already in evidence. According to Marilyn Barnewall, president of The MacGruder Company, a financial consulting firm in Colorado, this need will continue to grow in the future. In discussing the impact of change on this industry and the increasing need for intuitive skills in management she said, "The banking industry and the whole economy are changing drastically. If you aren't relying on intuition regarding the future and aren't able to see things as they might be rather than as they have been in the past, you're at a real disadvantage. I think women have been conditioned to rely more on their intuition in looking ahead. Some men, but very few, have learned to see things this way. Fortunately, one of the better things to have come out of the women's movement is a growing acceptance among men of their own intuitive abilities. Today there is more tolerance and greater acceptance of intuition among some men. Unfortunately, in attempting to imitate men by demanding facts, figures, etc., some women managers are losing their intuitive edge."

A male director of corporate planning for a major communications company also stressed the important role of intuition in successful long-range planning. He said, "I did a lot of work recently with a strategy group which depended on the ability to think 'holistically'—retrieving something that's approximately relevant without being able to articulate it in a fully rational process that might kill it. Men may have to unlearn some learned patterns of behavior. Women get into the intuitive part of their behavior more readily."

"The Intuitive Edge" is the title of a recent article in *Psychology Today* describing the research of Dr. Arthur Reber of Brooklyn College. According to his findings, humans have "an ability to know what to do in complicated situations without being able to explain exactly how we know." Although unconscious, this ability allows us to perform highly complex tasks and "when faced with exceptionally subtle tasks, people who 'feel,' or intuit their way through them actually have a competitive edge over those who consciously try to think their way through."[6]

THE VALUE OF NONTRADITIONAL THINKING

While some analysts would argue that intuition is a generic skill equally available to men and women, it is nonetheless true that each group has chosen to use this ability very differently. Although it seems likely that this difference will diminish over time, the need for intuitive skills is likely to grow at a much more rapid rate. In developing a nontraditional approach to problem-solving in organizations, the opportunity to use the input and expertise of feminine leaders exists today. While the task of changing the corporate culture to accommodate a more creative approach won't be easy, the consequences of not doing so will be disastrous. The accelerating pace of change demands an immediate response.

Envisioning how the intuitive approach of feminine leaders can help corporations solve complex problems may not be easy for some managers to do. It requires stepping outside conventional, rational bounds to see the advantages. In fact, it requires an intuitive leap to see how a more balanced, more feeling-centered approach to problem-solving would work in organizations, how it could promote creativity and improve the overall quality of many managerial decisions. Ironically, at a time when overreliance on logic has become a corporate way of life, organizations must begin to intuitively recognize the need for change. Now more than ever they must learn to trust their gut feelings and listen more closely to their most intuitive managers. Strategy and analytical approaches will not be enough. The wisdom needed to manage in this era of increasing change and economic uncertainty will require managers to use their hearts and their feelings as well as their heads.

Chapter Eleven
Managing Diversity, Stress, and Boundaries

Until the late sixties, when women managers finally became a recognized presence in many organizations, myths abounded about their behavior and the various traits they were presumed to possess. Among these was a widely held belief that women were obsessed with details. They were described as so involved in the nitty-gritty problems of everyday business that they were unaware of the big issues. What's more, their overdeveloped concern with details supposedly caused them to behave like corporate nit-pickers who were tough on employees.

Since few women were in managerial positions before the seventies, these myths were difficult to disprove. By and large, the people who were making these judgments had little or no contact with women. Yet, even though few employees had actual experience working for women managers, most had preconceived ideas about what it would be like.

WHAT'S IT LIKE TO WORK FOR A WOMAN?

One incident that demonstrated the power of preconceived ideas occurred during an executive seminar I conducted back in 1974. The focus of this program was the changing roles of men and women in organizations. As preparation for the conference, fifty participants were asked to conduct a series of four brief interviews with their colleagues. One question they were requested to ask during these interviews was, "As far as working for a man or a woman goes, do you have a preference? If so, which would you rather work for and why?"

On the opening day of the seminar, the group was asked to give a brief report on its findings. To the surprise of many, the data showed a strong preference for male leadership among men and women who had never worked for a woman. When asked to explain why they preferred to work for men, many of those interviewed stated, "because women are too picky." Interestingly, in cases where men and women had worked for managers of both sexes, there was no preference either way. In fact, some even referred to their female superiors as "well organized" and "buttoned down."

The data from these interviews show that employees who had actually worked for women had far less resistance to the idea, whereas those with no firsthand knowledge had the strongest and most negative attitudes about women as leaders. It is also worth noting that, throughout the next several years, as this seminar was offered again and again, this trend in the interview data remained very strong.

Since that time almost a decade ago, tens of thousands of people have learned from actual experience that women managers do, in fact, see both the forest and the trees. What's more, evidence suggests that women, as opposed to being "too picky," may simply be more ready and able to handle a variety of large and small tasks concurrently. This ability to juggle several things at the same time—without losing track of what is happening in any given area—seems to be a skill at which feminine leaders are particularly adept.

MANAGING DIVERSITY

If there is one observation employees and male colleagues repeatedly make about female executives, it is that they are particularly skillful in managing diverse tasks. According to the senior vice president of a large, California-based entertainment company, "Women are tenacious. They don't tend to forget about the details the way many of us males do. Sometimes it amazes me how many balls they can keep in the air at once.

"Right now, I have a personal aide who is a woman and she is really terrific at follow-up. The men who had the job in the past hated it. They got upset over the details. They wound up delegating everything away . . . and, oftentimes, things would slip between the cracks. . . .

"She is very different. She doesn't get as rattled by the minutiae. She seems to be able to stay on top of it all. I guess I think this is somehow related to the way we've been raised. Women are more attentive to details than most men. The small stuff doesn't drive them crazy. I know I could never do it."

Keeping track of many details is a big part of managing diversity effectively. The fact that women are often perceived as performing this function with ease raises questions about how their approach to diverse tasks differs from that of traditional managers. Let's take a few moments to look more closely at the evidence.

COMPLEXITY EQUALS STRESS

There is little doubt that rapid change and growing complexity have placed modern executives under increasing amounts of stress. While tolerance for stress seems to vary among individuals, there is also some indication that the two sexes have different reactions to prolonged exposure to stressful situations. According to the scientific evidence, women have more built-in hormonal protection that allows them to withstand chronic stress with less negative physiological consequences. Interestingly, it would seem that the less extreme reaction of women to stress might also be related to the apparent ability of female executives to manage diversity more easily than many of their male counterparts.

According to Dr. Estelle Ramey of Georgetown Medical School, "Physiologically, women don't cave in to stress as easily as men and that is why they live longer. They don't get as much adrenaline, which has very interesting effects on behavior. When you are threatened and you release adrenaline, it increases your level of irritability and anxiety even further. Under stress, women don't have as rapid an escalation of adrenaline, because it is testosterone that tends to increase adrenaline."

But hormonal structure is not the only biological difference that seems to relate to managing stress and diversity. Recently discovered evidence of differences in the organization of male and female brains also appears to have a bearing on the ability to manage diverse tasks. In discussing these findings, Dr. Ramey goes on to say, "As far as managing diversity goes, it would seem that women are ideally suited to this task because of their hormonal structure. The organization of the female brain may also account, in part, for this ability. Researchers calculate that women have about 40 percent more fibers running between the right and left sides.

"While it's difficult to separate the role of society and the role of the brain in shaping behavior, it looks as if the female brain is the kind of brain that should be able to handle several problems at once with less difficulty. In fact, it has long been one of the accepted characteristics of woman that she appears, with less internal pain, to be able to shift attention quickly from one thing to another. When her blood pressure goes up, she reduces the elevation more readily because she has a hormonal structure which releases more relaxing factor. She also has a brain which can shuttle information back and forth between hemispheres—both emotional and rational information that can help her solve problems and manage many tasks."

SOCIALIZED TO HANDLE STRESS

As is true in other areas of behavioral differences between the sexes, socialization plays an important part in shaping women's approach to managing diversity. According to many successful women executives, the skills required to effectively manage diversity are ones they began to learn very early in life as they observed their mothers handling the complex tasks that they themselves would one day have to perform. One such executive is Stephanie Solien, executive director of the Women's Campaign Fund in Washington, D.C. In recalling how she began to learn the importance of organization skills as a young girl she said, "As far as my own upbringing goes, I watched my mother have a career and run the household. I think I learned a great deal about how to manage many things at once and how to organize from seeing her do it. The demand to help isn't made so much on boys—so boys don't have as much responsibility early on and don't develop organizing skills.

I think that's starting to change, though, in some places."

In her work with many major organizations throughout the United States, Edith Whitfield Seashore, a successful organization consultant based in Washington, D.C., has also observed differences in the approaches used by women and men to manage diverse tasks. In her experience, men tend to address one issue at a time, whereas women seem more comfortable dealing with several matters concurrently. She describes the differences as follows: "Sometimes I have seen men become so focused on an issue that they lose their peripheral vision. At such moments, if you attempt to change the subject, they become disoriented. Women get focused but also have other 'to do' lists that they are working on at the same time. I'm often fascinated by just how many different agendas they can work off simultaneously.

"Some people perceive this as flightiness on the part of women. I think it's a real skill—this capacity that many women have to give their attention to a lot of diverse demands without losing the ability to focus in on a single item more closely. . . .

"I have a hunch socialization is what causes women to stay more alert to their environment because they are still responsible for many diverse family and professional tasks. As a group, they seem more able to make connections between seemingly disparate elements. They see the interrelatedness of things, actions, and people more clearly."

EMOTIONAL VENTING

Making connections between disparate elements is an ability many working women consider to be essential for survival in today's demanding world. As wives, mothers, and successful executives, they must often juggle a variety of conflicting demands on their time and their personal loyalties. One method many women use to reduce the stress that often accompanies such demands is emotional venting. By finding a safe outlet for the expression of their strong feelings when under stress, women are often able to discharge much of the tension and anxiety that can build up. Although the venting process offers only temporary relief, it is often enough to rejuvenate the spirit and refocus the energies of feminine leaders. Once they are able to discharge the emotional pressure, these women seem able, once again, to concentrate on the business at hand.

Whereas most women develop outlets for their strong feelings in order to reduce stress, this is often not the case for men. In situations where they are experiencing a stress buildup, many men react by ignoring the emotional signals. Instead of admitting to themselves or to others that they are operating under conditions of extreme stress, they have been taught to repress their feelings and to press on, regardless. As the partner of a large Dallas law firm stated, "It's not considered manly to admit you're working under stress. If any of the lawyers around here was to come down with an ulcer or some other telltale sign, I doubt seriously if he'd ever make partner.

"I think most men were brought up to believe the old adage about 'When the going gets tough, the tough get going.' We're not supposed to fall apart under stress. If we do, we have failed to live up to society's expectations of us as tough leaders—and our own expectations, too."

In attempting to live up to the masculine ideal, many men discover that being strong, in charge, and emotionally detached is a difficult role to play constantly. What's more, it is a role that does not allow one to seek help or to find outlets for tension in order to reduce the negative impact of chronic stress.

In the future, as more feminine leaders emerge in corporations—and greater acceptance and support for their style continue to grow—men may become more willing to acknowledge their feelings and share their concerns. Meanwhile they must learn to accept emotional venting as a healthy reaction to stress among feminine leaders. Although it may look out of control, it is not. In fact, for most feminine leaders it is an extremely useful way to clear the air.

As the female vice president of a large chain of women's apparel stores stated, "I need to blow off steam on occasion. When I do, I'm not expecting my boss to come in and fix the problem. I just want him to listen to me complain. A little sympathy and support is all I'm looking for—not a rescue. Then, once I've vented my feelings, I can take care of the problem myself."

ORGANIZATIONAL ABILITIES

In dealing with complexity and diverse tasks, feminine leaders also recognize the importance of thorough planning and organization. Nowhere is the need for organization more acute than among working mothers with successful, demanding careers. Not surprisingly, the demands placed on them as parents and professionals have forced these women to become efficient organizers of their time. According to a management study conducted by Dr. Lynn Offerman of George Washington University, "Women use time-management techniques, such as keeping a daily log of jobs to be done, organizing jobs by priority, and scheduling important jobs for times of peak energy more consistently than do men."

In discussing her findings at a meeting of the Eastern Psychological Association, Dr. Offerman was quoted as saying, "My best guess is that women perform a large share of household and child-rearing functions in addition to their job responsibilities, and this makes their time-management skills critical."[1]

Reflecting on her own situation as an executive director at Russell Reynolds, the international executive recruiting firm, Alice Early had this to say about women executives' organizational skills: "The women in this firm who have been extremely successful have also, as a group, been better organized. Maybe it's because we are also running families as in, 'I have to get on a plane to the coast but I also have to call a plumber before I leave and get dinner for the kids.' "

Managing multiple roles also requires paying careful attention to details. As Julia Goggin, an executive with Bankers Trust, points out, "Women managers are very attentive to detail. I think to a great degree this is because they must plan ahead—for meals, inoculations for the children, PTA meetings, etc. Because of the constant demands made on them by their families, their employers, and their communities, women are more used to thinking in these terms. They tend to be practical and future-oriented."

While the roles of father, husband, and manager are evolving in our society, they have yet to become the true counterparts of mother, wife, and manager. Today working mothers continue to bear the largest share of the child-care burden in most households and must manage the widest range of demands and responsibilities of any group in our society. No one who has ever observed a woman executive with young children plot her daily routine could possibly forget the intricate planning and tireless energy required to manage the day-to-day details of the home, the family, and the career. The term "superwomen," which is often used to describe this group, seems like a modest assessment of the multiple roles these women play.

SUPERWOMAN: PRO'S AND CON'S

In many respects, the role of superwoman is a part that has been unfairly imposed on working women in today's society. But in other respects, this role offers feminine leaders many satisfactions and rewards. Basically, the need to become a superwoman has been created by three interrelated phenomena. First, on the negative side, is the enormous gap that currently exists between the demand and the availability of institutional child-care support for working parents. As Muriel Fox of Carl Byoir & Associates points out, "We are still living in a society that makes greater demands on women. A wife working outside the home does twenty hours of work in the home while her husband does thirty minutes. Add children and it becomes infinitely harder on women since society has yet to address the problem of child care properly. . . . Women at the executive level must often sacrifice their sleep and leisure time in order to succeed as parents and as professionals."

A second negative factor identified by many women is the reluctance of organizations to support more sharing of parental responsibilities between men and women. Although many companies provide paternity leaves for men, there are still relatively few places where a male executive would not be criticized for taking time off from his work to be with a sick child. In the case of a long-term leave for child-care reasons, there appears to be virtually no support for men doing this within organizations.

As an executive recruiter with a major Chicago search firm stated, "To my knowledge we have never placed a single male executive who was reentering the job market after taking time off to raise a child. While it could happen, I think many of our clients would have some serious questions about that person. That sex stereotype would probably still prevail."

On the positive side, the role of superwoman provides its own special reward. Although the importance of work has begun to achieve a position of greater prominence in the lives of many feminine leaders, it has not supplanted the importance of home and family. On the contrary, many feminine leaders believe their careers have helped to enhance their personal lives and the quality of their relationships with friends and family. Playing multiple roles not only makes great demands on the energies of feminine leaders, it also offers them the challenges and satisfactions of being truly involved with their work and their homes.

The following comments from a development specialist at a Manhattan prep school are typical of the feelings of many women who are balancing the demands of a busy career with those of raising children: "When my first child arrived, I stopped working for two years. Then, when the youngest came, we really needed the income so I went back to work full-time. While there's no doubt that my time is more limited, I find that my work has added a new element of interest to my life. It's difficult to manage a household, two active children, and still be completely committed to a demanding career. But it's also a real challenge and allows me to use a lot more of my skills. I think my kids like it, too."

POSITIVE IMPACT ON HEALTH

There is also evidence that a connection exists between good health and multiple roles. In a paper examining the relationship between "Women's Social Roles and Health," Dr. Lois Verbrugge of the University of Michigan states, "It is common to cite the negative aspects of multiple roles and how they can cause role overload and role conflict. Overload refers to too many demands on time. Conflict refers to incompatible expectations from one's various roles. Both cause role strain.

"If this is true, the more roles a person has, the more role overload and negative consequences for health might be expected. . . . But multiple roles may also enhance health. People with multiple roles gain more privileges, security, resources, and feelings of self-esteem. They learn to use their time well. Their greater social involvement and achievement enhance feelings of satisfaction."[2]

Although there are negative consequences for working women who must manage multiple roles without adequate family, employment, and community support, when this support is available, multiple roles seem to have a beneficial effect on women's health. According to Dr. Verbrugge's findings: "The more roles women have, the better their health. Women with three major roles (employment, marriage, parenthood) tend to have the best health status and to engage in fewest curative actions. . . . It appears that multiple roles have an additive effect."[3]

In discussing the management of multiple roles, women often cite the importance of planning, organization, and attention to detail as being critical. Generally, these are skills that most feminine leaders are well practiced in by the time they reach the executive suite. But their ability to manage multiple roles is also related to another basic difference in perspective. This is the view feminine leaders have of the boundaries between their careers and their personal lives. Once again, in this area of setting boundaries, we see a noticeable difference in the approach used by feminine leaders and traditional managers to integrate and also to separate their work from their non-work lives.

ESTABLISHING BOUNDARIES

How can this difference be described? Simply stated, many traditional managers have more permeable boundaries between their work and their personal lives while the boundaries of feminine leaders are often more strictly defined. This translates into a difference in their outlook on many issues that impact both arenas.

According to many feminine leaders, the ability to manage multiple roles effectively is contingent on keeping the boundaries between them clearly in place. For some women, this may mean refusing to work overtime on an ongoing basis because of personal commitments or turning down a promotion in another city because acceptance would involve uprooting one's family. For others, it may simply mean preserving enough time to do the tasks associated with running a house or raising a family.

Who will ever forget Congresswoman Geraldine Ferraro's first encounter with the press after being chosen as the Democratic candidate for vice president? Surrounded by Secret Service men and women, she made her way up and down the aisles of her local supermarket buying groceries as she discussed her political beliefs. It was an interview like no other in the history of U.S. politics and pointed out the many roles some successful women continue to play regardless of their career aspirations.

Unlike many traditional managers, who believe that work priorities must come before personal needs and that competing for the next promotion means sacrificing time with friends and family, feminine leaders have a very different perspective on striking the proper balance between one's work and personal life. Although it is clear that women managers place a high value on their work and are serious about their careers, many are unwilling to support traditional organization norms regarding transfers, job-related travel, and other activities that interfere with day-to-day life. To a great degree, the importance feminine leaders place on family life precludes them from doing so.

But this reluctance among feminine leaders to allow their work to control their lives goes beyond the importance they place on the family. It has to do with building and maintaining personal relationships, on staying connected to other people, and on avoiding the social distance and resultant impersonality they associate with being too focused on work.

Colombe Nicholas of Christian Dior, New York, believes that a rich, multifaceted life can enhance the potential for business success. In a recent speech she said, "I think the fact that a good many successful managers are workaholics has fostered the idea that to succeed one has to neglect other aspects of living. You don't. Being a workaholic may help promote a career. Certainly it will limit one's non-work involvements. But it is not necessary to be a workaholic to succeed. In fact, multifaceted people have a better chance of succeeding in top executive positions."

IMPORTANCE OF FAMILY AND QUALITY OF LIFE

The boundaries women place around their work and personal lives help to preserve the unique aspects of each arena. In addition, these boundaries reduce the risk of isolation that comes from focusing too much energy on work and too little on personal interests and relationships. In a sense, this insistence on setting limits seems to allow feminine leaders to grow and develop in both personal and professional terms.

The different priorities given to work and personal commitments by men and women executives were also reflected in a recent study conducted by Korn/Ferry International. In comparing the work histories of three hundred men and women senior executives, several differences stood out. According to the findings, the "composite female executive spends an average of 33 days out of town per year, considerably less than the male average of 52 days. . . . Nearly half spend less than 20 days away on business in contrast to only 21% of the males." In addition to differences in job-related travel, the study also showed that although one third of the women had been asked to relocate, only 21 percent agreed to as compared to an 81 percent relocation rate among the men.[4]

Speaking about her own experiences managing the boundaries between work and family life, Barbara Fiorito, a vice president at Chemical Bank, said, "Many men still seem to care more about their material, 'up the ladder' achievements than the quality of the lives they are living. I think women executives are inclined to consider all areas. For example, during my children's early years I have avoided constant travel on occasion and make it a point to be home at a reasonable hour at night.

"As the mother of two young children and three stepchildren, I have a very busy life. Until the youngest turned three, I had little social life—I spent my days managing and the time from 6 P.M. on being a mother. It was important to me to meet my commitments in both areas. I don't think many men would be so focused on these priorities.

"Although I try not to let my family responsibilities interfere at the office, I do take my children's birthdays off and regard them as important as national holidays. Many of the men I have worked with might take time off for a golf tournament or a sailing date, but not for something like this. They just don't put the same emphasis on family as women do."

The decision of feminine leaders to set limits on the sacrifices they are willing to make in the name of career success is a difficult one for some organizations to accept. Yet many women managers believe that a great number of men would like to follow their lead. Jean Gleason, a partner with Fulbright & Jaworski, a prominent law firm in Washington, D.C., noted, "I know that a lot of my male contemporaries are as interested as I am in more time off to be with their children, but most of them talk about it as if it were impossible. None will admit publicly to wanting this. . . . If ever a [male] member of a law firm were to admit that he would like three months off, he would also have admitted, in essence, to a lack of being fully committed."

Although most men may not be ready to take long leaves to raise their children, many are thinking twice before going along with other corporate decisions that interfere with family life. Having watched their colleagues deal with the stress and disruption of frequent transfers, many male managers are weighing the advantages against the disadvantages before agreeing to relocate. One man who credits feminine leaders for this change in male attitude is Rusty Renick, a division manager of human resources at New York Telephone. In discussing this change he said, "Women have begun to broaden choices for all of us. Years ago men never questioned transfers. If they were told that their job was in New York today and in Buffalo tomorrow, they just saluted, took their families, and went. Women came along and said, 'Wait a minute.'

"Then some men started picking up on the same themes and said, 'The women are right.' While many men always felt strongly about their family values, they weren't sure they should ever mention this out loud. Now that's starting to change.

"Today I see more men who are making the decision to do a good job for their company, but not put twelve hours in every day. I think a lot of men are discovering they really have obligations and interests elsewhere."

More than in any other single area, the impact of feminine leadership has already had a significant influence on many organizational practices pertaining to executive mobility. Ten years ago most executives were resigned to relocating whenever and to wherever their corporations sent them. Today more and more men and women believe they have a choice. In addition, as more men followed the lead of women and refused to make arbitrary moves, corporations discovered they could find more humane alternatives to staffing problems—alternatives that did not breed resentment or force many talented managers to leave the business.

Jim Hennessy is executive vice president of the Nynex Corporation, a business with major offices from Maine to New York. During his career he has moved several times, frequently as a result of promotion. Although he believes that experience in different geographic locales is an important prerequisite to moving up in a large organization, he thinks that many companies failed to recognize the sacrifices relocation policies demanded of many executive families in the past. He also believes that women have had a positive, tempering effect on relocation policies throughout industry. As he states, "Unlike some times in the past, management today really thinks things through: 'Is this the move we really want to make? Is this the kind of person we really want to move ahead and is this the right kind of experience for that individual?' The process is much more selective. Today, when a relocation takes place, it's the kind of assignment which will benefit the person as well as the company."

MORE FLEXIBLE POLICIES

Despite some lingering resistance to change, corporations are beginning to recognize the need for more flexible policies that allow managers to balance career demands with personal interests and family responsibilities. Although in many organizations managers are still expected to subordinate their personal lives to corporate interests, more companies are starting to recognize the negative impact that workaholism has on executives. Not only can this narrow focus lead to chronic stress, isolation, and family problems, it can cause serious organizational problems as well.

By emphasizing both their career and personal interests, feminine leaders are helping organizations develop a cure for workaholism. They are demonstrating that the price of success need not include isolation from friends and family. As a result of their actions, some long-standing corporate traditions are beginning to change and the quality of life at work and beyond is improving for others as well.

To feminine leaders, a full, diverse life beyond the office is critically important and something they are working hard to preserve as they move up within organizations. We can only hope that as their influence continues to grow, this idea will become an accepted reality for all managers and receive more enthusiastic support from organizations. For today as never before, effective leadership requires more than hard work, ambition, and devotion to corporate goals. It requires staying in touch with our own humanity as well.

Chapter Twelve

Pitching In and Professional Development

P icture yourself in this situation: You have a detailed, last-minute report to present to the CEO tomorrow morning and your secretary is out sick. The copy machine just overheated and the typed material, which came back from the word-processing unit two hours late, still needs to be proofed and edited. It's now 4:30 and tonight is bowling night for the other secretaries. You've asked for a volunteer to stay but no one has offered. What would you do?

PITCHING IN

When faced with a crisis like the one just described, a woman manager might very likely step out of her normal role and pitch in—do whatever is required to get the job done. Obviously, women executives are not paid to do clerical work. Yet, there are times when such work is all that is

217

required to complete an important project and no one else is available to do it.

Confronted with the choice of either waiting for help to arrive or helping themselves, most women managers will choose the latter. When it comes to understanding the workings of an office, how to get a report produced, where to go to find a particular form, or how to clear the copier, most women are able to function effectively without help, whereas a large number of their male counterparts are either unwilling or unable to do so. What accounts for this stylistic difference? Three reasons come to mind.

The first has to do with office image. While many traditional managers believe that pitching in can tarnish their image as professionals, feminine leaders are less concerned about being seen at the typewriter or the copy machine. In fact, most regard clerical support as vital to their work rather than as menial labor. Because they view the efforts of all team members as significant, feminine leaders are willing to help out wherever help is needed.

A second reason for this willingness to pitch in relates to the performance pressure many women managers feel in organizations where they, as yet, have not been accepted. As Gerry Tabaczyk of Peter Rogers Associates points out, "Based on some of my past experiences at larger agencies, I don't think there is any doubt that women are more willing to pitch in to get things done while most men will go to the secretary. Today a woman's performance in management is still under the microscope. So to be sure that everything is done well, women are required to get more involved and to stay more involved. I think it's a survival issue for many women, this idea of pitching in."

Another male manager who agrees with this assessment is John Sheedy of Simon and Hilliard. In discussing the style women use to manage shortages of help and tight deadlines he stated, "Women are definitely more willing to get their hands dirty. Not only have I seen this, I've also seen more women than men putting in longer hours or working on weekends to meet a deadline. When I was vice president of marketing at Bristol-Myers, I used to work on the weekends. The only other people I ever saw in the office on a Saturday or a Sunday were women. The work ethic seems to be stronger among this group."

Pressure to perform well certainly accounts for some of the interest that feminine leaders have in pitching in. Because many women still believe they are being judged by tougher, more exacting standards than their male peers, they simply refuse to let anything fall between the cracks. But there is another reason pitching in seems to be easier for many women than for men. This ability is a function of the background and experiences many successful women had early in their careers. As Alice Early of Russell Reynolds remarked, "I think women are not as reliant on secretaries and not at a loss when a key person isn't available. Perhaps this is because so many of us started in very junior positions where, because we didn't have staff people to help us, we had to function on our own."

The phrases used to describe feminine leaders, such as "stronger work ethic" and "getting one's hands dirty," call to mind the image of the hardworking, first-generation immigrant. In many ways, this image aptly describes the attitudes, work spirit, and behavior of feminine leaders today. Although their methods may be viewed as unorthodox by some, they make the best use of their backgrounds and experiences to do what needs to be done.

But although most women managers feel comfortable dealing with office emergencies because of prior experience, this ability can become a drawback as well. Alice Early points out, "Most women are comfortable with almost any office task you can think of because at some point in their past, they had to learn how to do all those things. Now when they step in to solve a crisis, they run the risk that those who would like to hamstring them will say, 'Since you're so good at this why don't you take care of it from now on.' "

Many women who have had such experiences believe they run a risk each time they cross the line between manager and worker in emergencies. At the same time, they recognize that this line is often arbitrarily drawn and can get in the way in situations where a real team effort is required to accomplish a task.

In some organizations, feminine leaders have found that pitching in can create role confusion when it challenges long-established behavioral norms. As one woman manager stated, "Around here if you're a woman and you answer your own phone, the person calling automatically thinks you're the secretary not the manager." Yet, despite the confusion that their less formal, more fluid style can cause, most feminine leaders still regard the ability to pitch in as a useful managerial skill. Many women maintain that pitching in, although it is not always easy, helps them contain office crises. More important, they believe that a willingness to get one's hands dirty can help to narrow the gap that sometimes exists between management and employees. Diann Rohde, assistant director for field development at the National Multiple Sclerosis Society, is a proponent of pitching in. In her view, this ability helps women managers respond quickly and more appropriately to many situations. She states, "When responding to office crises, women will often look beyond the general facts to individual needs. They are able to perceive those needs downward through many layers of the organization and tend to know what help is required and how to move in and get things done even at the secretarial level."

PROFESSIONAL DEVELOPMENT

In addition to pitching in, many feminine leaders also display an unusually strong interest in professional development for themselves and their work groups. Although some analysts have attributed this to a lack of self-confidence, these women describe it differently. They say that excellent credentials can sometimes help to overcome resistance to women in leadership roles—resistance that might otherwise cost a woman manager an important promotion. Commenting on this point Dr. Donna Shalala of Hunter College said, "What women are doing today is what first-generation Irish immigrants did when they came to this country. They know they need an extra edge to overcome the barriers they face and they're willing to invest the time to get it.

"I tell women, 'Get yourself first-class training. Do everything you can so that no one can ever tell you that you are lacking something.' One of the reasons why I became president of Hunter College, instead of going back to the classroom which I love, was because I never wanted anyone to be able to say, 'She doesn't have executive experience.' Now I have addressed all the key issues that could be raised about my professional background. I've had all the experiences one is 'supposed to have' for a top job."

The emphasis placed on professional credentials by many women is often a direct reaction to the lingering doubts that still exist in many organizations regarding women's ability to manage. To overcome such reservations, women are willing to invest considerable time and energy pursuing advanced degrees and building their "technical" knowledge in new areas. Remarking on this drive for education and training, Jill Considine of The First Women's Bank said, "Most women, when they get a promotion, will work hard to demonstrate that they deserve it. Many men, on the other hand, begin immediately to look toward the next job. Women are the ones who will work much harder to get the background and try to learn."

Lydia Sarfati, president and development director of Sarkli-Repechage, Ltd., a manufacturer of skin care products, also believes that women have a particularly strong interest in this area. She sees competition from male managers as one of the principal reasons for this and states, "I think women are more willing to take courses and to develop themselves professionally. Particularly in the United States, a woman feels she has a great deal of competition from men and sees a key to her success being greater knowledge as well as management skill and experience."

Barbara Blum, president and CEO of The Women's National Bank in Washington, D.C., also sees a marked difference in the approach that women take to professional development. She expressed it this way: "I haven't worked with any women—even those with three children at home—who weren't willing to take a course or read a book if they thought that it would help them on the job or learn a skill to help improve their performance. Although it is easier for most men to take courses, because they don't have to go home and fix dinner for the family at night, it is women who are more likely to do this."

Whether they are new to the business of managing or seasoned veterans, it appears that many women place particular importance on the value of educational credentials and professional development. According to the findings in one recent AMA study of middle managers, women stressed the importance of seminars in technical and personal skill development far more frequently than men.[1] As opposed to many traditional managers, who place greater emphasis on career development—using each job as a springboard to a better opportunity elsewhere—women see a greater need for special skills and training as they progress up the professional ladder.

Because they are still relatively new to the world of middle management and are often in the position of having to prove their ability to skeptical colleagues, women place greater emphasis on acquiring professional credentials. For many, the advanced degree is indisputable evidence of technical competence—making it easier for women to speak up and use their influence.

Commenting on this point, Rusty Renick of New York Telephone observed, "While men are interested in career development, women want to develop expertise in their fields. They need to be able to back up their opinions with facts—to dispel any questions that people might have about their ability to manage effectively. If men don't know something, they are much more likely to make up the answer. Because women are always being challenged to prove their competence, they don't do this. Instead, they come at you with a full set of credentials."

In discussing the emphasis many women place on earning credentials, Rosemary Pooler, commissioner of the New York Public Service Commission, offered this thought: "Many of my women colleagues and I have said for a long time that true equality will finally be here when women have the right to be as ordinary and mediocre as some of the men we see in management. In truth, I haven't seen the Age of Mediocrity for women arrive yet. Even among younger women I still find that, where a man in the same job will have one degree she will have two; if the man is in the top third of his class she will be in the top ten percent. . . . In many cases, there is a dramatic difference in background, credentials, verbal ability, and thoughtfulness that is readily apparent."

If one takes into account the above, one might assume all

this extra effort and interest in professional development is paying off in greater promotional gains for more women today. But you'd be wrong if you were to make this assumption. The fact remains that women still do not get the same promotional considerations as men, even in cases where their credentials are equal. In one study of three hundred middle and senior managers, women with the same credentials as their male counterparts were found to be promoted more frequently but, despite this, still held lower-level positions within their companies.[2]

In another recent study conducted among men and women with equivalent educational credentials, women managers were shown to be losing the salary race as well. According to the results of Dr. Mary Anne Devanna's research at Columbia University involving two hundred men and women with MBA's, the salary gap between the sexes seems to widen over time. Dr. Devanna's findings show that women started out their careers with salaries equal to those of male peers. However, ten years later, women with equal educational credentials and training were being paid an average of 81 percent of what their male counterparts received. In addition, Dr. Devanna found that none of the commonly held theories about why women do not earn as much as men (such as marriage and child-care responsibilities) could adequately account for this gap.[3]

Although efforts to enhance professionalism have helped some women move further up the career ladder, it appears that for most women, professional development is still not enough to close the gender gap that exists in management. The findings of the Columbia study show that women managers are still the victims of negative attitudes and unfair practices even where their educational credentials are equal.

Yet, ironically, many male executives believe that a lack

of educational credentials is responsible for the slow progress being made by women. For example, in a survey conducted among 1,654 men in managerial positions (more than half of whom were in senior management jobs), 59 percent stated there were a limited number of women in their organizations with the qualifications to become managers. This same group cited education as a major deficiency preventing women from moving ahead.[4]

In looking at the professional development issue, one can readily see the many dilemmas facing women managers today. First there is the problem of tying professional development to career development. In many organizations there seems to be a very weak connection between the educational credentials of women managers and their salary and advancement potential. There is also a tendency to use this issue as an excuse for women's slower advancement in some companies, regardless of whether the facts support this reasoning or not. In addition, there seems to be no clear definition of what constitutes enough development in many organizations. Consequently, there is no way for women to judge whether they meet the criteria or not.

But perhaps the most difficult task facing feminine leaders today is judging what constitutes real professional development and distinguishing it from what is nice to know and just plain irrelevant. As women continue to search for solutions to the complex issues they face as professionals, many are finding that much of the advice being offered doesn't work. Most of these solutions ignore the need for organizational change and assume that the problems facing women executives today can be solved in a vacuum and corrected with cookbook approaches.

But as Barbara Blum, among other women executives, recognizes, "What we need to do is institutionalize change and that has got to happen in many different ways. The answer is not in encouraging women to take up golf so they can be included in the informal decision-making process. There has to be more emphasis placed on meaningful development and less on superficiality."

For many women managers, professional development continues to be an important goal unto itself. For others it is a means to an end—a potential pathway to advancement and greater career opportunity. But regardless of the personal motivation, it is clear that feminine leaders share an eagerness to learn and a willingness to invest the time and the effort required to improve their skills. What is not evident, as yet, is a serious commitment on the part of many organizations to fully utilize the talents that women already possess or to tie their professional development needs to specific job requirements.

Until stylistic differences between feminine leaders and traditional managers are fully understood and supported throughout corporations, much of what is called professional development for women will continue to focus on changing women's management style rather than on enhancing their technical skills. While this approach may create more homogeneity within management, it will not tap the vast potential of feminine leaders or solve the corporate crisis.

Status quo solutions are not the answer. Working together —using all the special skills and insights we have to offer as men and women—is the only solution.

PART

III

Chapter Thirteen

Making a Real Difference: What Women Can Do

A mong those who consider themselves knowledgeable on the subject of women in management, there is a popular theory known as critical mass. According to this point of view, the impact of women and their leadership skills will become obvious in organizations once the number of women managers has achieved a critical mass. Over the years, this mass has been estimated at about 30 percent of the total management group.

Recently, however, the proponents of this theory suffered a substantial setback when the percentage of female managers crossed over this critical point and nothing really noticeable happened. It was pretty much business as usual within corporations and back to the drawing boards for these management pundits.

Despite the current situation, I continue to believe there is something to the critical mass idea. But if a critical mass is really necessary for leadership change, why haven't the talents of feminine leaders described in the preceding chapters been more widely embraced and acknowledged within organizations? Why is this alternate management style still struggling for recognition in many companies?

The problem is that one essential element has been left out of the equations used to calculate the required critical mass. It is not just the mass itself that is important; the perceptions and actions of the mass also matter. Unlike atoms, women managers will not automatically burst out in a chain reaction once a certain density is achieved. For a chain reaction to be started on behalf of feminine leadership, more than the mere presence of women in management is required. These women must actively embrace and support this new style of management within their companies. What's more, their activities must be carefully considered and directed. Otherwise, they run the risk of a meltdown, both in terms of winning support for their natural management style and in the advancement of their own careers.

Women in management today are at distinctly different points when it comes to an awareness of feminine leadership and the benefits it offers. In the face of mounting evidence, some women continue to deny the very existence of feminine leadership. What is behind their resistance? The answer is a complex one. First, many women managers believe that the acknowledgment of differences will precipitate a regression in our society regarding acceptable roles for women. Such an admission, they fear, would demonstrate that women cannot function effectively as leaders. But concrete proof of the effectiveness of feminine leaders already exists in corporations throughout this country. Supported by this proof, women must have the confidence to point out the differences and the benefits of their unique style.

Then, there are those successful women who have learned to accommodate and now see themselves as different from other women. By virtue of their special status, such women are not anxious to see feminine leadership thrive. Nor are they willing to acknowledge that this style is appropriate, since so many of them were compelled to give up their own identities as women in order to succeed.

Finally, some women managers are truly unaware of any differences in management style because their own natural style is more adaptive or more traditional than nontraditional. Since they have found their transition into the executive world to be an easy one, it is difficult for many within this group to relate to the experiences of other women who have not found this to be the case. Nonetheless, these women must begin to recognize that feminine leadership is an effective alternative for many other women—whether they themselves choose to use this style or not.

Then there are the women who identify with the feminine leadership style. They are the ones I would like to address most directly in this chapter, for they represent a growing segment of corporate society—a segment that has the potential to bring about positive change for men and women, as well as for organizations. How can they make a difference? How can they convert the critical mass into a quality mass that will effectively work for change? The answers are simple, but not necessarily easy.

In working to promote the acceptance and utilization of feminine leadership skills within organizations, a number of basic actions can be taken:

1. LEARN ABOUT THE ISSUES

The first and most critical step is to learn about the issues. Too often I have observed women managers shrug off the need for education about the important matters they face. It's easy to understand why they think they already know enough but it's also self-defeating.

In order to build on a strong foundation of fact, women must find out the answers to questions such as these: What are the statistics on hiring and promotion of women into management in their own organizations? How many women are currently in senior management positions? What is the company's attitude toward women in managerial roles? How do corporate policies support this attitude?

In addition, women who are committed to changing attitudes must start by developing their own personal awareness. They must be willing to ask themselves a series of soul-searching questions such as: What is the impact of corporate masculinism on them as women? How does it affect their view of themselves as feminine leaders? When have they observed it affecting other women? How open and honest are their relationships with male coworkers? with other women? In what ways have they been expected to accommodate in order to succeed in management? What have they gained as a result? What have they lost?

Aside from helping women sort out their own positions on the issues, staying aware gives them important information about the corporate climate. The impact of corporate masculinism is not easy to assess. It takes careful, critical analysis as well as some personal soul-searching to see and appreciate its effects on feminine leaders. But this analysis is necessary if women are ever to achieve recognition as nontraditional leaders.

2. RENEGOTIATE COLLUSIVE RELATIONSHIPS

One of the sad but unavoidable aspects of developing greater awareness is the discovery that some of our oldest and closest relationships are the most resistant to change. But once awareness is heightened, we begin to experience a need for redefining old relationships and updating them so that they remain honest, current, and consistent with our new image of ourselves and the world around us. As women managers start to recognize the accommodating and unproductive roles they have played in the past and to be uncomfortable with them, some also discover that friends and colleagues continue to exert pressure on them to play these roles.

In order to maintain old attitudes, men must consciously or unconsciously rely on women to ignore or silently cooperate with their assumptions. When women managers are no longer willing to accommodate by playing their prescribed roles, the familiar rules of the male-female game suddenly change. Sometimes, men with a developing awareness are able to recognize the value of renegotiating outdated relationships with women, but many men are not.

For emerging feminine leaders, the choice of remaining in role or of risking the dissolution of a relationship is difficult but not impossible to make. With support from others and the knowledge that accommodation is not a long-term strategy for success, most women are able to begin renegotiating collusive relationships.

By starting with the least threatening ones first, and developing skills to deal with more difficult people over time, women can succeed in modifying their own behavior and the expectations of others. Once they recognize that collusion helps perpetuate the problem of corporate masculinism by delivering mixed or misleading messages, aware women can work for congruency between their thoughts, feelings, and actions. Where they encounter strong resistance to change, many also discover they are better off letting the relationship go since the personal cost of maintaining it is so high.

3. ESTABLISH A CORPORATE SUPPORT SYSTEM

Today, there is a deeper sense of support for feminine leadership among many successful women than ever before. After years of managing in and adapting to an alien culture, these women recognize the need for support and reinforcement in order to be effective agents of change. As Ruth Downing Karp of J. Walter Thompson states, "Today I see more women looking out for each other than I have seen in the past. I think there is a need for small local sisterhoods in every company where women can find support for being themselves and I think the seeds have finally been sown for this."

Carol Foreman, who was recently involved in organizing the Mondale-Ferraro campaign, also believes that there is a greater depth of feeling among women today than in the past. She states, "Most women out there are working together and protecting each other. What's more, there is a sense of pride that we feel as women in the accomplishments of each other. My success is felt by those around me. Gerry Ferraro's success belongs to us all."

Probably the best way of working together for the mutual benefit of all feminine leaders is through network development. Although the concept of networking is not new, the need for it today is as great as ever. As women try out new roles and take greater, more visible risks, many are discovering the importance of sharing their experiences with others who have similar concerns. Even when male colleagues are supportive, many women find it difficult to talk openly about their problems.

Since men do not encounter the same issues in organizations, they are often unaware of the problems and are unable to offer the type of assistance that feminine leaders need. But with the help of local networks, many women are finding the internal strength to stay themselves and the confidence to succeed as feminine leaders.

Obviously, this kind of cooperation and support doesn't just happen. It takes time, care, and commitment to build a network that really works. Unless a woman is willing to make a commitment to helping other women, she should forget about joining a network. Today, a lot is being written about how networks can help women find better jobs, make new friends and social contacts. But while it's fine to pursue these goals through networking, women must also be willing to give a great deal to others if they want the experience to be meaningful. Without a strong commitment to improving opportunities for all women in the organization, a network can become superficial and not much more than an elitist club.

4. BE A SUPPORTIVE ROLE MODEL

At a conference of middle and senior women executives in one of the nation's largest companies, I was asked to participate in a panel discussion about the issues facing executive women in the 1980's. In my opening remarks I spoke about the need for activism among women professionals, particularly the important role they could play within their companies to effect a change in the nature of corporate leadership and increase opportunity for women.

At the end of the seminar, after much lively discussion, the highest-ranking woman manager present, and the only female officer in this company at the time, approached me. She said, "In the late sixties and early seventies, I was an activist on behalf of working women. I lobbied for change within this company and I even carried placards and marched in political rallies. I think I've done my part to help create positive change, yet you are suggesting that I should be doing more. At this point in my career, I prefer to be quietly supportive." Surprised by the comment, I asked her what quietly supportive meant. She replied, "Not getting in the way."

Although it is easy to understand why some women managers are reluctant to remain actively involved in the change process, there is no doubt that feminine leaders must do more than not get in the way. The most important task that faces women today is that of education through example. Others must see feminine leadership at work. Thus, it is up to feminine leaders to create enthusiasm and support for feminine leadership by setting a new example.

In discussions with many women managers about feminine leadership, concern is often expressed about the lack of support for this alternate approach among the so-called queen bees who have already achieved top management positions. Although it is not likely that such women will ever become active supporters of feminine leadership, acceptance for this style is beginning to increase among women at the top. Today, more senior women believe in and practice this approach and are willing to speak out on important issues. Unlike the queen bees of the past, many are welcoming the entry of more feminine leaders into executive circles.

Regardless of where a woman might be on the corporate ladder, there are always other women below her who want to know what her situation is like and who need to hear the truth. It's critical that women in management positions provide honest information and guidance. Why not talk about the need for support, for cooperation, and for developing stronger bonds among working women? Why not let others know your views about feminine leadership? In short, why not offer women a supportive and more realistic model to use in making their way up the corporate ladder?

What a relief it can be for other women to learn that others are up against the same problems that they are! And what a frustrating and confusing experience it is for these women to hear that their management role models seem to be operating in another stratosphere without any major obstacles or problems. To bring the issues of corporate masculinism to the surface, women managers must be willing to speak with honesty and clarity about the need for change. More important, they can demonstrate through their actions that a realistic alternative is available by remaining true to their own values, beliefs, and talents as feminine leaders.

Today, a growing group of successful women in management is willing to acknowledge that their style is different and that, contrary to popular opinion, it has not hurt them but has helped them succeed. Many of the women quoted in this book are examples of this nontraditional model. Their comments and experiences underscore the fact that while people are people, they are also men and women with unique perspectives and different operating styles. While traditional formulas have been useful for some women, the nontraditional approach favored by feminine leaders must be given more emphasis in women's groups and professional networks today. These women represent an exciting new success model, one that many other emerging feminine leaders would welcome and emulate.

While many men have been highly instrumental in helping women managers succeed, there are some lessons that can be learned only from others of like identity. Speaking about the importance of female role models, Walter Blass of AT&T states, "Looking at today's women, I suggest that you will find an increasing number for whom their mother or other women were a major influence.

"To compete with others in a male-dominated field, an achieving woman needs a fair dose of masculine qualities such as assertiveness and willingness to take dangerous leadership positions. Conversely, to sense herself as a woman rather than a man in a woman's body, she needs to feel comfortable with her individual physical and mental endowment, her capabilities, and her sisterhood with all women, past and present. I stress this point because there is so much adulterated junk in books these days telling women to dress in suits like men, to talk like men, to master sports in which they have little interest . . . and to lose devotion, tenderness, and other ways of caring that seem natural to themselves."

For emerging feminine leaders, role models are in short supply. Nonetheless, they do exist. In searching for examples of this approach within organizations, women managers must first recognize that feminine leaders are likely to look and to act somewhat differently from their successful male counterparts and many of their successful female counterparts as well. While they may be softer, less out-front, and less visible by comparison, a closer examination will reveal that they are equally effective.

5. MAXIMIZE FEMININE LEADERSHIP STRENGTHS: BE YOURSELF

Today, women managers have an opportunity to put their natural management style to work for their companies and for themselves. But in order to do this, they must first become comfortable with their own feminine style. Unlike many other change efforts that require the learning of new behaviors, this one requires women simply to be themselves. They must use their natural strengths—their interpersonal skills, their feelings, and the problem-solving tools that have worked for them throughout their lives. They must practice trusting their own instincts and intuitions. Instead of ignoring emotional data or rationalizing their own reactions, they must work with what they think and feel. Based on their own experiences, they know that what feels right usually is right. Why should they stop trusting those feelings from nine to five? Why should they underutilize their special abilities to solve problems once they walk through an office door?

While some women argue that the corporate world is not yet ready for feminine leadership, I would argue that American industry is more ready today than it has ever been for this approach. The problem is one of recognition. Businesses simply have not yet recognized the contribution that women managers can make. They will become more receptive to this nontraditional style only when more women demonstrate a willingness to use it.

But first, women executives must be aware of the qualities that differentiate feminine leadership from the traditional masculine approach and use these in an open and out-front way to manage. In order to raise awareness within organizations of the benefits of feminine leadership, women who identify with this approach and see it as a more natural extension of the way they function must begin to use more of their skills instead of holding back and accommodating. While there is always a chance that others will disapprove, how great is the risk when compared to the negative consequences of playing accommodating roles? More important, how much can potentially be gained from being yourself and using all your talents and strengths to manage more effectively?

The importance of being yourself is an idea that today's successful feminine leaders stress as critical. As entrepreneur Deborah Fields says, "I feel strongly that instead of following a stereotype, women must rely more on being their unique selves. They can bring a great deal of added value to the business world if they do this."

In her work with large corporations, organization consultant Edith Whitfield Seashore has also seen the positive impact of this nontraditional style within businesses. Based upon her experiences, she believes that "as women move up in organizations they need to be aware of their own style. They need to be clear about the special qualities they have which would be useful for them to hold on to—and useful for their organizations as well."

Does this mean that women should not adapt their style to suit the particular environment they work in? Certainly not. All managers, regardless of gender, must adapt to organizational norms. It is a fact of corporate life that some stylistic differences must be de-emphasized in order to succeed within management. But for many women managers this process of adaptation has gone too far, causing them to give up their basic identities and values. Although compromises are necessary for survival and success in a complex organization, trading away one's own identity is not. Not only is this self-destructive, in most cases it does not lead to managerial success.

Today's feminine leader must see her own activism as a steady, persistent effort to develop awareness and acceptance for nontraditional leadership. This is best accomplished through behavior modeling and thoughtful discussion. The action must be deliberate, reasoned, and natural, without placards and protests. Above all, it must openly acknowledge that many women, when encouraged to be themselves, manage differently yet effectively.

Lynda Confessore, public relations director for Levenstein and Gaines Advertising, is a feminine role model who has worked hard to raise awareness and promote change throughout her own successful career. As she states, "Only as more women move up and maintain their own style of managing will we see real change. As others see more women managers who are dedicated to their work and who have a different view of leadership, they will take us seriously. I have seen it happen but I also know that this takes a lot of effort and a long time."

Wendy Fleder, a marketing executive with Nynex Corporation, also believes that feminine leaders must focus on setting a new example in order to bring about change. She says, "Throughout business, women are constantly reinforced for behaving like men. Now it is up to us to call attention to the fact that there is another way. Women have so much to offer, particularly in the area of working effectively with others. Those of us who know we operate differently and take pride in those differences must go public. We must be more willing to let others see us manage this way and hear from us.

"At first, just the mere mention of the word 'difference' will raise hackles. But I think we can get past this by staying focused on what we have to offer and making others more aware of how our different style works. We're not trying to fight the system. We're trying to improve it. Right now, I think we can do a lot to help organizations manage more effectively."

6. RAISE THE CORPORATE CONSCIOUSNESS

So far, we have talked about how feminine leaders can promote positive change by being themselves, by encouraging other women to develop their natural management style, and by serving as nontraditional leadership models. But there is another equally important task that women must continue to perform, a task that can open new doors for many men as well.

Today, the impact of corporate masculinism, with its emphasis on competition and careerism, is of growing concern to many male managers who want to achieve greater balance and satisfaction in their work lives and their personal lives. As more men question some of the traditions and values that have shaped the corporate culture, feminine leaders can serve as catalysts for change. By demonstrating that there is more than one effective leadership style, women can increase the range of options available to men as well.

Throughout many corporations, there is a growing interest among some men in the principles and qualities of feminine leadership. Unlike more traditional managers, these men recognize the advantages of this leadership approach and prefer to operate in much the same way as feminine leaders. But their ability to gain acceptance for their preferred style is limited by the role expectations others have of them as masculine leaders. Ironically, in many companies, these men have less freedom to break with the long-standing traditions of masculinism than do women. Consequently, many look forward to the time when feminine leadership is more widely recognized in their organizations, since greater freedom and support for women's skills will pave the way for new masculine leadership models as well.

PERSISTENCE AND VISION

In talking with feminine leaders about their personal vision for the future, it is clear that they also look forward to a time when organizations will encourage both men and women to put all their skills and perspectives to effective use within management. Yet they also recognize that developing a greater range of acceptable options for both sexes will come only after feminine leaders are acknowledged within organizations as serious and effective managers.

Changing the managerial norms within the masculine corporate culture to include feminine leadership skills is not an easy task. But it is not an impossible dream either. Throughout the corporate world, more and more women are succeeding by being themselves. In some places, as women come to appreciate and use their different style, the value that feminine leadership adds to the managerial mix is becoming more evident to men and women managers and to some businesses. While this change process takes time, there are encouraging signs that it is beginning to have an impact. What is needed now is persistence, vision, and the personal conviction required to maintain the momentum.

For corporate America, the pursuit of excellence through new leadership is both a worthy and critical goal. For feminine leaders, it must continue to be an ongoing personal commitment as well. Today, as never before in our industrial history, women managers have an opportunity to make an important difference within their organizations. Not only can they become a more powerful critical mass, they can also bring new meaning to the concept of humanizing the workplace. By setting a new example, they can inspire other women to follow their lead and open new avenues for men. Dr. Sharon Connelly of the University of Southern California sums up the challenge when she states, "There is a need for vision and passion in leadership today. To inspire people to risk and create, leaders must be future oriented—focusing on new relationships between elements and people. I think that's a very feminine quality."

Chapter Fourteen

Making a Real Difference: What Men Can Do

U nlike the other chapters in this book, this one is written especially for men, particularly for those men who support the concept of feminine leadership and would like to see it develop further within their organizations. During the past several years, I have met hundreds of male managers in corporations across the country with an enthusiastic interest in this subject. Some are working with women who use this feminine leadership style to manage and, as a result, have a real investment in seeing it develop. Others are men who believe in the idea and instinctively understand its utility but, as yet, have not seen it put into practice.

Regardless of the origins of their interest, these men recognize the potential for change that this emerging leadership style represents. They understand that greater freedom and support for women to use their own style as leaders will ultimately lead to greater latitude and choice for men as well. For feminine leadership is built upon a strong belief in the benefits to institutions and individuals of a pluralistic corporate culture—one that encourages all people to use their creativity and their unique skills to help themselves, their colleagues, and their organizations grow and prosper.

With this ultimate goal in mind, there are several immediate steps men can take to support this new approach to leadership and help organizations redefine the parameters of acceptable managerial behavior. But before we explore these, let me offer this word of caution to my readers. The ideas outlined in this chapter speak directly to many issues that create serious problems in work relationships between men and women. Although most of these issues have been with us for many years, they continue to be difficult ones for both sexes to address openly and to manage. They are even difficult to discuss because, in the past, discussions have often led to blaming and excusing but no real resolution.

In developing this chapter, I have tried to outline several steps men can take to address issues created by the current emphasis on masculinism within corporations. My suggestions are based upon more than fifteen years of work in organizations studying these problems, as well as discussions with thousands of men and women managers focusing on their resolution. The intent here is not to cast blame. Instead, it is to speak candidly about the current corporate climate that exists in most complex organizations and to enlist support among thoughtful men for change. Although my description of the current climate of masculinism may seem harsh to some readers, it is because I believe that this climate creates serious problems for many women managers that I am addressing it here. The situation facing women in corporations today demands an honest and critical exploration if it is ever to change for the better. And change it must if our organizations are to survive.

In talking with men and women about the need for

change, many have described strategies they have used successfully in their own organizations to establish a supportive climate for change. Among the strategies mentioned, several seem to be universally supported in places where real change is occurring and where feminine leaders are emerging as an influential force within management. These strategies help to create the climate required by feminine leaders in order to develop their own, natural management style.

A solid foundation for change is required within complex organizations—one that supports the concept of pluralism and paves the way for feminine leadership. In order to create that foundation, here are several key steps that men can take:

1. ACKNOWLEDGE THE BASIC ISSUES

Throughout this book, we have discussed the negative impact corporate masculinism has on many women and the ways in which it limits their ability to function effectively in leadership roles. We have also talked about the consequences to women managers of being forced to play accommodating roles and the resultant loss of creativity within organizations. Since the negative consequences are apparent to many people, why does this situation persist?

The main reason is an insistence within our society that equality must mean sameness; that being equal means not being different. It is a belief that, while opening some doors, has prevented women from establishing a separate identity and developing a style of leadership in organizations reflecting their values, personal views, and way of relating to their environment.

Today, for women to be equal to men in corporations and other formal institutions, it is believed they must be treated in exactly the same way as men. They must behave in similar ways and think similarly. They must live by the same rules and honor the same traditions despite the fact that they are very different.

The problem with this thinking is that it ignores many basic facts about men and women which point to stylistic differences and oversimplifies the current situation women face in seeking career opportunities and success within organizations. Moreover, it assumes that identifying differences will ultimately lead to greater conflict and inequity instead of mutual respect and increased understanding between the sexes.

While the development of this belief in equality as sameness was somewhat useful as a short-term change strategy in the sixties and seventies, it is time to recognize the obvious limitations and inaccuracies of this idea and look to the reality in organizations today.

My conversations with many male executives have convinced me that most men do, in fact, believe that women manage using a different style. Yet, there is a great reluctance to acknowledge this difference because of a concern about stereotyping. As one man stated, "It has been ingrained in us not to think in terms of differences in order to avoid being sexist. While I do think women operate differently, I'm reluctant to say so. I don't think they're inferior managers, in fact I think some women around here are better than any of the men. But if I say they're different, then I run the risk that people will accuse me of being unfair."

Because negative stereotyping and gender differences have been so confused in the past, it is difficult to separate them today. But it is critical that both men and women cut the Gordian knot that has been created by twenty years of equality as sameness and oversimplification of the issues. Clearly, after almost two decades in managerial roles, women as a group have demonstrated their competence.

Whereas calling attention to differences could have damaged their chances for success in the past, before they had established a record of competence and success, this is not the case today.

It is time for enlightened men to initiate a dialogue within their organizations about the differences between men and women. It is time to begin building awareness among others about the impact of corporate masculinism on feminine leaders. Even if it means risking one's image as an enlightened male manager, it is time to move on for the sake of feminine leaders and the future.

2. LEARN ABOUT DIFFERENCES

If men haven't done so already, they can begin to learn about the differences in the style of feminine leaders by reading the second part of this book. Then, they will need to use their own observation skills in the office to find examples of these differences in action. As they embark on this exploration, they must keep in mind that they are looking for leadership behaviors which are different yet effective. This means being careful not to judge the actions of feminine leaders but, instead, letting the consequences of their actions serve as the final measure of their effectiveness.

Within most organizations, it is likely that some feminine leaders would willingly talk with male colleagues about the differences of which they are aware. However, male managers should not expect every woman to jump at the chance to discuss this topic. Just as it is difficult for men to address these issues, remember that most women are convinced they must accommodate to be accepted as managers and believe that calling attention to differences will alienate the men with whom they work.

In looking for opportunities to increase their awareness of the impact of masculinism on feminine leaders, men must accept that they are probably less conscious of the negative consequences than many women are. Although some men may not like all aspects of the masculine corporate culture, their ability to function effectively within this environment is still far greater than that of many women. Hence, the worst possible step a male manager can take in discussing masculinism with feminine leaders is trying to convince them that their problem is his problem, or that the issue isn't as serious as many women think it is. Instead of trying to win these women over (by using a competitive approach to conflict resolution), it will be far more illuminating for men to listen to what feminine leaders have to say. In this way, male managers can begin to see and understand what the corporate climate is truly like for many women.

It is also quite probable that some women managers will find this topic difficult to discuss. First, they may need some time to think through their own ideas and feelings. In such cases, patience is required. One must keep in mind that women have also been encouraged not to think about these differences, but that it is never too late to start.

3. REDEFINE MODELS OF EFFECTIVE LEADERSHIP

Although the need for a change in leadership style within American business is the subject of much discussion today, there is little recognition of the important role feminine leaders can play in this critical area. The need for a change in leadership is still widely interpreted to mean a modification of the traditional masculine model.

Recognizing the feminine leadership model as an alternative to traditional management is the first step in redefining what effective leadership in American business is. It is the initial step in a change process that can eventually lead to greater options and latitude for all managers, both men and women. While the feminine leadership model is based upon the socialization and biological makeup of women, other management models are needed for men who feel restricted by corporate masculinism—models that offer more behavioral choice while still allowing them to maintain their masculine traditions and their own identity.

While the concept of androgynous management is an interesting one, it, too, tends to oversimplify and trivialize the real and immutable differences that exist between the sexes. As men and women, we cannot be the same. Our biology and socialization are quite different and have given us each separate legacies.

As a concept, androgyny points up the benefits to organizations of using the widest possible range of leadership skills available, both masculine and feminine. But this idea does not translate into a realistic management style for the vast majority of men and women. Rather than establish a uniform but unattainable goal for themselves by trying to become androgynous managers, men and women would be better served by acknowledging their own styles and learning more about how they are similar and different.

By dealing with reality rather than with an unattainable ideal, it is far more likely that both men and women will come to understand and respect each other and function as different but equal partners in the world of work.

4. BUILD AWARENESS AMONG MEN

In the early days of the feminist movement, some men took pride in being called male chauvinists and viewed feminism as a passing fad. Over time, as more women began to speak out about sexism, many male managers grew confused and defensive. Why were they being attacked for the sins of their forebears? What was the big deal about using the term "girl" to describe a woman? Why were some women so touchy about these things while others insisted they were not bothered at all? As the responses to these questions became stronger, yet less consistent among women managers, some men gave up trying to understand and grew weary of the debate and discussion. Unfortunately, they tired long before the problems were resolved.

Today, with the help of other men, some traditional male managers are rejoining the discussion. Although they are still reluctant to acknowledge the problems corporate masculinism creates for many women, they are curious as to why some other men see the situation differently. In discussions with men who support feminine leadership, traditional managers are discovering that this idea need not diminish their style or create divisiveness. Instead, it can help men and women work more effectively together by increasing awareness of and respect for stylistic differences.

One of the most important steps that aware men can take in order to promote change is raising the consciousness among other men about the issue of corporate masculinism. Unlike women, aware men are often better able to communicate with traditional managers without raising defensiveness. By providing support as well as a degree of confrontation, aware men can help other men change and grow. In addition, they can also make the point that corporate masculinism isn't a problem for women only, but instead is an issue that affects men and requires their energy and commitment to resolve.

5. PROMOTE INTEGRATION, NOT ACCOMMODATION

Today, there is increasing recognition among many men of the added value feminine leaders can bring to their role as managers. But recognition alone will not create the climate needed for change. If these women are ever to reach their true level of achievement as competent professionals, men must begin to act in ways that support their nontraditional leadership style. They must encourage feminine leaders to be themselves as well as recognize and call attention to their contributions as managers.

More important, men must work to influence policies and organizational practices that force women to accommodate to masculine norms and to ignore their leadership skills. In short, they must support the integration of feminine leadership into the corporate culture and encourage other men to do the same.

Within their own work groups, men must strive to replace tokenism with real teamwork. They must make every effort to include their women colleagues in the decision-making process and must be aware that women are sometimes excluded even by men with the best intentions. As Barbara Blum, bank president and former government official, observed, "Women are often excluded from power no matter where they are. For example, when I was the deputy director of the Carter-Mondale campaign in 1976, I often found that decisions were made among the guys, off in a motel room somewhere, drinking beer, with their feet up on the bed. I'd hear about it all afterwards."

When more men begin to include women as members of the team, they may be surprised by the quality of their contributions. Women have a different view of problems and organization dynamics. When they are encouraged to offer their reactions and ideas, they are often the source of insightful, nontraditional solutions. Men can also expect to hear the truth from their women team members, provided they make it clear that they want the truth, for one important trademark of feminine leaders is that they have difficulty modifying the truth to fit the occasion. They are far more comfortable with straight talk than with double-talk.

For women to become fully integrated members of the management team, men must begin to listen carefully to their ideas, value their contributions, and stop discounting so-called emotional reactions. It is not enough simply to bring women managers into the organization; serious efforts must be directed at maximizing their strengths. Only then will women be positioned by their organizations to live up to their true potential as feminine leaders.

6. DEVELOP PROFESSIONAL RELATIONSHIPS WITH WOMEN

Despite the interest of many men in developing legitimate peer relationships with their female colleagues, some have been unable to abandon their old masculine notions about what a relationship with a woman should be. For example, many men are turned off by women managers whom they don't find physically attractive, regardless of how irrelevant it might be to getting the job done. Although they are reluctant to admit it, sexuality still plays an important part in their relationships with women at work. Such men seem to enjoy working with women only when there is some sexual chemistry and the unstated possibility of a future sexual encounter.

Whether or not the woman is interested in sharing the fantasy seems to be of little consequence. In fact, in many cases, men prefer working with women who are not at all interested in them to avoid any serious complications. However, the complications that this attitude creates for women are still very serious.

As long as these men continue to treat women as sex objects in the office, they cannot hope to relate to them as equals. While there is always an element of sexuality to be managed in a male-female relationship at work, sex appeal

253

should not be a qualifier or disqualifier for any management position. Until men learn how to separate out their sexual feelings and evaluate women for their skills and competence as managers, they will continue to do a disservice to every woman they encounter, regardless of whether they choose or reject her as a fantasy lover.

In discussions with male executives, I am often struck by the concern that many men express for their working wives and daughters who are struggling to achieve success in the corporate world. If all men would strive to treat their women colleagues with the same consideration and professional attitude that they would want for their loved ones, what a dramatic difference we would see in many companies!

7. BECOME AN ACTIVE ADVOCATE

Finally, men can make a real difference in the acceptance of feminine leadership by becoming active advocates for the women in their organizations. They cannot sit back and be silent when top female executives receive substantially lower salaries than their high-performing male counterparts. Instead, they must begin to speak up. They can no longer allow only men to receive the choice assignments in their organizations. They must make sure that these assignments are assigned on the basis of merit and that women get their fair share of the rewards. They cannot permit a woman to be passed over for an important promotion because someone thinks that she might eventually get pregnant and leave the company. They must point out that some of America's most effective managers are working mothers who manage both career and family roles with poise and excellence.

In American business today, men still control the overwhelming majority of power and influence. To a very large extent, the advancement of feminine leaders and the acceptance of the feminine leadership style depend on their active support and advocacy. For influential male managers, an enlightened attitude is just not enough. Feminine leaders need their assistance and cooperation to truly succeed. For those men who respond by getting involved, the potential for positive change will surely become a reality and lead to increased quality in their working lives—a secondary but worthwhile achievement.

Chapter Fifteen

Making a Real Difference: What Organizations Can Do

So far in this section, we have focused on the actions that individual women and men can take to promote feminine leadership within corporations. But if this change in managerial style is to become a permanent part of the organization culture, more than the impetus of individuals will be required to sustain it. It will also require the active, ongoing support of institutions. In addressing what organizations can do to support feminine leadership, this chapter will focus on the types of formal policies, programs, and procedures that can be put into place to help institutionalize this alternate management style.

But before we examine the specific steps corporations can take to encourage the wider use of feminine leadership, let's take a moment to consider one other attitudinal change that must first occur within corporations, specifically within top management. If feminine leadership is to become a powerful force within industry, senior executives must first be convinced of the value to their organizations of utilizing a more participative management style. While there is still a degree of skepticism among many executives regarding this approach, today there are also countless examples to persuade them of the positive impact that participative management methods are having on productivity and morale throughout industry.

Once this conviction develops and participative programs take hold within organizations, a corresponding shift in management style also begins to occur. In many cases one sees greater willingness to relinquish tight control in favor of increased employee involvement; greater emphasis on cooperation rather than competition among employees; a shift in emphasis away from authoritarian tactics toward the development of interpersonal skills; and greater support for intuitive, nontraditional problem-solving processes and procedures. As each of these shifts in managerial behavior occurs within organizations, the receptivity of top management to the feminine leadership style also increases. As more and more women managers demonstrate the effectiveness of this alternate approach, many also gain the respect and approval of their male peers. Although their style may be nontraditional, it is difficult for even the most traditional executive to argue with success.

While examples of this evolutionary process are still rare, there are a few organizational examples, notably Hunter College, a public educational institution in New York City with an enrollment of 14,000 undergraduates. Dr. Donna Shalala, president, spoke about the attitudinal change that has occurred at the top levels of management as a result of her efforts to institutionalize the feminine leadership approach within this organization. She said, "Some of the most traditional, even chauvinistic managers in this institution have become strong supporters of this strategy because they believe it increases productivity. . . . If someone told them today that this was a feminist strategy, they'd say, 'That's not just a feminist strategy, that's a good management strategy.' They've become believers because they've seen results."

With the active support of senior management, feminine leadership can become an accepted, valued, and lasting part of the organizational culture. By developing formal policies and processes to deal with the most blatant aspects of masculine bias and to ensure that women managers are encouraged to contribute at the highest levels of which they are capable, the qualities that characterize feminine leadership can be woven into the fabric of organization life. In some companies, efforts are already under way to promote this change in leadership. Among the many activities that have been instituted to support feminine leadership, these are the ones many men and women in management believe are having the most far-reaching impact:

1. RECRUIT AND HIRE WOMEN

Although the number of women in management has increased dramatically in recent years, the impetus for this massive change was largely the result of legislation and government-backed affirmative action programs. Since 1980, however, federal enforcement of equal opportunity legislation has been greatly relaxed. According to an official publication of the League of Women Voters, "While the past two decades were marked by the gradual expansion of the government's commitment to enforce equal employment opportunity, the policies of the last few years have called that commitment into serious question. . . . At the EEOC, litigation challenging equal opportunity violations has fallen off dramatically in the last few years. . . . Budget cuts and staff reductions throughout the agency have also hampered the EEOC's enforcement efforts."[1]

Increasingly, it has fallen on the shoulders of corporate officers themselves to be certain their companies continue to uphold both the letter and the spirit of the law. As stated in a *Working Woman* study on sex discrimination in business, "The key to success in affirmative action is the commitment of the chief executive officer. If the CEO is lukewarm, the program will flounder. If the CEO really wants it to work, the middle managers will see that it does."[2] In today's less regulated environment, the backing of senior management is absolutely necessary if the influx of competent women into management is to continue. What's more, this commitment to equal opportunity must go beyond the hiring step. It must be used to develop policies and practices that protect the rights of all employees at all levels within the organization and encourage them to fully utilize all their skills.

2. REVISE PERFORMANCE APPRAISAL SYSTEMS

One of the most powerful signs of organizational support for feminine leadership can occur when a company redefines its management appraisal process to incorporate feminine leadership skills. In organizations where this has occurred, characteristics such as interpersonal competence, effective teamwork, nontraditional approaches to innovation and problem-solving, and the capacity to manage diverse, pluralistic work groups fairly and effectively are often included in the management evaluation process along with more traditional management skills. All managers, both male and female, are rated and rewarded for their effectiveness in these areas. At Texas Instruments in Dallas, a formal evaluation system is used to help prohibit discrimination against women in nontraditional jobs. These comments from a female electrical engineer were reported in a recent interview. "In addition," she says, "while some of [my] male superiors clearly feel threatened by the presence of women in traditionally non-female lines of work, instances of discrimination are not taken lightly by management. A twice-a-year performance review of all salaried employees acts as a kind of insurance against discriminatory attitudes."[3]

In cases where an organization's masculine tradition is especially strong, employees may also be asked to comment on their immediate supervisors' ability to manage women and minorities objectively. Such employee review processes can help organizations identify those managers with the skills and perspectives required to manage diverse work groups most effectively.

3. RECTIFY INEQUITIES IN SALARIES AND PROMOTIONS

In a recent interview, a woman vice president at one of the nation's leading financial institutions said: "Although the personnel director will deny it, I would bet my annual salary that many of the women managers within this institution are receiving the minimum salary for their positions while most of the men are getting the maximum. Because many of us started out at lower-level positions as secretaries and management assistants, our salary base has remained lower. Even after several promotions and years within management, there are still many women who haven't caught up. They are doing the same work as their male peers, but they are getting much less for it."

Corporations committed to promoting feminine leadership and realizing its benefits cannot permit inequities in salary and promotion policies to go unresolved. From the standpoint of fairness as well as from the perspective of providing a motivating incentive for outstanding performance, a firm policy of equal pay for equal work must be conscientiously enforced. Moreover, this policy cannot apply only to entry-level positions; it must be applied in all job classifications throughout the organization. Instead of earning 59 cents for every dollar received by their male counterparts, working women must draw comparable salaries for comparable work.

Likewise, high-performing feminine leaders must also begin receiving the same number and quality of promotions as high-performing men. Company-sponsored promotion tracking programs can help make certain that equitable treatment takes place. Such a program has been established by the 3M Company of St. Paul, Minnesota, and was described in a feature article in *Savvy* titled "Corporations of the Year: The Annual Report on Corporations Where Success Is Based on Merit not Gender." According to the article, "A more dramatic example of 3M's progressive review system is the 'high-potential employee' identification program. Managers single out employees who appear to have exceptional abilities—'with special attention now being given to women and minorities,' according to one manager—and present a tracking plan for that employee to an executive resources committee. The chairman of the committee is L. W. Lehr, 3M's chairman and chief executive officer. The progress of promising employees is carefully followed to make sure they are given the opportunity to advance."[4]

4. APPOINT OUTSTANDING WOMEN TO CORPORATE BOARDS

Another effective method for ensuring that the contributions of feminine leaders are recognized within corporations is the appointment of prominent women to serve as members of the board of directors. According to a recent study conducted by Catalyst, a nonprofit organization that works for the advancement of women in the corporate world, women currently fill only 455 (or about 3 percent) of the 14,000 directorships that exist within the Fortune list of the nation's 1,000 leading businesses. Ironically, while this number is extremely small, it still represents a major increase over the 46 women who were directors on an expanded Fortune list of 1,350 companies back in 1969.[5] But progress continues to be slow for women as corporate directors.

Colombe Nicholas, president of Christian Dior, New York, is a successful senior manager with a strong opinion on this subject. She says, "I personally feel very strongly that every major corporation should have at least one woman on the board. The presence of women encourages the men to stop and think about the question, 'Do our decisions really include consideration for women?' I believe that when women are on boards, companies make better products and provide better services. Which leads to better bottom-line figures. And at an insignificant cost, especially when the cost is compared to the benefits."

Alice F. Emerson, president of Wheaton College, serves as a director on the boards at both The Bank of Boston and The Penn Mutual Life Insurance Company. She has seen firsthand how the presence of a female director can advance opportunities for women and direct greater corporate attention toward the needs of feminine leaders. She relates, "Having asked once or twice or three times as we reviewed senior promotions how many women were in the pool of candidates, they now routinely report that. I also try to have lunch every so often with the head of human resources, informally. Other board members may not be doing that since they have other areas of special concern to them."[6]

In addition to the insights that a woman director can

provide in policymaking situations, a female presence in this top management group can also provide an important psychological lift for other women within the organization. A female director demonstrates tangible corporate commitment to advancing opportunities for women managers and the woman herself can serve as an important role model for other women looking to move ahead in the company. Moreover, because so many male executives have little ongoing contact with women in collegial roles, the female director can also build greater awareness and support for feminine leadership by demonstrating how this style works to other senior executives who have limited exposure to women in executive decision-making roles.

5. CREATE EXECUTIVE WOMEN'S COUNCILS

In organizations that recognize the need for ongoing, direct communication between senior management and female employees, councils of women managers have been established to serve as the interface between these two groups. Such councils serve a number of important purposes. First, they offer input to top management on issues that affect all women within the organization and ensure that policy changes and new procedures do not have an unusually adverse impact on this group. They can also be used to solicit comments and reactions from other women regarding corporate policies and operating methods and call attention to any problems that seem to be unfairly limiting equal opportunities for women.

Just as the presence of women on corporate boards assures that a feminine viewpoint will be considered when corporate decisions are being made, executive women's councils can also focus attention on the special concerns of working women. They can solicit opinions and generate continuous feedback for corporate leaders regarding the problems and opportunities that confront women on a day-to-day basis within organizations.

6. COMMUNICATE ORGANIZATIONAL COMMITMENT TO FEMININE LEADERSHIP

Another important method for reinforcing a corporation's formal commitment to feminine leadership is regular, official employee communications on this subject. Newsletters, company magazines, and closed-circuit television broadcasts are all popular and effective methods for communicating change within organizations. In addition, informal meetings in which senior executives comment on important organizational changes and corporate priorities also provide ideal opportunities for endorsements by top management for an expanded approach to leadership. In some companies, where consistent, clear messages from senior management are regarded as critical for effective implementation of any major change, "evergreen statements" are prepared for senior executives summarizing the current status of major changes under way within the organization. These statements are continuously updated to remain "evergreen," and managers are encouraged to refer to them during formal meetings and informal visits with employees at all company locations. Such communications from the top can be used effectively to reinforce the corporate management philosophy and to signal others of the need for change.

Where there is a strong corporate commitment to enhancing the accepted style of management, such communications can do much to clarify the organization's position and build understanding and support for change among all employees. Every informal discussion, speech, and piece of printed material that is circulated helps to reinforce the idea that management is serious about promoting this alternate leadership approach.

7. COMMUNICATE CORPORATE COMMITMENT TO CLIENTS OF THE ORGANIZATION

While support for feminine leadership has to start inside corporations, it must also be made visible to outside organizations. In dealing with suppliers, client companies, and customers, businesses can make use of the approach of feminine leaders to improve service and product quality. They can also promote this style by acknowledging the organizational benefits derived from encouraging women to be themselves.

Within service industries and companies with a strong sales orientation, there is an additional step that can be taken to heighten customer awareness of the benefits of the feminine leadership style. While it may be difficult to overcome initial resistance, organizations convinced of the advantages of this approach can actively promote the placement of women managers in client service positions. In many cases, once clients have personally observed the professional competence of women managers and the important contributions they can make to the overall team effort and the success of the business, they become avid supporters of the very women they at first resisted.

The problem of client prejudice toward women executives was discussed in the advertising industry publication *Adweek.* In an article titled "The Client Barrier: Why So Few Women Reach the Top," the pressure felt by many organizations to please clients at the expense of talented women employees was highlighted. The article stated, "Only a handful of women occupy senior management offices at major agencies. While more than half of all agency employees and a third of all agency professionals are women, huge disparities exist between men and women in pay and position. Client attitudes and prejudices are the principal reasons."[7] When it comes to dealing with client attitudes that unfairly discriminate against any employee or group of employees, corporations must be willing to stand their ground. While the risk of losing an account may increase as a result, the negative consequences of colluding with unreasonable or unfair client demands and allowing unfair practices to influence corporate decisions can be far more damaging to long-term productivity and morale.

8. UPDATE CORPORATE POLICIES

Many companies are also recognizing that some traditional operating procedures are no longer in the best interest of the organization or the employees. As demands for flextime have continued to increase, some companies which resisted the idea initially are discovering that many jobs can be performed at lower cost and peak efficiency outside the traditional nine-to-five workday schedule. In addition, improved technology is being used to close the gap between career and family demands by some women managers. With the help of personal computers, more feminine leaders are discovering that work at home can be more than an unrealistic dream. It can be a practical reality.

Another tradition that has begun to change is the corporate approach to executive transfers which, in the past, had such a disruptive effect on family life. As more men and women refuse to move because of second income and quality of life considerations, companies are beginning to reconsider and redesign promotion and transfer systems to better meet the personal needs of managers and their families.

One recent policy innovation geared to protect the rights of working women concerns the issue of sexual harassment.

Once considered a non-issue by many managers, today most executives and many corporations take this problem very seriously. Rather than attempt to protect the guilty, some companies are responding with sensitivity and concern for the victims and taking punitive action where required. Nancy Crossman, special counsel to the Options Division of the American Stock Exchange, believes that it is important for companies to take a firm stand on the sexual harassment issue. She says, "Although I see signs of positive change, this is still a rather old-fashioned male-dominated industry in which many talented and accomplished women have problems being accepted. Consciousness-raising must go on constantly. Employees must be reminded that demeaning remarks, etc., are not tolerable. Women should be hired regardless of their attractiveness or lack thereof. Although these may seem like small things, they should not be ignored by corporations. They should be as important as other issues which companies emphasize with their employees."

Another critically important area where policy changes are still needed is that of pregnancy leave. Currently, federal rulings legislate that a woman may take leave from her job for up to four months to care for her newborn child. However, many believe that women who request more extended leaves should still be able to return to their corporation with no loss of seniority or accumulated benefits. One progressive chief executive of a major food company expressed his willingness to consider these types of policy changes in an interview with researchers from Cornell University's Institute for Women and Work. He said, "We need to spend more time developing life plans. What are the skills needed for each rung of the ladder? How does that work with a woman's personal plans? Can we work out ways to give a woman time off for child-bearing, with provisions for her return after two or three years to the same job level, with no loss in such things as pensions?"[8] A policy covering extended pregnancy leave is one key way to ensure that companies continue to reap the long-term benefits of their substantial investments in the training and development of skilled feminine leaders.

9. REVISE CORPORATE BENEFIT PLANS

Although the majority of businesses still have fixed benefit plans that do little to address the needs of single workers, single parents, dual career families, etc., more companies are beginning to respond with flexible plans that offer a greater variety of options to employees. In some cases, provisions for day care (in the form of on-premise corporate facilities as well as financial assistance) are now being offered to working parents. Naturally, these new options have been enthusiastically welcomed by many employees and have been credited for improvements in attendance and productivity in some organizations.

But the diverse needs of today's employees are still going largely unrecognized in most businesses. According to an article titled "Changing Policies for Changing Families," published by Catalyst, "Corporate benefits programs need to be redesigned just as government policies need to be re-examined to take into account working families. Most corporate benefit programs are designed to accommodate the traditional single-income family, despite estimates that this family type now accounts for only 20 percent of the U.S. labor force. This means that corporations are spending money on benefits that in many cases are duplicative while at the same time failing to meet other critical employee needs. For example, in the two-income family where both are employed by different corporations, the family may be covered by two identical medical plans, only one of which is usable. The single employee without a family may be receiving unwanted life insurance. In both these cases, the employees are not receiving the full value of their benefits package. Given that benefits can account for up to 30 percent of an employee's compensation, this loss is substantial. The employer is also not receiving the best value for each benefit dollar and is not reaping the less tangible, but important benefit of employee satisfaction and appreciation."

The article continues, "A few employers have realized the cost of the mismatch between employees and benefits and have switched to a flexible benefits plan. There are many ways of implementing flexible benefits and plans may vary in what they offer, but the key to their effectiveness is their ability to meet the needs of a wide variety of employees. Switching to a flexible benefits plan is a first big step towards recognizing the true nature of today's work force."[9]

At present, few companies have yet to act in an area of critical interest to working parents—provisions for child day care. The vacuum that currently exists in this vital area has created a situation in which many women managers are forced to work under unnecessary stress to meet the demands of both job and family. Commenting on this situation, cosmetics company president Lydia Sarfati said, "I would very much like to see corporations provide some type of child care so that women with serious career ambitions can compete equally with men. In the business world today, being a mother is a great handicap for a woman. More cooperation would really help to alleviate the mental wear and tear that results within women."

10. SPONSOR CORPORATE NETWORKS

As organizations become more aware and less defensive about the need for support among women managers, a few have begun offering corporate facilities, clerical support, speakers, and even funding to assist women in establishing companywide networks. While most groups continue to meet out of hours and to operate independently, such formal recognition by the organization legitimates the need for women's support groups, promotes goodwill among women employees, and costs companies a minimal amount of time and money.

As we have discussed, the benefits to feminine leaders of establishing networks for discussion and problem-solving can be enormous. To understand the impact of masculinism on their style of management, women must have opportunities for discussion and exploration of this important issue in a safe environment. They must have access to other women who are succeeding by using this nontraditional approach. By exposing women to a variety of management models including feminine leadership, networks can do much to build awareness and support for this nontraditional style and relieve some of the ongoing pressure to conform to masculine norms that many women feel. In short, networks can reassure women that a choice does exist.

11. INITIATE AWARENESS SEMINARS

There is a widely held belief within organizations today that attitude change, where possible, is an extremely slow, tedious process. Yet each of us can attest that when we are exposed to new ideas, learn more about the facts, or have a powerful emotional experience, our attitudes about many issues do change and often change radically.

Today we live in an environment where change is a pervasive, accepted fact of life. Because of the depth and frequency of change, it is impossible for any of us to maintain a rigid, fixed set of beliefs and still function effectively. As the world around us continues to change, challenging us to think and act in new ways, our attitudes must also change. Organizations can help managers deal effectively with change—and the important role that feminine leadership can play—by offering seminars to raise awareness and increase understanding of today's leadership issues.

Can you imagine any organization selecting a sophisticated new data processing system, installing it throughout the company, but not training its employees to operate the system correctly? When introducing technological change, most companies go to considerable lengths to retrain employees. The need for reeducation and employee support for technological change is widely understood and accepted within business. Yet in the case of moving women into management, this equally dramatic change is one for which few companies thought to prepare their employees at all. Instead of assuming that some education and support-building would be required among members of the organization, only the women themselves were singled out for reeducation. In most corporations it was assumed that any real attitude change among men was not required or else would take a very long time.

But this assumption was far from correct. Since the late sixties, when women first began to move into leadership roles, the importance of building support among all employees for this major change has become much more evident. In organizations where this need has been recognized, women are not only surviving as managers, they are also prospering. Some are recognizing the special contributions that they can make as women and are receiving encouragement from colleagues and the formal organization to use their own natural leadership style.

For feminine leadership to be recognized and fully developed within organizations, real attitude change must first occur among both men and women. Accommodation must be replaced with policies and practices that promote integration. Organizations have to recognize the enormous untapped potential that exists today among women whose skills have yet to be put to full use. Contrary to popular opinion, this change in attitude doesn't have to take years. In fact, once the commitment to support feminine leadership is in place within a company, such a change can take root within a few short months.

An activity that can make a great difference in accelerating the pace of attitude change is one often overlooked by corporations—management development. For women managers and the feminine leadership style to achieve equal status in executive circles, corporations must rethink their approach to executive training and development. In addition to focusing affirmative action efforts on more inclusive policies and procedures, organizations must begin providing awareness seminars for managers to help them understand and support the need for leadership change. These seminars can be used to raise the level of awareness among managers about the damaging effects that corporate masculinism can have on many women. In addition, they can also help individuals sort out their own feelings and reactions to this sensitive and complex issue and prepare them to accept change.

In companies where awareness training is offered, sessions focus on the impact of masculinism on the work environment. The issue is examined at two levels: within the corporate culture and within the individual world of each participant. Through small group discussions, exercises, and provocative films and articles, managers increase their awareness and understanding of the many issues that influence and shape their management style. By creating a nondefensive environment for discussion and reflection, seminar leaders help both men and women explore, probe, question, and participate to the fullest.

Topics such as socialization, managing sexuality at work, the norms and traditions of corporate masculinism, masculine and feminine leadership styles, the use of power, and the need for accommodating roles are defined and explored within small group discussions. Participants are encouraged to examine their thoughts and feelings about the issues in an effort to gain greater clarity about their own positions and to determine how they are similar to and different from the views expressed by others. As this process unfolds, an awakening occurs. For many men and women, strong feelings that have long been buried and suppressed begin to come into clear focus. In some cases, this new awareness leads to catharsis, while in others it leads to confrontation. With the help of new insights and information, men and women begin to reexamine old attitudes and beliefs. In some cases, they may decide that personal change is required in order to meet the new demands of their roles as managers, parents, spouses, friends, and colleagues.

Because of the personal nature of awareness seminar training, it is not unusual for participants to develop insights and powerful new learnings in a very short period of time. Even though most programs last only three or four days, it is quite common to observe dramatic growth in participants during this period. For many, these three or four days represent a rare opportunity for reflection. It is the first time that most managers are able to really examine the issues rather than just react to them. For some, the experience is like a breath of pure oxygen. Ideas begin to gel: Issues that had been confusing are suddenly much clearer, and old problems and concerns become less difficult to resolve. It is the rare person who leaves unaffected by the experience or unwilling to work for change and greater acceptance of women within the organization.

By institutionalizing the policies, programs, and development activities described in these pages, organizations can create a more supportive corporate climate for women managers and the feminine leadership style. Instead of focusing all efforts on recruitment and hiring, a more multifaceted approach is required. The need for changes in policies, practices, and performance standards that support greater diversity must be addressed at all levels of the organization, not just the entry level. As these changes take place, there will be corresponding changes in morale, productivity, and the general quality of work life. Although the focus of this book has been specifically on women managers, the activities described will not only have a favorable impact on feminine leaders but, more important, will affect virtually every employee within the corporate structure. The steps required to bring about this change are simple and straightforward. They require energy and commitment from individuals and organizations, but they need not take a lifetime to implement. Where feminine leadership is viewed as a worthy goal, today's efforts can produce results immediately.

Chapter Sixteen

Feminine Leadership and the Future

At a recent conference, the chief executive officer of one of the nation's largest corporations was asked where he thought he would be today if he had been born a woman. Without a moment's hesitation he replied, "Exactly where I am right now!" While the sincerity of his response cannot easily be challenged, its accuracy certainly can be. In survey after survey and study upon study, the statistics and the experiences of thousands of women managers continue to disprove his statement.

Despite the obstacles that currently exist, his comment will undoubtedly be true one day. With women now constituting more than 40 percent of the work force and hundreds of thousands of female managers holding responsible positions within corporations, the ultimate acceptance of feminine leadership has become inevitable. But to say that this is inevitable does not guarantee it will happen quickly. Will the acceptance of feminine leadership take place soon enough to benefit this generation of women managers or even the next? Will corporations reap the rewards of this alternate leadership style in this decade or by the end of the century?

While the answers to these questions are as yet unclear, one thing is certain. The full potential of feminine leadership will be realized only when large numbers of women managers begin to assert their true identities, utilize their special talents, and commit themselves to the task of creating positive change within corporations. To achieve this goal, they must also be joined by enlightened male managers working to institutionalize change within their companies.

"BUSINESS AS USUAL"

Today corporations are at an important crossroads regarding the future of women managers. If they choose to follow a business-as-usual philosophy, then feminine leaders are certain to lose out. If enlightened men and women wait for others to take the lead in managing this leadership change, an entire generation of talented women managers may well be sacrificed. In a recent study of women's salaries, the Rand Corporation predicted that by the year 2000, women will be earning only 74 cents for every dollar earned by men.[1] This is an indication of what talented, dedicated, and hardworking women have to look forward to if change continues at the current rate.

Other statistics also underscore the gender gap that continues to persist in corporations. An article in *Time* points out, "More than a third of all candidates for M.B.A. degrees are women. But only 5% of the executives in the top 50 American corporations are women: the numbers numb."[2] While it is certainly true that women managers have come a long way, it is equally apparent that their journey is far from over. Equality will be achieved only when organizations acknowledge feminine leadership as an acceptable alternative to the traditional style of management.

ORGANIZATIONAL BENEFITS OF FEMININE LEADERSHIP

By encouraging women to use all their skills and abilities to manage effectively, organizations can increase their capacity to solve problems and improve productivity. As Jim Hennessy of Nynex states, "The addition of more women in management raises the average. Everybody works smarter as a result." As the pool of feminine talent increases within management, companies have greater human resources to tap into. The flow of creative ideas also increases as men and women approach problems from their own unique perspectives.

Dr. Estelle Ramey of Georgetown Medical School describes this increase in creative potential: "Scientists know that there is nothing more valuable than having different kinds of thoughts brought to bear on a problem, particularly a very complex problem. If the rare genius that resides in human brains, including female brains, had been utilized, might we have a cure for cancer or a cure for the aging of male blood vessels? Excellent minds are so rare. Can we afford to waste any?"

Clearly, the answer to her question is no. Yet, given the present course of events in organizations, the reality is that the abilities of many women *are* being wasted. Moreover, business itself is the biggest single loser, for homogeneity within management does not lead to increased productivity. It simply maintains the status quo and, in some areas, actually decreases the potential for creativity.

HUMANIZING THE WORKPLACE

Much has been said about the special role women can play in humanizing the workplace. By increasing the value placed on building relationships as well as by balancing work priorities with other interests and personal pursuits, feminine leaders can make an important contribution. They can demonstrate that career success and a satisfying personal life can be achieved simultaneously.

By following the example set by feminine leaders in this area, men also have much to gain, for the masculine model of executive success has often constrained and confined many men, leaving little room in their lives for much beyond their work. As John Kenneth Galbraith commented in a recent essay on "Corporate Man," "Any consideration of the life and larger social existence of the modern corporate man . . . begins and also largely ends with the effect of one all-embracing force. That is organization. . . . It is to this, at the expense of family, friends, sex, recreation and sometimes health and effective control of alcoholic intake, that he devotes his energies."[3]

There is little doubt that today's corporate man and woman both can benefit from a redefinition of effective leadership—one that emphasizes feminine skills as well as traditional masculine qualities. Moreover, organizations stand to make the most significant gains of all when this change is fully implemented. But the pace of this change and the benefits to be derived from it will depend upon the effort of individuals and institutions.

To promote feminine leadership, nothing less than total commitment will be required. In order to succeed, this change will require the constant attention and support of enlightened men, women, and institutions. While the potential benefits are great, the challenges will also be considerable.

For women, the challenge will come from finding their own voice within organizations and infusing institutions with their values. As Dr. Donna Shalala states, "In the 1980's, women in power who expect to be counted must be more than role models—they must make a difference for women, for minorities, for the poor. A woman in power must bring new sensitivity to her position. We are expected to foster change—to humanize the institutions for which we are responsible."

For men, the challenge lies in understanding the meaning of different but equal and then acting accordingly. Walter Blass of AT&T put it this way: "The answer to Freud's question 'What do women want?' is, I believe, to be equal but different. Equal in the sense of being treated as such; by parents in terms of opportunity to risk . . . in education by being allowed to take shop or math or engineering or surgery; in management by being allowed to do line as well as staff jobs. . . .

"But different in the sense that their style may differ from the men we are used to; the language, the dress, the conduct of meetings or supervisory relations. Those of us [men] who have worked overseas have learned that some of our American methods travel well while others have to be radically adapted to local customs. Increasingly we are learning from foreigners. . . . We may yet recognize that right in our midst we have a subculture that has much to teach us, if we can recognize their equality and difference."

Today, recognition of the different but equal impact of feminine leadership is increasing in many corporations. But to grow and prosper, this emerging style will need the active support of all enlightened managers and institutions. Similarly, to grow and prosper in the future, industry will need the active involvement of all of its employees—including its feminine leaders. The time has come for men, women, and corporations to act. The talents and potential of this group can no longer be ignored. For the sake of our future, feminine leadership must be encouraged and developed now.

Notes

CHAPTER 1: LEADERSHIP IN TRANSITION

1. Louise Bernikow, "We're Dancing as Fast as We Can," *Savvy* (April 1984), p. 42.

2. Wendy Cooper, "Conquering Wall Street: Women Investment Bankers," *Working Woman* (January 1984), p. 66.

3. "Poll Says Most Women Perceive Job Sex Bias," *The New York Times* (Aug. 15, 1982), p. 28.

CHAPTER 2: MASCULINISM IN THE CORPORATION

1. Betty Friedan, "Twenty Years After the Feminine Mystique," *The New York Times Magazine* (Feb. 27, 1983), p. 35.

2. Betty Lehan Harragan, *Games Mother Never Taught You: Corporate Gamesmanship for Women* (New York: Warner Books, 1978), p. 38.

3. Michael Maccoby, *The Gamesman: Winning and Losing the Career Game* (New York: Bantam Books, 1978), pp. 40–41.

4. Harragan, *op. cit.,* p. 55.

5. Maccoby, *op. cit.,* p. 41.

6. Steve Farnsworth, "Women Fill One-Third of Executive Posts," *The Washington Post,* Part I (April 11, 1984), p. 16.

7. Susan Fraker, "Why Women Aren't Getting to the Top," *Fortune* (April 16, 1984), p. 40.

8. *Ibid.*

9. Natasha Josefowitz, *Paths to Power* (Reading, Mass.: Addison-Wesley, 1980), p. 46.

10. Jay Cocks, "How Long Till Equality?" *Time* (July 12, 1982), p. 23.

11. Patricia O'Toole, "So You Want to Start a Business," *Vogue* (November 1982), p. 90.

CHAPTER 3: THE CRISIS IN THE CORPORATION

1. Robert B. Reich, *The Next American Frontier* (New York: Times Books, 1983), p. 118.

2. Robert B. Reich, "The Next American Frontier," *The Atlantic Monthly* (March 1983), p. 45.

3. Daniel Yankelovich, "New Rules in American Life: Searching for Self-Fulfillment in a World Turned Upside Down," *Psychology Today* (April 1981), p. 78.

4. William Serrin, "Study Says Work Ethic Is Alive but Neglected," *The New York Times* (Sept. 5, 1983), p. 8.

5. Ann Crittenden, "The Age of 'Me First' Management," *The New York Times,* Section 3 (Aug. 19, 1984), p. 1.

6. George E. Breen, "Middle Management Morale in the '80's,"

AMA Survey Report (New York: AMA Publications Division, 1983), p. 12.

7. Reich, "The Next American Frontier," *op. cit.,* p. 49.

8. Rosabeth Moss Kanter, *The Change Masters: Innovation for Productivity in the American Corporation* (New York: Simon & Schuster, 1983), p. 41.

9. William G. Ouchi, *Theory Z: How American Business Can Meet the Japanese Challenge* (Reading, Mass.: Addison-Wesley, 1981), p. 43.

10. Kanter, *op. cit.,* p. 167.

11. George F. Telfer, "Motorola Gears Up Productivity to Meet the Japanese Head-On," *The Journal of Commerce* (Aug. 3, 1981), p. 1A.

12. John Naisbitt, *Megatrends: Ten New Directions Transforming Our Lives* (New York: Warner Books, 1982), p. 14.

13. Michael Maccoby, "Management and Leadership," *The Mitre Lecture Series* (McLean, Va.: The Mitre Corporation, April 8, 1980), p. 13.

14. James MacGregor Burns, *Leadership* (New York: Harper & Row, 1979), p. 455.

15. Michael Maccoby, "The Leader," *The Sloan Management Review* (Cambridge, Mass.: Fall 1983), p. 61.

16. Lynn Rosener and Peter Schwartz, "Women, Leadership and the 1980's: What Kind of Leaders Do We Need?" *The Report: Round Table on New Leadership in the Public Interest* (New York: NOW Legal Defense and Education Fund, Oct. 29, 1980), p. 25.

17. *Ibid.,* p. 26.

CHAPTER 4: THE CASE FOR FEMININE LEADERSHIP

1. John Naisbitt, *Megatrends: Ten New Directions Transforming Our Lives* (New York: Warner Books, 1982), p. 182.

2. *Ibid.,* pp. 159–60.

3. Thomas J. Peters and Robert H. Waterman, Jr., *In Search of Excellence: Lessons from America's Best-Run Companies* (New York: Harper & Row, 1982), pp. 45–46.

4. Jacklin and Maccoby are quoted in Francine E. Gordon and Myra H. Strober, *Bringing Women into Management* (New York: McGraw-Hill, 1975), p. 25.

5. Jo Durden-Smith and Diane DeSimone, *Sex and the Brain* (New York: Arbor House, 1983), p. 59.

6. Gordon Allport, Philip Vernon, and Gardner Lindzey, *Study of Values Manual* (Boston: Houghton Mifflin, 1970), p. 12.

7. *Ibid.*

8. Carol Gilligan, *In a Different Voice: Psychological Theory and Women's Development* (Cambridge, Mass.: Harvard University Press, 1982), p. 29.

9. Betty Friedan, "Twenty Years After the Feminine Mystique," *The New York Times Magazine* (Feb. 27, 1983), p. 56.

10. Lois Wyse, *The Six-Figure Woman (and How to Be One)* (New York: Linden/Simon & Schuster, 1983).

11. "Life at the Top," *Vogue* (August 1983), p. 282.

12. *Ibid.,* pp. 375–76.

13. Michael Korda, "Emotions in a Woman's Briefcase," *SELF* (September 1983), p. 60.

CHAPTER 5: THE USE OF POWER

1. Lynn Rosener and Peter Schwartz, "Women, Leadership and the 1980's: What Kind of Leaders Do We Need?" *The Report: Round Table on New Leadership in the Public Interest* (New York: NOW Legal Defense and Education Fund, Oct. 29, 1980), p. 26.

CHAPTER 6: SETTING PERFORMANCE STANDARDS AND TAKING RISKS

1. Anne Harlan and Carol Weiss, "Moving Up: Women in Managerial Careers," Wellesley College Center for Research on Women, Working Paper #86 (Wellesley, Mass.: September 1981), p. 58.

2. Louise Bernikow, "We're Dancing as Fast as We Can," *Savvy* (April 1984), p. 42.

3. George E. Breen, "Middle Management Morale in the '80's," *AMA Survey Report* (New York: AMA Publications Division, 1983), p. 40.

4. Barry Posner and Warren Schmidt, "Managerial Values in Perspective," *AMA Survey Report* (New York: AMA Publications Division, 1983), pp. 17–19.

5. "Profile of Women Senior Executives," Publication of Korn/ Ferry International (New York: 1982), pp. 9–23.

CHAPTER 7: TEAMWORK AND PARTICIPATIVE MANAGEMENT

1. Margaret Hennig and Anne Jardim, *The Managerial Woman* (New York: Pocket Books, 1978), p. 51.

2. Betty Lehan Harragan, *Games Mother Never Taught You: Corporate Gamesmanship for Women* (New York: Warner Books, 1978), p. 67.

3. Carol Gilligan, *In a Different Voice: Psychological Theory and Women's Development* (Cambridge, Mass.: Harvard University Press, 1982), p. 63.

4. J. Clayton Lafferty and Alonzo Pond, *The Desert Survival Situation* (Plymouth, Mich.: Human Synergistics, 1974).

5. Rosabeth Moss Kanter, *The Change Masters* (New York: Simon & Schuster, 1983), p. 257.

CHAPTER 8: INTERPERSONAL EFFECTIVENESS

1. Thomas J. Peters and Robert H. Waterman, Jr., *In Search of Excellence: Lessons From America's Best-Run Companies* (New York: Harper & Row, 1982), p. 289.

2. William Hunter, "The Visible Manager," *Savvy* (December 1983), p. 72.

3. Mary Kay Ash, *On People Management* (New York: Warner Books, 1984), p. 6.

4. Mary Brown Parlee, "Getting a Word in Sex-Wise," *Across the Board* (New York: The Conference Board, Inc., September 1984), p. 8.

5. D. H. Zimmerman and C. West, "Sex Roles, Interruptions and Silences in Conversations," in B. Thorne and N. Henly (eds.), *Language and Sex: Difference and Dominance* (Rowley, Mass.: Newbury House, 1975), p. 105.

6. Robert Rosenthal, Judith A. Hall, Robin M. DiMatteo, Peter L. Rogers, and Dane Archer, *Sensitivity to Nonverbal Communication: The Pons Test* (Baltimore: The Johns Hopkins University Press, 1979), p. 153.

7. *Ibid.,* p. 163.

8. Jo Durden-Smith and Diane DeSimone, *Sex and the Brain* (New York: Arbor House, 1983), p. 73.

9. William G. Ouchi, *Theory Z: How American Business Can Meet the Japanese Challenge* (Reading, Mass.: Addison-Wesley, 1981), p. 108.

10. Michael Maccoby, *The Gamesman: Winning and Losing the Career Game* (New York: Bantam Books, 1978), p. 189.

11. Margaret Hennig and Anne Jardim, *The Managerial Woman* (New York: Pocket Books, 1978), pp. 205–6.

12. Mary Brown Parlee, "Getting a Word in Sex-Wise," *Across the Board* (New York: The Conference Board, Inc., September 1984), pp. 7–8.

13. Ouchi, *op. cit.*, p. 9.

14. Lorraine Davis, "Between Us," *Vogue* (March 1983), p. 172.

15. Barry Posner and Warren Schmidt, "Managerial Values in Perspective," *AMA Survey Report* (New York: AMA Publications Division, 1983), p. 17.

16. *Ibid.*, p. 18.

CHAPTER 9: CONFLICT MANAGEMENT

1. Ralph H. Kilmann and Kenneth W. Thomas, "The Thomas-Kilmann Conflict Mode Instrument" (Tuxedo, N.Y.: Xicom, 1974)

CHAPTER 10: INTUITION AND PROBLEM-SOLVING

1. Weston H. Agor, *Intuitive Management: Integrating Left and Right Brain Management Skills* (Englewood Cliffs, N.J.: Prentice-Hall, 1984), p. 3.

2. Thomas J. Peters and Robert H. Waterman, Jr., *In Search of Excellence: Lessons from America's Best-Run Companies* (New York: Harper & Row, 1982), p. 31.

3. Patrice Steadman, "Hotel Chief Tells How to Survive," *El Paso Times* (November 1982).

4. Agor, *op. cit.*, p. 25.

5. Michael L. Johnson, "Women: Born to Manage," *Industry Week* (Aug. 4, 1975), pp. 22–26.

6. Michael A. Guillen, "The Intuitive Edge," *Psychology Today* (August 1984), p. 68.

CHAPTER 11: MANAGING DIVERSITY, STRESS, AND BOUNDARIES

1. Jeff Meer, "Organized Women Managers," *Psychology Today* (August 1984), p. 71.

2. Lois M. Verbrugge, "Women's Social Roles and Health," eds. P. Berman and E. Ramey, NIH Pub. No. 82-2298 (Bethesda, Md.: National Institute of Child Health and Human Development, April 1982), p. 56.

3. *Ibid.,* p. 65.

4. "Profile of Senior Women Executives," Publication of Korn/ Ferry International (November 1982), p. 9.

CHAPTER 12: PITCHING IN AND PROFESSIONAL DEVELOPMENT

1. George E. Breen, "Middle Management Morale in the '80's," *AMA Survey Report* (New York: AMA Publications Division, 1983), p. 18.

2. Carol A. Bridgewater, "Women's Puny Promotions," *Psychology Today* (February 1983), p. 16.

3. K. J. Wills, "What's New at the Columbia Business School: Losing the Salary Game," *The New York Times,* Section 3 (Feb. 20, 1983), p. 27.

4. Martha G. Burrow, "Developing Women Managers: What Needs to Be Done?" *AMA Survey Report* (New York: AMA Publications Division, 1978), p. 12.

CHAPTER 15: MAKING A REAL DIFFERENCE: WHAT ORGANIZATIONS CAN DO

1. "Women and Work: Looking for Jobs and Justice," *National Voter* (Spring 1983), pp. 3–4.

2. Claire Safran, "Corporate Women: Just How Far Have We Come?" *Working Woman* (March 1984), p. 99.

3. Jaye Scholl, "Savvy Corporations of the Year," *Savvy* (June 1983), p. 37.

4. *Ibid.*

5. Tamar Lewin, "Women in Board Rooms Are Still the Exceptions," *The New York Times* (July 5, 1984), p. C1.

6. *Ibid.,* p. C8.

7. Michael Cooper and Maria Fisher, "The Client Barrier: Why So Few Women Reach the Top," *Adweek* (Nov. 8, 1982), p. 38.

8. Safran, *op. cit.,* p. 103.

9. "Changing Policies for Changing Families," *Catalyst Career and Family Bulletin* (Fall 1981), pp. 1–2.

CHAPTER 16: FEMININE LEADERSHIP AND THE FUTURE

1. William Serrin, "Experts Say Job Bias Against Women Persists," *The New York Times* (Nov. 25, 1984), p. 32.

2. Jay Cocks, "How Long Till Equality?" *Time* (July 12, 1982), p. 20.

3. John Kenneth Galbraith, "Corporate Man," *The New York Times Magazine* (Jan. 22, 1984), p. 39.

Index

Accommodation approach to
conflict management,
170–71, 174
Accommodation of female
managers, *see* Adaptation
of female managers
Accountability, 94, 115
Across the Board, 148–49
Adaptation of female managers,
21, 22–23, 29–36, 68, 70,
71–72, 147, 232
the fallacy of, 37–40
promoting feminine style of
leadership instead of,
230–31, 239, 240
renegotiating collusive
relationships, 232–33
Stage I: Fraternity Pledging,
30–32
Stage II: Making the First
String, 30, 32–34
Stage III: Splendid Isolationism,
30, 34–36
Advice offered female managers,
6, 28–29, 31, 61, 225

self-help literature, 10–11,
112
on standards of performance,
104–105, 112
on suppressing emotions, 147,
148–49
Adweek, 265
Affirmative action policies, 6–7,
19–20, 21–22, 258–59
Aggressive behavior, 25, 33, 65,
73, 99, 163
Agor, Dr. Weston, 189–90
Air Force Academy, 21
Allocation of resources, position
power over, 85
Alpha style leaders, 56, 57
American Express
Communications Division,
94, 110, 193
American Management
Association, 45, 102, 106,
152, 222
American Stock Exchange, 267
Analytical thinking, 25–26, 28,
60, 61, 71, 75

Analytical thinking (*cont'd*)
  intuitive thinking as opposed
    to, 183, 184, 185–86, 187,
    190, 195, 196, 197–98
  overreliance on, 184–86
Androgynous management, 250
Anger, 141, 162
Annapolis, 21
Aptitudes, gender differences in,
    63–65
Arthur Andersen & Company,
    172
Ash, Mary Kay, 93, 137, 153
Assertiveness, 25, 83–84
Assertiveness training, 28, 83
Assessing personal impact, 135,
    152–56
AT&T, 191, 237, 279
Attitude changes among top
    management, 256–58
Attitudes of employees, *see*
    Employee attitudes
Authoritarian management,
    24–25, 55, 92, 257
  versus consensus-building,
    124–25
  resentment of, employee, 43–44
Automobile industry, 43, 46
  participative management in
    the, 52–53
Avoidance response to conflict
    management, 165–67, 174
Awareness seminars, 270–74

Bach, J. S., 183
Bankers Trust, 207
Bank of Boston, 262
Barnewall, Marilyn, 196
Bellamy, Carol, 75
Bell Telephone System,
    Male-Female Awareness
    Workshop, 5–6
Beta style leaders, 56–57
Biological differences between the
    sexes, 11, 91, 163–64, 250

affecting aptitudes, 63–65
affecting intuitive thinking,
    191–92
affecting managing diversity,
    202–203
conflict management and, 168,
    171
in handling stress, 65, 163, 171,
    202
interpersonal skills and, 118,
    144–45
Blass, Walter, 191, 237–38, 279
Blum, Barbara, 222, 225–26,
    252
Board of directors, appointment
    of women to, 261–63
Body language, *see* Nonverbal
    cues
Boundaries between career and
    personal life, setting,
    210–16, 278
Brain:
  gender differences, 64–65,
    144–45, 191–92, 202–203
  intuitive thinking as
    right-hemisphere skill, 188
Bristol-Myers, 219
Brooklyn College, 196
Burns, James MacGregor, 55

Capital-intensive industries,
    42–43, 45, 46, 47
  participative management in,
    52–53
Career development, 222, 223,
    225
  see also Promotions
Caress, Gilhooly & Kestin, Inc.,
    67
Carl Byoir & Associates, Inc., 74,
    97, 208
Carter-Mondale campaign,
    252
Catalyst, 17, 262
Census Bureau, U.S., 36

Change Masters: Innovation for Productivity in the American Corporation, The (Kanter), 47, 51–52, 130
Charisma, power derived from, 88, 89, 95, 96
Chartwell & Company, 108, 194
Chemical Bank, 122, 213
Chemical companies, 46
Children, *see* Family
Christian Dior, New York, 95, 212, 262
Civil Rights Act of 1964, Title VII of, 19, 36
Clerical work, pitching in with, 217–20
"Client Barrier: Why So Few Women Reach the Top, The," 265–66
Clients, communicating support of feminine leadership to, 265–66
Collaboration approach to conflict management, 169–70, 171, 174, 180
Columbia Business School Club, 95
Columbia University, 224
Communication:
  with clients supporting feminine leadership, 265–66
  expression of feelings as part of, 142
  internal corporate, supporting feminine leadership, 264–65
  nonverbal, 135, 137, 138, 142–43, 145
  performance feedback, 151–52
  two-way, in participative management, 127–28, 131
Competition, 23, 24, 25, 33, 120, 180

behind male approach to conflict management, 165–68, 179
  versus cooperation, 120–22, 126
  with foreign products, 41, 42–43, 45–46
  for position power, 86
Competitive response to conflict management, 165–66, 174
Compromise approach to conflict management, 167–69, 171, 174
Computer technology companies, 46, 47, 50, 51
Conciliation, 162
Conference Board, The, 148
Confessore, Lynda, 240–41
Conflict management, 158–81
  competitiveness in, 165–68, 179
  defining conflict, 159
  five modes of, 164–71
    accommodation, 170–71, 174
    avoidance response, 166–67, 174
    collaboration, 169–70, 171, 174, 180
    competitive response, 165–66, 174
    compromise, 167–69, 171, 174
  gender differences in, 162–64, 165–81
    biological reasons for, 163–64, 168, 171
    socialization and, 162–63, 171–72
  intergroup conflict, 160–61, 175–79
  interpersonal conflict, 161, 175–79
  NTL Institute seminar, 175–79
  range of behaviors required for, 173–75, 180–81

Conflict management (*cont'd*)
sources of organizational
conflict, 159–60
valuing relationships in, 169,
170–73
Connelly, Dr. Sharon, 105, 137,
243
Consensus-building, 76, 124–25,
130, 169, 176
see also Cooperation, fostering
Considine, Jill, 110, 194–95,
221–22
Consular Corps, 110
Control of resources, position
power derived from, 85, 99
Cooperation, 74, 76, 92, 94, 106,
130
versus competition, 120–22, 126
see also Consensus-building
Cornell University's Institute for
Women and Work, 267
"Corporate Man," 278
Corporations:
authoritarian management of,
see Authoritarian
management
conflict management within,
158–62, 179–81
crisis faced by U.S., 40, 41–57
changes in organizational
structure, 46–48
changing worker attitudes,
43–44
declining confidence in
management, 44–45
foreign competition, 41,
42–43, 45–46, 185
new concept of leadership,
54–56
participative management,
48–54
role of feminine leaders,
56–57
the service sector, 53–54
shift away from heavy
industry, 45–46

feminine style of leadership
and, 4, 40
conflict management, 179–81
the future for, 275–80
high performance standards,
112–13
humanizing the workplace,
278–79
integration of, in the
corporate culture, 251–52
interpersonal skills, 149,
157
intuitive thinking, 184–85,
192, 193, 197–98
lack of recognition of, 15,
68–70, 98, 239
resistance to, 16–18
setting boundaries between
career and personal life,
210–16, 278
steps organizations may take
to promote, *see* Feminine
style of leadership,
corporations' role in
promoting
flexible organization of, 46–48
hierarchical organization of,
24–25, 48, 55, 56, 85, 87,
115, 185
hiring practices, 232
affirmative action policies,
6–7, 19–20, 21–22, 258–59
intuitive thinking used in
problem-solving in,
184–85, 193, 194, 195–96
masculine corporate culture of,
22–27, 69–70, 87, 232,
233, 237, 245, 248, 251,
272
as alien to women, 27, 70
raising corporate
consciousness about,
241–42
values of, 24–26
participative management in, *see*
Participative management

policies affecting family life, 266, 267–68
  child care, 208, 268, 269
  flexible benefit plans, 268–69
  increasing flexibility in, 215–16
  job-related travel, 211, 212–13
  paternity leave, 208
  pregnancy leave, 267–68
  transfers, 211, 213, 214, 215, 266
  working at home, 266
promotions within, 224, 225, 232, 254, 260–61, 266
salary gap between the sexes, 224, 225, 254, 260–61, 266, 276
traditional style of leadership expected by, 8, 16–18, 19, 68–70, 242
  see also Traditional style of leadership
"Corporations of the Year: The Annual Report on Corporations Where Success Is Based on Merit not Gender," 261
Councils of executive women, 263–64
Creative problem-solving, 61, 72, 193
  see also Intuitive thinking
Credentials, professional, 221–26
Critical mass theory, 229–30
Criticism, direct, 153
Crossman, Nancy, 267

Day care, 268, 269
"Deep sensing," 136
Delegation of work, 91
Details, attention to, 199, 200–201, 207, 210
Devanna, Dr. Mary Anne, 224
Diplomacy, 153

Diversity, managing, 199–210
  attention to details, 199, 200–201, 207, 210
  emotional venting, 204–206
  multiple roles and good health, 209–10
  organizational ability, 203–204, 206–207
  reaction to stress and, 202–204
  role of superwoman, 208–209
Dressing for success, 28, 77

Early, Alice, 207, 219–20
Eastern Psychological Association, 206
Ecton, Donna, 151
Educational credentials, 221–26
"Egg-catching contest" at NTL Institute seminar, 175–79
Einstein, Albert, 183
Electronics companies, 46, 51
Emerson, Alice F., 262
Emotional involvement with people, 28, 61, 62, 76–77, 135, 238–39
  management of feelings, 135, 139–49
  personal power and, 88–89
  traditional leadership's view of, 26, 139, 140, 141, 148–49
Emotional venting, 204–206
"Emotions in a Woman's Briefcase," 76–77
Empathy, 135, 137, 140–43, 147, 152
Employee attitudes:
  changes in, 43–44, 59
  surveys of, 44, 139
Employee morale, 15, 39–40, 41, 59, 60, 78, 130, 257
  feminine style of leadership to raise, 3, 274
  middle management's, 45
Employee satisfaction, 26
  participative management and, 51
Empowerment, 92, 119, 120

Entrepreneurs, women as, 39, 108–109

Equal Employment Opportunity Commission (EEOC), 258–59

Equality as sameness, dispelling belief of, 246–48, 279

Ethics of management, decline in confidence in, 44

Executive career counselors, 67

Executive Order No. 11375, 20

Executive women's councils, 263–64

Facilitation skills, *see* Process and facilitation skills

Fairness issue, *see* Performance appraisal system; Promotions; Salary gap between the sexes

Family:
corporate policies regarding, 266, 267–68
child care, 208, 268, 269
flexible benefit plans, 268–69
increasing flexibility in, 215–16
job-related travel, 211, 212–13
paternity leave, 208
pregnancy leave, 267–68
transfers, 211, 213, 214, 215, 266
working at home, 266
establishing boundaries between career and, 210–16, 278
multiple roles and health, 209–10
organizing skills, 206–207
superwoman, role of, 207–209

Federal government, sex discrimination and, 20, 21, 258–59

Feedback, 89, 134, 135, 145, 151–55
on performance, 151–52
quality of, 152–55

Feelings, management of, 135, 139–49
see also Emotional involvement with people; Emotional venting

Feminine style of leadership:
balancing, with traditional style of leadership, 75–76, 77–79, 98–99, 126, 132, 157, 174–81, 193, 197–98, 277
Beta leadership style, 56–57
the case for, 58–79
conflict management, 162–81
corporations' role in promoting, 256–74
appointing outstanding women to corporate boards, 261–63
attitudinal changes, 256–58
communicating corporate commitment to clients, 264–65
communicating organizational commitment to feminine leadership, 264–65
creating executive women's councils, 263–64
initiating awareness seminars, 270–74
recruiting and hiring women, 258–59
rectifying inequities in salaries and promotions, 260–61
revising corporate benefit plans, 268–69
revising performance appraisal systems, 259–60
sponsoring corporate networks, 269–70

updating corporate policies,
    266–68
defining the, 61–63
development of a model of,
    11–13
confirmation of the model,
    13–14
future for, 275–80
increase in awareness of,
    71–77
need for, 5, 17–18, 68–70
interpersonal skills, *see*
    Interpersonal skills
intuition and problem-solving,
    56, 60, 61, 72, 75, 145,
    182–98
managing diversity, 199–210
men's role in promoting,
    244–55
    acknowledging the basic
        issues, 246–48
    becoming an active advocate,
        254
    building awareness among
        men, 250–51
    developing professional
        relationships with women,
        253–54
    learning about differences,
        248–49
    promoting integration, not
        accommodation, 251–53
    redefining models of effective
        leadership, 249–50
origin of concept of, 3
performance standards,
    setting, 92–93, 100–109,
    112–13
persistence of, 4–5
pitching in, 217–20
power, use of, 83–99
professional development,
    221–26
questions raised about, 9–10
review of the literature, 10–11
risk-taking, 109–11

setting boundaries between
    career and personal life,
    210–16, 278
teamwork and participative
    management, 76, 114–32
underutilization of, 7, 16, 40,
    180, 226, 277
women's role in promoting,
    229–43
    becoming a supportive role
        model, 235–38
    establishing a corporate
        support system, 234–35
    learning about issues, 231–32
    maximizing feminine
        leadership strengths: being
        yourself, 238–41
    persistence and vision,
        242–43
    raising the corporate
        consciousness, 241–42
    renegotiating collusive
        relationships, 232–33
    see also Corporations;
        Traditional style of
        leadership
Ferraro, Geraldine, 111, 211, 234
Fields, Deborah, 120, 195, 239
Fields, Randy, 195
Financial results:
    interpersonal skills balanced
        with interest in, 157
    as measure of managerial
        effectiveness, 26
    participative management's
        impact on, 51, 53, 60
Financial services industry, 196
Fiorito, Barbara, 122, 213
First Women's Bank, The, 110,
    194, 221
Fleder, Wendy, 241
Flexible production companies,
    46–48
Flextime, 266
Foreign competition, 41, 42–43,
    45–46, 185

Foreman, Carol, 111, 234
Fortune, 36–37
Fortune 500 companies, senior management at, 36, 37
Fox, Muriel, 74, 97–98, 110, 208
"Fraternity Pledging" stage of adaptation, 30–32
Friedan, Betty, 22, 69–70
Fulbright & Jaworski, 213–14

Galbraith, John Kenneth, 278
Gallup survey, 18
Gamesman, The (Maccoby), 24, 25, 146–47
Games Mother Never Taught You (Harragan), 23, 24–25, 117
Gender differences, evidence of, 11, 61, 63–68
General Foods, 95
General Motors, 52–53
Inland Division, 52–53, 166
Georgetown Medical School, 65, 163, 202, 277
George Washington University, 206
Gilligan, Dr. Carol, 67–68, 119
Gleason, Jean, 213–14
Godwin, Judy, 166
Goggin, Julia, 207
Gottlieb, June, 150
Graham, Katharine, 36
Group process skills, *see* Process and facilitation skills
GTE, 92, 102

Haffner, Noreen, 91–92, 169–70
Hard work, *see* Performance standards, setting; Work ethic
Harlan, Anne, 101
Harragan, Betty Lehan, 23, 24–25, 117
Harvard University, 22, 46, 67, 69–70, 143
Business School, 151
Health care, 36

"Heart," having, 146–47, 149
Heidt, Julie, 166
Hennessy, Jim, 215, 277
Hennig, Dr. Margaret, 115
Hewlett-Packard, 50
Hierarchical organization of corporations, 24–25, 48, 55, 56, 115, 185
position power derived from, 85, 87
High-technology industries, 46, 47
participative management in, 50–51, 53
Hiring practices, 232, 258–59
affirmative action policies, 6–7, 19–20, 21–22, 258–59
Home, working at, 266
Hormonal differences between the sexes, 65, 191
in reaction to stress, 65, 163, 202
Housing and Urban Development, U.S. Department of (HUD), 107
Human Synergistics, 125–26
Hunter College, 107, 169, 221, 257–58

Immigrant work ethic, 106, 219, 221
Innovation, intuitive thinking leading to, 186, 187, 195
In Search of Excellence (Peters and Waterman), 59–60, 136, 185
Intergroup conflict, 160–61
"egg-catching contest" experiment, 175–79
International Association of Quality Circles, 53
International Harvester, 172
Interpersonal conflict, 161
"egg-catching contest" experiment, 175–79

Interpersonal skills, 59, 61, 72, 75, 90, 133–57, 238, 257
   assessing personal impact, 135
   to foster teamwork, 120
   having "heart," 146–47
   for holistic management, 157
   intimacy and authenticity, 135, 149–51
   intuition and, 145, 187, 238
   listening skills, 134, 135, 137–39
   management of feelings, 62, 135, 139–49
   personal power derived from, 88–89, 92–93, 94, 95, 99
   process and facilitation skills, 143–46
   sensing skills, 73, 74, 88–89, 135, 136–37
   sensitivity training, 154–56
   setting boundaries between career and family and, 212
   use of feedback, 89, 134, 135, 151–55
   valuing relationships in conflict resolution, 169, 170–73
Intimacy and authenticity, 135, 149–51
"Intuitive Edge, The," 196–97
Intuitive Management (Agor), 189–90
Intuitive thinking, 56, 60, 61, 72, 75, 182–98, 238, 257
   benefits of, 186–87
   biological basis of, 188, 191–92
   creative solutions arising from, 195–97
   experience of female managers using, 193–95
   negative stereotypes linked with, 182–84
   personal power and, 88–89
   reading of nonverbal cues as root of, 145
   renewed interest in, 184–85
   role of socialization in use of, 190–91

the value of, 197–98
   women managers' use of, in problem-solving, 188–90
Isolation, risk of, 212, 216
"Splendid Isolationism" stage of adaptation, 30, 34–36

Jacklin, Carol, 63–64
Japan, 46, 49, 59, 130, 150, 184
Jardim, Dr. Anne, 115
J. C. Penney Company, 51–52
Johns Hopkins University, 143
Johnson, Arlene, 17
Johnson O'Connor Research Foundation, Inc., 192
Jones, Dr. Janice, 108–109, 194
Josefowitz, Dr. Natasha, 37
Journalism, 36
Journal of Commerce, The, 53
Junior Leagues, 173
J. Walter Thompson Company, 193, 234

Kanter, Dr. Rosabeth Moss, 47, 51–52, 130
Karp, Ruth Downing, 193, 234
Korda, Michael, 76–77
Korn/Ferry International, 107, 212–13
Kuzukian, Edward, 67

Labor Department, U.S., 53–54
Lazard Frères and Co., 189
"Leader, The," 55–56
Leadership, 60
   new concept of, 54–56, 112
   redefining models of effective, 249–50
   see also Feminine style of leadership; Management; Traditional style of leadership
Leadership (Burns), 55
League of Women Voters, 258
Lehr, L. W., 261

Levenstein and Gaines
    Advertising, 240
Levin, Amy, 131, 153
Levy, Jerry, 144–45
Listening skills, 134, 135, 137–39
Long-range outcomes, approach
    to use of power and, 94,
    98–99
Long-term corporate goals, 62,
    73, 76
Lou Harris poll, 44

McCabe, Jewel Jackson, 74
Maccoby, Eleanor, 63–64
Maccoby, Michael, 24, 25, 54–56,
    146–47
McCoy, Christine, 168
MacDonald, Randy, 92, 102
MacGruder Company, The, 196
McGuinness, Diane, 64
Mademoiselle, 131, 153
Mahoney, Sister Colette, 111,
    172–73
"Making the First String" stage
    of adaptation, 30, 32–34
Male leadership, see Traditional
    style of leadership
Management:
    decline in confidence in, 44–45
    hierarchical, 24–25, 48, 55, 56,
        85, 87, 115, 185
    mass entry of women into, 16,
        18
    statistics on, 36, 277
    Title VII of the 1964 Civil
        Rights Act and, 19–22
    new concept of leadership,
        54–56, 112
    participative, see Participative
        management
    redefining models of effective
        leadership, 249–50
    study of values of men and
        women in, 106
    see also Feminine style of
        leadership; Middle

management; Senior
    management; Traditional
    style of leadership
"Management and Leadership,"
    54–55
Managerial functions, 12
Managerial Woman, The (Hennig
    and Jardim), 115, 148
Managing diversity, see Diversity,
    managing
Marriott, J. W., 187
Marriott Corporation, 187
Martens, Michelle, 93
Mary Kay Cosmetics, 93
Marymount College, 111, 172
Masculine style of leadership, see
    Traditional style of
    leadership
Masculinism, 22–27, 69–70, 87, 116
    values of, 24–26
    see also Corporations, masculine
        corporate culture of
Mathematics, skills in, 63, 64
MBA Resources, 151
Mediator, role of, 162–63
Megatrends (Naisbitt), 58–59
Men's leadership style, see
    Traditional style of
    leadership
Men's role in promoting feminine
    style of leadership, 244–55
    acknowledging the basic issues,
        246–48
    becoming an active advocate,
        254
    building awareness among
        men, 250–51
    developing professional
        relationships with women,
        253–54
    learning about differences,
        248–49
    promoting integration, not
        accommodation, 251–53
    redefining models of effective
        leadership, 249–50

Meyer, Sandra, 94–95, 110, 193
Michigan Telephone Company, 166
Middle management, 6, 39
  lack of confidence in top management, 44
  professional development of, 222–23
  promotion to, 224
  salary gap between the sexes, 224
  visibility of women in, 102–105
Military, similarities between business and the, 23, 24, 60, 87, 91, 99, 116–17
Military academies, 21, 22
Milwid, Beth, 16–17
Mrs. Fields' Cookies, 120
Mondale-Ferraro campaign, 111, 211
Morale, *see* Employee morale
Motivating people, 74, 91, 93, 97, 193–94
Motorola, Inc., 53
"Moving Up: Women in Managerial Careers," 101
Multiple-role conflict:
  between career and personal life, 209
  in the corporate setting, 159–60
  see also Diversity, managing
Municipal Assistance Corporation, New York City, 189

Naisbitt, John, 58–59
National Coalition of 100 Black Women, 74
National Multiple Sclerosis Society, 220
National Park Service, 168
Negative stereotypes, 224, 247
  of overattention to details, 199, 200–201
  overcoming, 101–102
  of women's intuition, 182–84

Networks:
  teamwork based on building, 119
  women's, 234–35, 237, 269–70
New England Telephone Company, 169–70
"New Rules in American Life: Searching for Self-Fulfillment in a World Turned Upside Down," 43
New York City Council, 75
New York Public Service Commission, 223
New York Telephone Company, 91, 97, 214, 223
New York Times, The, 18, 44
New York Times Magazine, The, 69
"Next American Frontier, The," 42
Nicholas, Colombe, 95, 212, 262
Nonverbal cues:
  listening skills involving, 135, 138
  sensitivity to, 135, 137, 142–43, 145
NTL Institute seminar, 175–79
Nynex Corporation, 215, 241, 277

Objectivity, 26
Offerman, Dr. Lynn, 206–207
Ohio Bell Telephone Company, 168
Okada, Shigen, 184
One Minute Manager, The, (Blanchard), 151
Opinion Research Corporation poll, 44
Organizing skills, 203–204, 206–207, 210
  see also Diversity, managing
O'Shea, Dr. Lynne, 172
Ouchi, Dr. William, 49, 59, 146, 150

Participative management, 48–54, 58–60, 94, 129–32
advantages of, 49
collaboration approach to conflict management and, 170
employee attitudes toward, 43
feminine concept of teamwork and, 118–20, 126–28, 131
need to change management's attitude toward, 256–57
problems in implementing, 129–30, 131–32
within service industries, 53–54
success stories, 50–53, 59–60
see also Teamwork
Paternity leave, 208
Paths to Power (Josefowitz), 37
Penn Mutual Life Insurance Company, The, 262
People orientation in managing, see Interpersonal skills
Perceptions of a problem, conflict over differing, 160
Performance appraisal system, 102, 151–52, 259–60
Performance standards, setting, 92–93, 100–109, 112–13
high-performance entrepreneurs, 108–109
overcoming negative stereotypes, 101–102
pitching in and, 218–19
visibility factor, 102–105
work ethic, female, 106–108, 113, 219
working harder than men to succeed, 101, 105, 106, 218, 219
Personal computers, 266
Personal life, setting boundaries between career and, 210–16, 278
see also Family
Personal power, 87–90
components of, 87–89

factors influencing use of, 90–92
favored by feminine leaders, 90, 92–93, 96, 97–98
outcomes produced by, 94–95
Peter Rogers Associates, 104, 218
Peters, Tom, 59–60, 136, 185
Pharmaceutical companies, 46
Pitching in, 217–20
Pitney Bowes, 93
Planned Parenthood Federation of America, 74
Politics in the office, 105, 106, 107–108, 112, 113
Pooler, Rosemary, 223
Position power, 85–87
competition for, 86
factors influencing use of, 90–92
favored by traditional leaders, 86–87, 96–97
feminine leaders sparing use of, 90, 96
outcomes produced by, 94–95
sources of, 85–86
Power, use of, 83–99
assumptions about, 92–93
complementary approaches to, 96–97
corporate implications of, 97–99
definition of power, 84
factors influencing use of, 90–92
outcomes of, 94–95
perceptions of, 96
personal power, 87–92, 94–95, 96, 97
position power, 85–87, 90–92, 94–95, 96–97
understanding, 85
Preference for male or female manager, 200–201
Pregnancy leave, 267–68
Problem-solving and intuition, see Intuitive thinking

Process and facilitation skills, 142, 143–46
Productivity, 39–40, 41, 59, 60, 78, 106
  employee attitudes and crisis in, 43, 44
  feminine style of leadership to improve, 3, 15, 71, 258, 274, 277
  participative management and, 51, 53, 257
Professional development, 221–26
Professional managers, 128–29
Professional relationships between the sexes, 253–54
"Profile of Women Senior Executives," 106–107
Promotions, 232
  inequity in, 224, 225, 254, 260–61, 266
Psychological differences between the sexes, 11
Psychology of Sex Differences, The (Jacklin and Maccoby), 63–64
Psychology Today, 196
Public administration, 36

Qualitative thinking, 56
Quality circles, 53
  see also Participative management
Quality control, 51, 53

Ramey, Dr. Estelle, 65, 163–64, 171, 202–203, 277
Rand Corporation, The, 276
Rational thinking, *see* Analytical thinking
Reber, Dr. Arthur, 196–97
Reich, Robert, 42, 46–47
Relationships, importance of, *see* Interpersonal skills
Relocation, *see* Transfers

Renick, Rusty, 91, 97, 214, 223
Retailing industry, participative management in the, 51–52
Risk-taking, 109–11
Rohatyn, Felix, 189
Rohde, Diann, 220
Role conflict, *see* Multiple-role conflict
Role confusion, 220
Role models, women managers as, 102–105, 235–38, 240–41, 263, 279
  see also Support among female managers
Role overload, 209, 210
Role strain, 209
Rosener, Lynn, 56–57, 96
Russell, Dr. Yvonne, 72–73
Russell Reynolds, 207, 219

Salary gap between the sexes, 224, 225, 254, 260–61, 266, 276
Santa Clara Valley Hospital, 72
Sarfati, Lydia, 222, 269
Sarkli-Repechage, Ltd., 222
Savvy, 16–17, 261
Scarce resources, conflict over, 160
Schwartz, Peter, 56–57, 96
Seashore, Edith Whitfield, 204, 239–40
Secretarial work, pitching in with, 217–20
Self-employment, *see* Entrepreneurs, women as
SELF, 76–77
Senior management, 6, 72
  attitude changes needed among, 256–58
  barriers preventing women from reaching, 17, 36–37
  communication of commitment to female leadership, 264–66

Senior management (cont'd)
  to clients, 265–66
  to employees, 264–65
  competition for position power, 86
  executive women's councils and, 263–64
  hiring practices of, 259
  intuitive thinking relied on by, 190
  lack of confidence in, 44–45
  promotions to, 224, 232
  salary gap between the sexes, 224
  "Splendid Isolationism" stage of adaptation, 30, 34–36
  visibility of women in, 102–105
  see also Feminine style of leadership; Management; Middle management; Traditional style of leadership
Sensing skills, 73, 74, 88–89, 135, 136–37
Sensitivity to Nonverbal Communication: The Pons Test, 142–43
Sensitivity training, 154–56
Service sector, participative management in the, 53–54
Sex and the Brain (Durden-Smith and DeSimone), 64, 144
Sexism in the workplace, 6
  building awareness of, 249–50
  Title VII of the 1964 Civil Rights Act and, 19–22
  see also Corporations, masculine corporate culture
Sexual harassment, 266–67
Sexuality and professional relationships, 253–54
Shalala, Dr. Donna, 107, 169, 189, 221, 257–58
Sheedy, John, 96, 218–19
Simon and Hilliard Advertising, 96, 218

Six-Figure Woman (and How to Be One), The (Wyse), 73
Socialization process and gender differences, 11, 61, 65–68, 75, 112, 250
  in conflict-management styles, 162–63, 171–72
  in expression of feelings, 140, 141
  in intuitive thinking, 190–91
  in listening skills, 138
  in managing diversity, 203–204
  in risk-taking, 101
  in sensitivity to nonverbal cues, 143
  in use of power, 90–91
Sole, Dr. Kenneth, 175n.
Solien, Stephanie, 127, 203–204
Sorensen, Gillian Martin, 110, 162–63
Southern New England Telephone Company, 91
"Splendid Isolationism" stage of adaptation, 30, 34–36
Sports, analogies between business and, 23–24, 28, 114–15, 116, 117, 120–22, 179
Standardized production, 42
Stanford University, 64
Steel industry, 46
Stereotypes, see Negative stereotypes
Stewart, Martha, 120
Strategic thinking, 25–26, 28, 90
  see also Analytical thinking
Straus, Ellen Sulzberger, 137
Stress, 65, 163, 171, 202–204, 205, 216
"Study of Values, The," 66–67
Superwoman, role of, 207–209
Support among female managers, 234–35, 269–70
  lack of, 32–34, 35
  see also Role models, women managers as

Tabaczyk, Gerald, 104, 218
Task competence, 106
    personal power derived from,
        88, 89, 94, 95, 99
Team units, *see* Participative
    management
Teamwork, 76, 114–32
    control versus
        consensus-building, 124–25
    cooperation versus competition,
        120–22
    differences in male and female
        views of, 114–16, 179
    feminine concept of, 118–20
    integration of women team
        members, 252–53
    ownership in the final decision,
        125–26, 178
    problems with professional
        managers, 128–29
    traditional definition of, 116–17
    wilderness survival problem,
        122–23, 126
    see also Participative
        management
Ted Bates Advertising, 150
Telecommunications companies,
    46
Texas Instruments, 260–61
T-groups, 155–56
*Theory Z: How American Business Can
    Meet the Japanese Challenge*
    (Ouchi), 49, 59, 146
"Thomas-Kilmann Conflict Mode
    Instrument," 164–65, 174
3M Company, 261
Time, 276
Time-management skills, 206–207
Title VII, *see* Civil Rights Act of
    1964, Title VII
Tokenism, 33, 252
Trade, international, 41, 42–43,
    45
Traditional style of leadership, 4,
    5, 58, 61
    adaptation of female managers

    to, *see* Adaptation of
        female managers
    advice for women to follow, *see*
        Advice offered female
        managers
    Alpha style leaders, 56, 57
    balancing, with feminine style
        of leadership, 75–76,
        77–79, 98–99, 126, 132,
        157, 174–81, 193, 197–98,
        277
    conflict management by,
        165–68, 174
    "egg-catching contest"
        experiment, 175–79
    need for a range of
        behaviors, 173–75, 180–81
    corporate bias toward, 8, 16–18,
        19, 68–70, 242
    development of a model of,
        11–13
    confirmation of the model,
        13–14
    difficulty of, in implementing
        participative management,
        127–30
    discomfort of female managers
        with, 7–9, 71–72, 149
    emotional detachment in, 26,
        130, 140, 141
    imitated by female managers,
        7, 8, 22, 32–33, 35, 70,
        71–72, 196, 230–31
    interpersonal skills used in, 133
    intuitive thinking and, 184–85,
        190, 192, 193, 194, 195–96
    masculinism and, 22–27,
        69–70
        as alien to women, 27, 70
        values of, 24–26
    pitching in and office image,
        218
    power, use of, 83–99
    teamwork and, 116–17
    see also Corporations; Feminine
        style of leadership

Tragash, Dr. Harold, 50, 51
Training, professional, 221–26
Transfers, 211, 213, 214, 215, 266
Travel, job-related, 211, 212–13

United Nations, 110, 162
University of California, 143
University of California at Los Angeles, 107
University of Chicago, 144
University of Michigan, 209
University of Southern California, 105, 137, 243
University of Texas at Galveston, 72

Values:
conflict over differing, 160
gender differences, 66–68
among managers, 106, 107–108
of women managers, 106–108, 152
Verbal skills, 63, 64, 192
Verbrugge, Dr. Lois, 209–10
Visibility of women managers, 102–105
"Visible Manager, The," 136
Visual-spatial abilities, 63, 64, 192
Vogue, 74

Wage discrimination, 20
Washington Post Company, The, 36
Waterman, Bob, 59–60, 136, 185
Wattleton, Faye, 74–75

Weiss, Carol, 101
Wellesley College Center for Research on Women, 101
Wells, H. G., 19
West Point, 21
"What Kind of Leaders Do We Need?," 56–57
Wheaton College, 262
Wilderness-survival problem, 122–23, 126
WMCA Radio, 137
Wolan-Martin, Elaine, 168
Women as managers, see Feminine style of leadership
Women's Campaign Fund, 127, 203
Women's National Bank, The, 222
"Women's Social Roles and Health," 209
Workaholics, 212, 216
Worker attitudes, see Employee attitudes
Work ethic, female, 106–108, 113, 219
Working hard, see Performance standards, setting; Work ethic
Working mothers, see Family
Working Woman, 17, 259
"Work spirit," 105, 219
World economy, changes in, 42–43
Wyse, Lois, 73
Wyse Advertising, 73

Xerox Corporation, 50–51

Yankelovich, Daniel, 43